# COMMON CORE ACHIEVE

## Mastering Essential Test Readiness Skills

## TASC Test Exercise Book

### READING & WRITING

Mc
Graw
Hill
Education

Bothell, WA • Chicago, IL • Columbus, OH • New York, NY

**MHEonline.com**

Send all inquiries to:
McGraw-Hill Education
8787 Orion Place
Columbus, OH 43240

ISBN: 978-0-02-143264-6
MHID: 0-02-143264-3

Printed in the United States of America.

2 3 4 5 6 7 8 9 RHR 17 16 15 14

# Table of Contents

Congratulations! If you are using this book, it means that you are taking a key step toward achieving an important new goal for yourself. You are preparing to take the TASC Test Assessing Secondary Completion™, one of the most important steps in the pathway toward career, educational, and lifelong well-being and success.

*Common Core Achieve: Mastering Essential Test Readiness Skills* is designed to help you learn or strengthen the skills you will need when you take the TASC test. The *Reading & Writing Exercise Book* provides you with additional practice of the key concepts and core skills required for success on test day and beyond.

## How to Use This Book

This book is designed to follow the same lesson structure as the Core Student Module. Each lesson in the *Reading & Writing Exercise Book* is broken down into the same sections as the core module, with a page or more devoted to the key concepts covered in each section. Each lesson contains at least one Test-Taking Tip, which will help you prepare for a test by giving you hints such as how to determine where to find the answer to a question, or strategies such as how to approach multiple-choice questions. At the back of this book, you will find the answer key for each lesson. The answer to each question is provided along with a rationale for why the answer to each concept-based question is correct. If you get an answer incorrect, please return to the appropriate lesson and section in either the online or print Core Student Module to review the specific content.

## About the TASC Test for Reading and Writing

The TASC test for Reading assesses across two content categories (approximate percentage of test questions in each category is shown in parenthesis): Informational Literature (75%) and Literary Language Literature (25%). There are a total of 50 questions on the test, all of which are in multiple-choice format. Test-takers have 75 minutes to complete all the questions

The TASC test for Writing assesses across four content categories (approximate percentage of test questions in each category is shown in parenthesis): Organization (15%), Sentence Structure (30%), Usage (30%), and Mechanics (25%). There are 50 multiple-choice questions in the Language Ability section of the test and an essay prompt asking test-takers to respond to passages in the Writing Essay section. Test-takers have 55 minutes to complete the Language Ability section and 50 minutes to complete the Writing Essay section.

## Item Formats

### Multiple-Choice Items

All the questions on the TASC test for Reading and the Language Ability section of the Writing test are in multiple-choice format. Each multiple-choice question contains four answer choices, of which there is only one correct answer. When you encounter a multiple-choice question, eliminate any possible answers that cannot be correct based on the information given so you can focus on the relevant information to answer the question.

### Essay Question

The Writing Practice in each lesson is designed to help you prepare for writing the essay for the TASC test for Writing. Writing prompts and passages guide you to produce responses that reflect the types of writing addressed in the essay question. Your essay response will be scored based on the development of your main idea through supporting reasons, examples, and details; clear organization of ideas; language use; and clarity and correctness of writing conventions. The Writing Practice activities will help you practice and master these areas of writing competency.

# Strategies for Test Day

There are many things you should do to prepare for test day, including studying. Other ways to prepare you for the day of the test include preparing physically, arriving early, and recognizing certain strategies that can help you succeed during the test. Some of these strategies are listed below.

- **Prepare physically.** Make sure you are rested both physically and mentally on the day of the test. Eating a well-balanced meal will also help you concentrate while you take the test. Staying stress-free as much as possible on the day of the test will make you more likely to be focused than you would be if you are stressed.

- **Arrive early.** Arrive at the testing center at least 30 minutes before the beginning of the test. Give yourself enough time to get seated and situated in the room. Keep in mind that some testing centers will not admit you if you are late.

- **Think positively.** Studies have shown that a positive attitude can help with success, although studying helps even more.

- **Relax during the test.** Stretching and deep breathing can help you relax and refocus. Try doing this a few times during the test, especially if you feel frustrated, anxious, or confused.

- **Read the test directions carefully.** Make sure you understand what the directions are asking you to do and complete the activity appropriately. If you have any questions about the test, or how to answer a specific item using the computer, ask before the beginning of the test.

- **Have a strategy for answering questions.** For each question, read the question prompt, identifying the most important information needed to answer the question. If necessary, reread the information provided as well as the answer choices provided.

- **Don't spend a lot of time on difficult questions.** If you are unable to answer a question or are not confident in your answer, move on and come back to it later. If you are taking the paper and pencil version of the TASC test, mark your test booklet so you can easily find questions you have skipped. If you are taking the computer-based version of the TASC test, the testing software includes a tool that allows you to mark questions and move on to the next question. Answer easier questions first. If time permits at the end of the test, review and answer questions you have marked. Regardless of whether you have skipped questions or not, try to finish with around 10–15 minutes left so you have time to check your answers.

- **Answer every question on the test.** If you do not know the answer, make your best guess. You will lose points leaving questions unanswered, but making a guess could possibly help you gain points.

Good luck with your studies, and remember: you are here because you have chosen to achieve important and exciting new goals for yourself. Every time you begin working within the materials, keep in mind that the skills you develop in *Common Core Achieve: Mastering Essential Test Readiness Skills* are not just important for passing the TASC test; they are keys to lifelong success.

This lesson will help you practice determining the main ideas and supporting details in two types of texts. Use it with Core Lesson 1.1 *Determine the Main Idea* to reinforce and apply your knowledge.

## Key Concept

The main idea is the most important idea in a paragraph or passage. A main idea can be found in many different kinds of text.

## Core Skills

- Determine Main Ideas
- Identify Main Ideas in Various Texts

## Main Idea in Informational Text

Informational texts explain, describe, instruct, or try to persuade. The main idea often states the purpose of the document. The supporting details of the text give facts, opinions, examples, and explanations to support the main idea.

**Directions:** Read the text. Then do Numbers 1–6.

# New Purchasing System

**To All Employees,**

As you should be aware, the Purchasing Tracker (PT) system has been rolled out and must now be used for all purchasing. This new system will allow our company to easily organize and track all orders in one system and to cut back on the number of steps required to process an order. As with any new system, it will take some time to perfect the operation. However, to ensure that we realize the full benefit of PT, please start using these guidelines immediately.

**Use of PT**

Use of PT is mandatory for all new service orders. If you feel you have a special situation that cannot be accommodated in the system, let the PT team know immediately so the problem can be solved in a way that does not delay the project.

**Purchase orders to vendor prior to project start**

Corporate policy mandates that suppliers may not start work on a project without a fully approved PT purchase order. A contract does not replace this requirement. If a contract is required for the project, it must be attached to the PT order. Suppliers can start the project only after receiving the approved purchase order (with attached contract, if applicable).

**Use of rates in PT**

If a service category in PT has associated rates, then the PT order must be built using the applicable rate-based line items. This means the order should include a line specific to each rate-based item. Lump sums, combined totals, or use of "miscellaneous" items are not acceptable. Proper breakout of the order ensures that the company has full visibility of what we are purchasing and that our reporting is meaningful.

**Change orders**

Orders should be created based on your original estimate. If the project specs or scope change, the order should be updated via the Change Order process before the supplier submits an invoice. Suppliers may not begin work on additional scope items until they have received the updated purchase order. Do not pad your requisitions in an attempt to avoid change orders. Additional funds on a purchase order open the door for the supplier to invoice for these funds.

1. Which text feature best helps you identify the main idea of each section?
   - A  headings
   - B  passage title
   - C  last sentence
   - D  first sentence

2. Which detail supports the main idea that vendors must have a purchase order before starting work?
   - F  Let the PT team know immediately so the problem can be solved in a way that does not delay the project.
   - G  Suppliers can start the project only after receiving the approved purchase order.
   - H  Lump sums, combined totals, or use of 'miscellaneous' items are not acceptable.
   - J  Additional funds on a purchase order open the door for the supplier to invoice for these funds.

3. What is the main idea of the section titled "Use of rates in PT"?
   - A  Orders should be based on estimates.
   - B  PT must be used for all service requests.
   - C  Contracts do not replace purchase orders.
   - D  Rates must be listed for each rate-based item.

4. In which section would you expect to find details about additional work on a project?
   - F  Use of PT
   - G  Purchase orders to vendor prior to project start
   - H  Use of rates in PT
   - J  Change orders

5. Read this sentence.

   This office memo is about a company's new purchasing system. The text explains to company employees how to use the system when making purchases for their departments.

   Which term identifies the statement?
   - A  main idea
   - B  perspective
   - C  point of view
   - D  supporting detail

6. Why might the writer of this informational text state the topic sentence at the beginning of the passage?
   - F  to make sure the reader knows what the passage is about
   - G  to provide information in least-important to most-important order
   - H  so that the reader does not have to read the entire passage to understand it
   - J  because the reader would not understand the passage without the topic sentence

## Main Idea in Literary Text

Fiction writers invent a self-contained world where imaginary events unfold. The writers also create characters who play roles in these events. Main ideas are presented in paragraphs and longer passages. As you read, look for the main idea and details. The main idea may be directly stated in a topic sentence, but it is more likely to be implied in a longer passage.

**Directions:** Read the text. Then do Numbers 7–12.

# From "To Build a Fire"

### by Jack London

1    But all this—the mysterious, far-reaching hair-line trail, the absence of sun from the sky, the tremendous cold, and the strangeness and weirdness of it all—made no impression on the man. It was not because he was long used to it. He was a newcomer in the land, a *chechaquo*, and this was his first winter. The trouble with him was that he was without imagination. He was quick and alert in the things of life, but only in the things, and not in the significances.

2    Fifty degrees below zero meant eighty-odd degrees of frost. Such fact impressed him as being cold and uncomfortable, and that was all. It did not lead him to meditate upon his frailty as a creature of temperature, and upon man's frailty in general, able only to live within certain narrow limits of heat and cold; and from there on it did not lead him to the conjectural field of immortality and man's place in the universe. Fifty degrees below zero stood for a bite of frost that hurt and that must be guarded against by the use of mittens, ear-flaps, warm moccasins, and thick socks. Fifty degrees below zero was to him just precisely fifty degrees below zero. That there should be anything more to it than that was a thought that never entered his head. . . .

3    At the man's heels trotted a dog, a big native husky, the proper wolf-dog, gray-coated and without any visible or temperamental difference from its brother, the wild wolf.

4    The animal was depressed by the tremendous cold. It knew that it was no time for travelling. Its instinct told it a truer tale than was told to the man by the man's judgment. In reality, it was not merely colder than fifty below zero; it was colder than sixty below, than seventy below. It was seventy-five below zero. Since the freezing-point is thirty-two above zero, it meant that one hundred and seven degrees of frost obtained.

5    The dog did not know anything about thermometers. Possibly in its brain there was no sharp consciousness of a condition of very cold such as was in the man's brain. But the brute had its instinct. It experienced a vague but menacing apprehension that subdued it and made it slink along at the man's heels, and that made it question eagerly every unwonted movement of the man as if expecting him to go into camp or to seek shelter somewhere and build a fire. The dog had learned fire, and it wanted fire, or else to burrow under the snow and cuddle its warmth away from the air.

**7.  What is the main idea of this excerpt?**
- **A**  The man has more knowledge than the dog.
- **B**  The man and dog share the same experiences.
- **C**  The man and dog are dependent on each other.
- **D**  The dog has survival instincts that the man lacks.

8.  **Which detail from the passage shows that the man is not prepared for the environment?**

F  he was long used to it

G  he was without imagination

H  He was quick and alert in the things of life

J  Such fact impressed him as being cold

9.  **Read this excerpt from the text.**

> The animal was depressed by the tremendous cold. It knew that it was no time for travelling. Its instinct told it a truer tale than was told to the man by the man's judgment. In reality, it was not merely colder than fifty below zero; it was colder than sixty below, than seventy below. It was seventy-five below zero. Since the freezing-point is thirty-two above zero, it meant that one hundred and seven degrees of frost obtained.

**What is the main idea of this excerpt?**

A  The dog is like a wild wolf.

B  The dog trusts the man's judgment.

C  The dog knows how cold it really is.

D  The dog can tolerate the cold better than the man.

10.  **Which phrase would best express the main idea of the passage?**

F  happiness or sadness

G  instinct or knowledge

H  mortality or immortality

J  experience or inexperience

11.  **Read this sentence from the text.**

> The animal was depressed by the tremendous cold.

**What does the word tremendous mean as it is used in this sentence?**

A  excellent

B  extreme

C  large

D  vast

12.  **Which of these statements is true about the main idea of the passage?**

F  The reader can infer the main idea through details.

G  The writer wants the reader to provide the main idea.

H  The writer directly states the main idea in a topic sentence.

J  The main idea is obvious and, therefore, does not need to be stated.

---

### ✔ Test-Taking Tip

The more you practice reading different types of texts of different lengths, the better prepared you will be to read and understand passages presented in reading tests. A good way to practice is to read as much as you can about subjects that interest you. Not only will you become a better reader when taking a test, you will also increase your enjoyment of reading.

---

# Language Practice

Commas are used in a number of situations, such as to separate items in a series, to separate introductory information, to separate independent ideas, and to separate text that provides additional details.

**Directions:** Read the draft of an article. Then do Numbers 13 through 16.

1    Reality television is not a new phenomenon. In fact reality shows like *Candid Camera* and *What's My Line* were hits in television's earliest days. PBS broke new ground in 1973 with *An American Family* by following the Loud family as they went about their everyday life and when the Louds decided on camera to divorce, millions of viewers were shocked.

2    By the 2000s reality television shows were common on nearly every network. The shows were clearly entertaining to viewers but they were also cheaper to make than scripted shows. A typical reality show uses a smaller crew, hires fewer performers, needs fewer sets, and requires very few writers. These less-expensive shows give networks a larger profit margin so hit reality shows mean big money.

**13.** **Which version of the first underlined sentence in Paragraph 1 is punctuated correctly?**

   **A** In fact, reality shows like *Candid Camera* and *What's My Line* were hits in television's earliest days.

   **B** In fact reality shows, like *Candid Camera* and *What's My Line* were hits in television's earliest days.

   **C** In fact reality shows like *Candid Camera* and *What's My Line* were hits in television's earliest days.

   **D** In fact reality, shows like *Candid Camera* and *What's My Line* were hits in television's earliest days.

**14.** **Which version of the second underlined sentence in Paragraph 1 uses a comma or commas to separate independent ideas?**

   **F** PBS broke new ground in 1973 with *An American Family* by following the Loud family as they went about their everyday life and when the Louds decided on camera to divorce, millions of viewers were shocked.

   **G** PBS broke new ground in 1973 with *An American Family* by following the Loud family as they went about their everyday life, and, when the Louds decided on camera to divorce, millions of viewers were shocked.

   **H** PBS broke new ground in 1973 with *An American Family* by following the Loud family as they went about their everyday life, and when the Louds decided on camera to divorce, millions of viewers were shocked.

   **J** PBS broke new ground in 1973 with *An American Family* by following the Loud family as they went about their everyday life. And, when the Louds decided on camera to divorce, millions of viewers were shocked.

15. **Which version of the first underlined sentence in Paragraph 2 makes proper use of commas to separate additional information?**

   A  The shows were clearly entertaining to viewers but they were also cheaper to make than scripted shows.

   B  The shows were clearly entertaining to viewers, but they were also cheaper to make than scripted shows.

   C  The shows were clearly entertaining to viewers but, they were also cheaper to make than scripted shows.

   D  The shows were clearly entertaining to viewers, but, they were also cheaper to make than scripted shows.

16. **Which version of the second underlined sentence in Paragraph 2 is punctuated correctly?**

   F  These less-expensive shows give networks a larger profit margin so hit reality shows mean big money.

   G  These less-expensive shows give networks a larger profit margin. So, hit reality shows mean big money.

   H  These less-expensive shows give networks a larger profit margin so, hit reality shows mean big money.

   J  These less-expensive shows give networks a larger profit margin, so hit reality shows mean big money.

---

### ✅ Test-Taking Tip

Some language questions may have phrases or sentences from a passage as answer choices. The answer choices may have subtle differences, such as the placement of a comma. Scan each answer choice to see how they differ. Then read the answer choices in the context of the passage to determine the correct answer.

---

# Writing Practice

As you have learned, writers at times do not directly state the main idea of a text in a topic sentence. Instead, the idea may unfold over the course of many paragraphs. It often is implied through text details rather than stated outright. This is true in nonfiction as well as fictional texts.

**Directions:** Write an explanatory text that clearly and concisely summarizes the following excerpt from an essay by sociologist and historian W.E.B. DuBois in your own words. Explain the implied main idea of the text, and effectively select and include details from the text that support that idea.

## From *The Souls of Black Folk*

*by W.E.B. DuBois*

And yet, being a problem is a strange experience,—peculiar even for one who has never been anything else, save perhaps in babyhood and in Europe. It is in the early days of rollicking boyhood that the revelation first bursts upon one, all in a day, as it were. I remember well when the shadow swept across me. I was a little thing, away up in the hills of New England, where the dark Housatonic winds between Hoosac and Taghkanic to the sea. In a wee wooden schoolhouse, something put it into the boys' and girls' heads to buy gorgeous visiting-cards—ten cents a package—and exchange. The exchange was merry, till one girl, a tall newcomer, refused my card,—refused it peremptorily [arrogantly], with a glance. Then it dawned upon me with a certain suddenness that I was different from the others; or like, mayhap, in heart and life and longing, but shut out from their world by a vast veil. I had thereafter no desire to tear down that veil, to creep through; I held all beyond it in common contempt, and lived above it in a region of blue sky and great wandering shadows. That sky was bluest when I could beat my mates at examination-time, or beat them at a foot-race, or even beat their stringy heads. Alas, with the years all this fine contempt began to fade; for the words I longed for, and all their dazzling opportunities, were theirs, not mine. But they should not keep these prizes, I said; some, all, I would wrest from them. Just how I would do it I could never decide: by reading law, by healing the sick, by telling the wonderful tales that swam in my head,—some way. With other black boys the strife was not so fiercely sunny: their youth shrunk into tasteless sycophancy [flattery of those with more power], or into silent hatred of the pale world about them and mocking distrust of everything white; or wasted itself in a bitter cry, Why did God make me an outcast and a stranger in mine own house? The shades of the prison-house closed round about us all: walls strait and stubborn to the whitest, but relentlessly narrow, tall, and unscalable to sons of night who must plod darkly on in resignation, or beat unavailing palms against the stone, or steadily, half hopelessly, watch the streak of blue above.

_____

_____

_____

_____

_____

_____

_____

This lesson will help you practice identifying supporting details in two informational texts. Use it with Core Lesson 1.2 *Identify Supporting Details* to reinforce and apply your knowledge.

| Key Concept | Core Skills |
|---|---|
| Supporting details are concrete ideas that develop the main idea in a passage. There are many types of supporting details. | • Identify Supporting Details<br>• Cite Details |

## Identifying Supporting Details

The main idea of a passage is its most important idea. Supporting details are ideas in sentences and paragraphs that support this main idea. The supporting details in a text may include facts, examples, reasons, and descriptions.

**Directions:** Read the text. Then do Numbers 1–5.

## Civilizations Begin To Interact

1    The Middle East and the coastal regions of the Mediterranean Sea, as well as the Nile Delta, were the locations for the beginning of many early civilizations, including Egyptian, Babylonian, Sumerian, Phoenician, Persian, and Greek. The close proximity of these civilizations allowed for trade and also created competition for land and resources. The interaction among various cultures created changes in and exchanges of traditions and technology

2    The classical civilizations that had the largest impact on the world's cultural development are the Greek and Roman Empires. Greek civilization continued the Egyptian priorities of art, literature, music, theater, architecture, and the sciences. The first major citizen participation in government occurred in ancient Athens, a powerful Greek city-state. All male citizens participated in the assembly, which determined laws and policies.

3    During the golden age of ancient Greece (500 BCE to 300 BCE, before the common era), many great philosophers and educators such as Socrates, Plato, and Aristotle shared their wisdom with the world. For the first time, the improvement of the mind and the body was viewed as an important priority for society. The challenge of improved physical fitness was the reason why the Olympic Games began in ancient Greece.

4    Eventually the Romans conquered the Greeks, copying their architecture, art forms, and poetry, and even some of their mythological gods. The Greeks and the Romans had maintained early people's practice of using myth to explain natural phenomena such as seasonal changes, flooding and severe weather, and success in agriculture. To make the myths easier to understand and appreciate, the Greeks and Romans had gods with human attributes. Greek and Roman mythology has continued to exist even after our understanding of the universe had outgrown the need for storylike explanations. Many of the planets, including Jupiter, Neptune, Mars, Venus, and Mercury, were named for Roman gods.

5    The Romans were interested in military strength and acquiring land for the empire. Thus, athletic competition and training for combat as a form of entertainment developed in Rome. The Roman government differed from the Athenian model. One, two, or sometimes three consuls were chosen by the Roman senate, a group of the wealthiest landholders, or patricians. The vast majority of the citizens were plebeians—the small farmers, tradesmen, artisans, and merchants.

*(Continued on next page)*

6    Wealth and connections among family members thus determined position in the social classes within Roman culture. This status determined whether a member of the society was considered to be worthy of having a vote. The Roman system of government was called a republic. The lower class of slaves and the common class of farmers and tradesmen were limited in their rights of marriage partners and land ownership.

7    One lasting contribution of the Romans was the calendar introduced by Julius Caesar in 46 BCE. Caesar made the months of unequal days and added leap years to make the reckoning more equal to an actual year. This Julian calendar, with some modifications, is still in use today.

1.  **Which term describes the type of details used in the passage to provide information about mythology and the calendar?**

    A  insignificant

    B  main

    C  precise

    D  supporting

2.  **Which detail supports the main idea that Greek and Roman empires contributed to the culture of the surrounding area?**

    F  The interaction among various cultures created changes in and exchanges of traditions and technology.

    G  For the first time, the improvement of the mind and the body was viewed as an important priority for society.

    H  The challenge of improved physical fitness was the reason why the Olympic Games began in ancient Greece.

    J  The vast majority of the citizens were plebeians—the small farmers, tradesmen, artisans, and merchants.

3.  **Read this excerpt from the text.**

    **Eventually the Romans conquered the Greeks, copying their architecture, art forms, and poetry, and even some of their mythological gods. The Greeks and the Romans had maintained early people's practice of using myth to explain natural phenomena such as seasonal changes, flooding and severe weather, and success in agriculture. To make the myths easier to understand and appreciate, the Greeks and Romans had gods with human attributes. Greek and Roman mythology has continued to exist even after our understanding of the universe had outgrown the need for storylike explanations. Many of the planets, including Jupiter, Neptune, Mars, Venus, and Mercury, were named for Roman gods.**

    **Which detail could be added to this paragraph to support its main idea?**

    A  When the Romans conquered the Greeks, much of Greek culture was destroyed.

    B  The Romans made many contributions to culture, including a series of roadways and aqueducts.

    C  Although Roman and Greek gods shared similar stories, they had different names and personalities.

    D  The Romans' astronomical discoveries included the discovery of several planets and the constellations.

4. **In which paragraph would you expect to find a supporting detail about the Greek government?**

   F   paragraph 2 (beginning with "The classical civilizations . . .")

   G   paragraph 3 (beginning with "During the golden age . . .")

   H   paragraph 4 (beginning with "Eventually the Romans conquered . . .")

   J   paragraph 5 (beginning with "The Romans were interested . . .")

5. **Which detail could be cited to support an idea about the structure of Roman society?**

   A   To make the myths easier to understand and appreciate, the Greeks and Romans had gods with human attributes.

   B   Thus, athletic competition and training for combat as a form of entertainment developed in Rome.

   C   One, two, or sometimes three consuls were chosen by the Roman senate, a group of the wealthiest landholders, or patricians.

   D   One lasting contribution of the Romans was the calendar introduced by Julius Caesar in 46 BCE.

## Using Details to Make Generalizations

Writers use many types of details to help readers understand a passage. By thinking carefully about these details, the reader can make generalizations, or broad statements about the topic of the text.

**Directions:** Read the text. Then do Numbers 6–9.

# From "Marshes"

*by the United States Environmental Protection Agency*

Marshes are defined as wetlands frequently or continually inundated with water, characterized by emergent soft-stemmed vegetation adapted to saturated soil conditions. There are many different kinds of marshes, ranging from the prairie potholes to the Everglades, coastal to inland, freshwater to saltwater. All types receive most of their water from surface water, and many marshes are also fed by groundwater. Nutrients are plentiful and the pH is usually neutral leading to an abundance of plant and animal life. . . . [W]e have divided marshes into two primary categories: non-tidal and tidal.

Marshes recharge groundwater supplies and moderate streamflow by providing water to streams. This is an especially important function during periods of drought. The presence of marshes in a watershed helps to reduce damage caused by floods by slowing and storing flood water. As water moves slowly through a marsh, sediment and other pollutants settle to the substrate, or floor of the marsh. Marsh vegetation and microorganisms also use excess nutrients for growth that can otherwise pollute surface water. . . . This wetland type is very important to preserving the quality of surface waters. In fact, marshes are so good at cleaning polluted waters that people are now building replicas of this wetland type to treat wastewater from farms, parking lots, and small sewage plants.

Non-tidal marshes are the most prevalent and widely distributed wetlands in North America. They are mostly freshwater marshes, although some are brackish or alkaline. They frequently occur along streams in poorly drained depressions, and in the shallow water along the boundaries of lakes, ponds, and rivers. Water levels in these wetlands generally vary from a few inches to two or three feet. . . . [S]ome marshes, like prairie potholes, may periodically dry out completely.

*(Continued on next page)*

TASC Test Exercise Book

11

It is easy to recognize a non-tidal marsh by its characteristic soils, vegetation, and wildlife. Highly organic, mineral rich soils of sand, silt, and clay underlie these wetlands. . . . [L]ily pads, cattails . . . , reeds, and bulrushes provide excellent habitat for waterfowl and other small mammals. . . . Prairie potholes, playa lakes, vernal pools, and wet meadows are all examples of non-tidal marshes.

Due to their high levels of nutrients, freshwater marshes are one of the most productive ecosystems on Earth. They can sustain a vast array of plant communities that in turn support a wide variety of wildlife within this vital wetland ecosystem. As a result, marshes sustain a diversity of life that is way out of proportion with its size. In addition . . . , non-tidal marshes serve to mitigate flood damage and filter excess nutrients from surface runoff.

Unfortunately, like many other wetland ecosystems, freshwater marshes have suffered major acreage losses to human development. Some have been degraded by excessive deposits of nutrients and sediment from construction and farming. Severe flooding and nutrient deposition to downstream waters have often followed marsh destruction and degradation. Such environmental problems prove the vital roles these wetlands play. This realization has spurred enhanced protection and restoration of marsh ecosystems. . . .

Tidal marshes can be found along protected coastlines in middle and high latitudes worldwide. They are most prevalent in the United States on the eastern coast from Maine to Florida and continuing on to Louisiana and Texas along the Gulf of Mexico. Some are freshwater marshes, others are brackish (somewhat salty), and still others are saline (salty). . . . [T]hey are all influenced by the motion of ocean tides. Tidal marshes are normally categorized into two distinct zones, the lower or intertidal marsh and the upper or high marsh.

In saline tidal marshes, the lower marsh is normally covered and exposed daily by the tide. It is predominantly covered by the tall form of Smooth Cordgrass. . . . The saline marsh is covered by water only sporadically, and is characterized by Short Smooth Cordgrass, Spike Grass, and Saltmeadow Rush. . . . Saline marshes support a highly specialized set of life adapted for saline conditions. . . .

Tidal marshes serve many important functions. They buffer stormy seas, slow shoreline erosion, and are able to absorb excess nutrients before they reach the oceans and estuaries. High concentrations of nutrients can cause oxygen levels low enough to harm wildlife. . . . Tidal marshes also provide vital food and habitat for clams, crabs, and juvenile fish, as well as offering shelter and nesting sites for several species of migratory waterfowl.

Pressure to fill in these wetlands for coastal development has lead to significant and continuing losses of tidal marshes, especially along the Atlantic coast. Pollution . . . also remains a serious threat to these ecosystems. Fortunately, most states have enacted special laws to protect tidal marshes, but much diligence is needed to assure that these protective measures are actively enforced.

6. **Read this excerpt from the text.**

   > Marshes are defined as wetlands frequently or continually inundated with water, characterized by emergent soft-stemmed vegetation adapted to saturated soil conditions. There are many different kinds of marshes, ranging from the prairie potholes to the Everglades, coastal to inland, freshwater to saltwater. All types receive most of their water from surface water, and many marshes are also fed by groundwater. Nutrients are plentiful and the pH is usually neutral leading to an abundance of plant and animal life. . . . [W]e have divided marshes into two primary categories: non-tidal and tidal.

   **Which generalization could be drawn from the details in this paragraph?**

   F Marshes are inhospitable to many animal and plant species.

   G Marshes are very fragile and highly susceptible to droughts and flooding.

   H Marshes can be found in many geographic locations across the United States.

   J Marshes, because of their plentiful water, provide an excellent location for the development of new housing.

7. **Which detail supports the generalization that marshes are important to water quality?**

   A We have divided marshes into two primary categories: non-tidal and tidal.

   B As water moves slowly through a marsh, sediment and other pollutants settle to the substrate, or floor of the marsh.

   C Tidal marshes can be found along protected coastlines in middle and high latitudes worldwide.

   D Pressure to fill in these wetlands for coastal development has led to significant and continuing losses of tidal marshes, especially along the Atlantic coast.

8. **Which detail provides an example to support the generalization that marshes have diversity in their ecosystems?**

   F They frequently occur along streams in poorly drained depressions, and in the shallow water along the boundaries of lakes, ponds, and rivers.

   G Water levels in these wetlands generally vary from a few inches to two or three feet. . . .

   H Lily pads, cattails . . . , reeds, and bulrushes provide excellent habitat for waterfowl and other small mammals.

   J Unfortunately, like many other wetland ecosystems, freshwater marshes have suffered major acreage losses to human development.

9. **Read this sentence from the passage.**

   > They buffer stormy seas, slow shoreline erosion, and are able to absorb excess nutrients before they reach the oceans and estuaries.

   **What does the word _absorb_ mean as it is used in this sentence?**

   A to take in or soak up

   B to occupy completely

   C to spread across a large area

   D to capture someone's attention

## Language Practice

A complete sentence must have a subject and predicate. It must be able to stand alone. When you write, check your text for sentence fragments. Change fragments into complete sentences.

**Directions:** For Numbers 10 through 13, read the questions and choose the best answer.

10. **Which of the following is a complete sentence?**
    F  One of my favorites is the distinctive octopus.
    G  One of my favorites, although it is hard to choose.
    H  One of my favorites, the incredibly flexible octopus.
    J  One of my favorites among the thousands of creatures I have seen.

11. **Which of the following is a complete sentence?**
    A  A gigantic head attached to eight wiggly arms, not to mention its squishy, flexible body.
    B  A gigantic head attached to eight wiggly arms makes the octopus different from many animals.
    C  A gigantic head attached to eight wiggly arms, large eyes, spotted skin, and incredible flexibility.
    D  A gigantic head attached to eight wiggly arms and the fact that it is found in oceans around the world.

12. **Which of the following is not a fragment?**
    F  Using specialized pigment cells, located in the muscles of its skin.
    G  Using specialized pigment cells, creating a variety of colors and patterns.
    H  Using specialized pigment cells, it can blend in with almost any environment.
    J  Using specialized pigment cells, changing the color of its skin to match its environment.

13. **Which of the following contains a subject and a predicate and can stand alone?**
    A  When it is discovered, great, thick clouds of black ink.
    B  When it is discovered, which does not occur frequently.
    C  When it is discovered, by a predator or even a diver like myself.
    D  When it is discovered, the octopus can release a puff of black ink.

### ✓ Test-Taking Tip

When you are taking a test, be an active reader. Underlining words in the passage or taking notes on scratch paper will help you find important details when you are answering questions. Later you can use your notes to determine a main idea or to make generalizations.

# Writing Practice

As you have learned, the main idea is the most important idea in a passage. Supporting details are facts, examples, reasons, and descriptions that reinforce the main idea. Both elements are essential to clear and effective writing.

**Directions:** Write an informative text about the lasting impact of cultural developments from ancient Greek and Roman civilizations, based on the information in the passage on pages 9 and 10. Include a clearly stated main idea and develop it by selecting the most significant and relevant supporting details from the passage, including facts, quotations, examples, and other information.

_____

_____

_____

_____

_____

_____

_____

_____

_____

_____

_____

_____

_____

_____

_____

_____

_____

This lesson will help you practice identifying directly stated main ideas and implied main ideas from supporting details. Use it with Core Lesson 1.3 *Identify Direct and Implied Main Ideas* to reinforce and apply your knowledge.

| Key Concept | Core Skills |
|---|---|
| The main idea may be stated directly in a topic sentence or sentences, or it may be implied. An implied main idea must be inferred from supporting details. | • Determine Implied Main Ideas<br>• Use Details to Deduce Central and Supporting Ideas |

## Direct and Implied Main Ideas

In some texts, the main idea may be directly stated. In others, the main idea is implied, or expressed indirectly, through the details in the text. To figure out the implied main idea, you need to think about what the details are about and how they are related to each other.

**Directions:** Read the text. Then do Number 1–4.

# Early Domestic and Foreign Policy

1    The years between 1791 and 1803 saw the United States expand geographically. Between 1791 and 1796, Vermont, Kentucky, and Tennessee were admitted to the Union under the administration of George Washington, the first president. In 1803, under President Thomas Jefferson, Ohio was admitted to the Union, and the largest acquisition of land for the United States occurred with the Louisiana Purchase. By paying France $15 million for the territory, Jefferson doubled the size of the country. He subsequently appointed Lewis and Clark to explore the acquired territory.

**The Monroe Doctrine**

2    A strong sense of nationalism developed after the War of 1812. For the first time the United States could afford to look inward and pay less attention to European affairs. As a result, westward expansion continued, with victories over several Native American tribes.

3    In 1823 President James Monroe proclaimed to the world that European powers would no longer be allowed to colonize the Americas. He indicated that the United States would remain neutral in European conflicts as long as the European powers left the emerging republics in North and South America alone. Known as the Monroe Doctrine, this foreign policy statement marked the appearance of the United States on the world political stage.

**Jacksonian Democracy and the Mexican War**

4    After Monroe left office, sectionalism became a problem for the United States. Sectionalism refers to the political, cultural, and economic differences among regions of the country—in this case the agricultural South and West and the industrial Northeast. The conflicting demands that each section put upon the government caused great political turmoil.

5    The first United States president elected to office as a result of these factional differences was Andrew Jackson in 1828. A Southerner and hero in the War of 1812, Jackson was considered to be a populist, a man who represented the interests of the common people. He believed that *all* people, not just the propertied few, should have a voice in deciding how the government should be run.

*(Continued on next page)*

6    As the champion of the common people, Jackson opposed the establishment of a national bank because he believed that it would benefit only the wealthy and because he feared the Eastern merchants and industrialists would control it. Under Jacksonian democracy, farmers and craftspeople gained a louder voice in government than they had had under previous administrations. Despite pressure to annex Texas during his second term, Jackson refused, fearing a war with Mexico.

7    President James Polk, Jackson's successor, had no such fear. Congress, agreeing to the demands of the Texans, annexed the Texas Republic in 1845. Thus, the expansionist fervor in the United States was renewed. Manifest Destiny—the drive to extend the borders to the Pacific Ocean—became a rallying cry. When President Polk was unable to purchase the territory that included New Mexico and California, the United States declared war on Mexico in 1846 as a result of a territorial dispute between the two countries.

8    The Treaty of Guadalupe Hidalgo that ended the war in 1848 resulted in the United States gaining the land that would later become California, Utah, Nevada, and parts of Colorado, New Mexico, Arizona, and Wyoming. Thus, the United States had set its continental boundaries.

1.  **Which sentence best describes how the main idea is expressed?**
    **A**  It is stated explicitly.
    **B**  There is no main idea.
    **C**  It is implied through details.
    **D**  The reader creates the main idea.

2.  **Which sentence best expresses the main idea of the entire passage?**
    **F**  The Louisiana Purchase doubled the size of the country.
    **G**  Exploration of new lands was a priority of early Americans.
    **H**  Relationships between the United States and Mexico were strained.
    **J**  United States domestic and foreign policies have changed through the years.

3.  **Which sentence best expresses the main idea of the first paragraph?**
    **A**  The years between 1791 and 1803 saw the United States expand geographically.
    **B**  In 1803, . . . the largest acquisition of land for the United States occurred with the Louisiana Purchase.
    **C**  By paying France $15 million for the territory, Jefferson doubled the size of the country.
    **D**  He subsequently appointed Lewis and Clark to explore the acquired territory.

4.  **Which part of the passage best implies the main idea that the United States expanded through a territorial war with another country?**
    **F**  "Early Domestic and Foreign Policy" section
    **G**  paragraph 1 (beginning with "The years between 1791 and 1803 . . .")
    **H**  paragraphs 5 and 6 (beginning with "The first United States president . . .")
    **J**  paragraphs 7 and 8 (beginning with "President James Polk, Jackson's successor . . .")

## Implied Main Ideas and Supporting Details

The main idea of a text may be directly stated, but it is often implied. To identify an implied main idea, look for sentences that contain key phrases and details. Think about how these details are related.

**Directions:** Read the text. Then do Numbers 5–9.

## From "The Golden Windows"

*by Laura E. Richards*

All day long the little boy worked hard, in field and barn and shed, for his people were poor farmers, and could not pay a workman; but at sunset there came an hour that was all his own, for his father had given it to him. Then the boy would go up to the top of a hill and look across at another hill that rose some miles away. On this far hill stood a house with windows of clear gold and diamonds. They shone and blazed so that it made the boy wink to look at them: but after a while the people in the house put up shutters, as it seemed, and then it looked like any common farmhouse.

The boy supposed they did this because it was supper-time; and then he would go into the house and have his supper of bread and milk, and [go] to bed.

One day the boy's father called him and said: "You have been a good boy, and have earned a holiday. Take this day for your own; but remember that God gave it, and try to learn some good thing."

The boy thanked his father and kissed his mother; then he put a piece of bread in his pocket, and started off to find the house with the golden windows.

It was pleasant walking[, for h]is bare feet made marks in the white dust, and when he looked back, the footprints seemed to be following him, and making company for him. His shadow, too, kept beside him, and would dance or run with him as he pleased; so it was very cheerful. . . .

After a long time he came to a high green hill; and when he had climbed the hill, there was the house on the top; but it seemed that the shutters were up, for he could not see the golden windows. He came up to the house, and then he could well have wept, for the windows were of clear glass, like any others, and there was no gold anywhere about them.

A woman came to the door, and looked kindly at the boy, and asked him what he wanted.

"I saw the golden windows from our hilltop," he said, "and I came to see them, but now they are only glass." . . .

"We are poor farming people," she said, "and are not likely to have gold about our windows; but glass is better to see through."

She bade the boy sit down on the broad stone step at the door, and brought him a cup of milk and a cake, and bade him rest; then she called her daughter, a child of his own age, and nodded kindly at the two, and went back to her work.

The little girl was barefooted like himself, and wore a brown cotton gown, but her hair was golden like the windows he had seen, and her eyes were blue like the sky at noon. She led the boy about the farm, and showed him her black calf with the white star on its forehead, and he told her about his own at home, which was red like a chestnut, with four white feet. Then when they had eaten an apple together, and so had become friends, the boy asked her about the golden windows. The little girl nodded, and said she knew all about them, only he had mistaken the house. . . .

*(Continued on next page)*

"Come with me, and I will show you the house with the golden windows, and then you will see for yourself."

They went to a knoll that rose behind the farmhouse, and as they went the little girl told him that the golden windows could only be seen at a certain hour, about sunset. . . .

When they reached the top of the knoll, the girl turned and pointed; and there on a hill far away stood a house with windows of clear gold and diamond, just as he had seen them. And when they looked again, the boy saw that it was his own home.

Then he told the little girl that he must go; and he gave her his best pebble, the white one with the red band, that he had carried for a year in his pocket; and she gave him three horse-chestnuts, one red like satin, one spotted, and one white like milk. He kissed her, and promised to come again, but he did not tell her what he had learned; and so he went back down the hill, and the little girl stood in the sunset light and watched him.

The way home was long, and it was dark before the boy reached his father's house; but the lamplight and firelight shone through the windows, making them almost as bright as he had seen them from the hilltop; and when he opened the door, his mother came to kiss him, and his little sister ran to throw her arms about his neck, and his father looked up and smiled from his seat by the fire. . . .

"[H]ave you learned anything?" asked his father.

"Yes!" said the boy. "I have learned that our house has windows of gold and diamond."


5. **The boy's words and his actions at the top of both hills can help you determine**
   A the main idea
   B figurative language
   C the author's perspective
   D the writer's point of view

6. **Which sentence best describes how the main idea is presented in this passage?**
   F The main idea is stated as a topic sentence.
   G The main idea is stated at the end of the story.
   H The writer wants the reader to provide the main idea.
   J The reader can infer the main idea through the details.

7. **Which statement best describes the main idea of this passage?**
   A Hard work always pays off in the end.
   B Things are not always the way we see them.
   C Sometimes friends are the best kind of family.
   D Sometimes home is not the easiest place to stay.

8.  **Which excerpt from the passage best supports the main idea?**

    **F**  One day the boy's father called him and said: "You have been a good boy, and have earned a holiday.". . .

    **G**  She bade the boy sit down on the broad stone step at the door . . . and bade him rest; then she called her daughter, a child of his own age. . . .

    **H**  The little girl nodded, and said she knew all about them, only he had mistaken the house. . . .

    **J**  It was dark before the boy reached his father's house; but the lamplight and firelight shone through the windows . . .

9.  **Read this sentence from the passage.**

    **One day the boy's father called him and said: "You have been a good boy, and have earned a holiday."**

    **What does the word holiday mean as it is used in this sentence?**

    **A**  celebration

    **B**  time of relaxation

    **C**  date on a calendar

    **D**  religious feast day

## Language Practice

Sentences contain at least one independent clause, but they may also contain dependent clauses and phrases. All clauses contain a subject and a predicate. The subject names the person or thing that the sentence is about. The predicate, which always includes a verb, tells what the subject is or is doing. Phrases are grammatical clusters of words. They include:

- infinitive phrases (words grouped around the word *to* and the infinitive form of a verb),

- participial phrases (words grouped with a participle, or a form of a verb used as a noun or adjective),

- gerund phrases (words grouped with a gerund, or a form of a verb that ends in *–ing* and functions as a noun),

- and prepositional phrases (a preposition, or a word that indicates the relationship between a noun and other words in a sentence, and the words that accompany it).

Phrases may contain nouns and verbs, but they do not contain both a subject and a predicate.

Both phrases and clauses may modify nouns or verbs; thus, they can form part of the subject or predicate of a sentence. A phrase or clause may also be the subject or object in a sentence.

**10. Read these sentences.**

> Devon listened intently. Someone was <u>in the upstairs bedroom</u>.

**What is the function of the underlined prepositional phrase?**

**F**  The phrase describes where Devon is in the house.

**G**  The phrase clarifies the idea described in the previous sentence.

**H**  The phrase modifies the subject, *someone*, to describe the intruder.

**J**  The phrase modifies the verb, *was*, to give the location of the intruder.

**11. Read this sentence.**

> He wondered <u>whether his wife had come home early</u> but discarded the idea.

**What is the function of the underlined clause?**

**A**  It modifies the noun *wife*.

**B**  It modifies the subject, *he*.

**C**  It modifies the verb, *wondered*.

**D**  It functions as the object of the verb.

**12. Read this sentence.**

> <u>Clutching a heavy iron poker</u>, Devon tiptoed upstairs.

**What is the function of the underlined phrase?**

**F**  It modifies the verb, *tiptoed*.

**G**  It describes the subject, *Devon*.

**H**  It acts as the predicate of the sentence.

**J**  It functions as the subject of the sentence.

**13. Read this sentence.**

> He didn't want <u>to make a noise and alert the intruder</u>.

**What is the function of the underlined phrase?**

**A**  It modifies the verb *want*.

**B**  It describes the subject, *he*.

**C**  It acts as the object of the verb.

**D**  It functions as the subject of the sentence.

## ✔ Test-Taking Tip

Keep an eye on the time as you are taking the test. Plan ahead. Think about how much time you should spend on each section or on each question. Allow time at the end of the test to check your answers. Check periodically to make sure that you are on target to finish.

## Writing Practice

In fiction, main ideas often are implied rather than stated. The author develops the main idea through character and plot details. Then readers must use these details to infer the main idea.

**Directions:** Write an explanatory text that clearly and concisely summarizes "The Golden Windows" on pages 18 and 19 in your own words. Explain the implied main idea of the text, and effectively select and include details from the text that support that idea.

_____

_____

_____

_____

_____

_____

_____

_____

_____

_____

_____

_____

_____

_____

_____

_____

_____

_____

_____

This lesson will help you practice summarizing details in two passages. Use it with Core Lesson 1.4 *Summarize Details* to reinforce and apply your knowledge.

## Key Concept

Explaining the most important ideas in a passage in a concise way is called summarizing. A summary includes the main idea and the key supporting details.

## Core Skills

- Summarize Key Information
- Summarize a Text

## Summarizing Key Information

To write a concise and effective summary, you must first identify the most important points. Begin by identifying the main idea. Then identify the most important supporting details. Once these details are identified, paraphrase by restating the main idea and important supporting details in your own words.

**Directions:** Read the text. Then do Numbers 1–5.

## From *Up From Slavery: An Autobiography*

### by Booker T. Washington

The first pair of shoes that I recall wearing were wooden ones. They had rough leather on the top, but the bottoms, which were about an inch thick, were of wood. When I walked they made a fearful noise, and besides this they were very inconvenient, since there was no yielding to the natural pressure of the foot. In wearing them one presented [an] exceedingly awkward appearance. The most trying ordeal that I was forced to endure as a slave boy, however, was the wearing of a flax shirt. In the portion of Virginia where I lived it was common to use flax as part of the clothing for the slaves. That part of the flax from which our clothing was made was largely the refuse, which of course was the cheapest and roughest part. I can scarcely imagine any torture, except, perhaps, the pulling of a tooth, that is equal to that caused by putting on a new flax shirt for the first time. It is almost equal to the feeling that one would experience if he had a dozen or more chestnut burrs, or a hundred small pin-points, in contact with his flesh. Even to this day I can recall accurately the tortures that I underwent when putting on one of these garments. The fact that my flesh was soft and tender added to the pain. But I had no choice. I had to wear the flax shirt or none; and had it been left to me to choose, I should have chosen to wear no covering. In connection with the flax shirt, my brother John, who is several years older than I am, performed one of the most generous acts that I ever heard of one slave relative doing for another. On several occasions when I was being forced to wear a new flax shirt, he generously agreed to put it on in my stead and wear it for several days, till it was "broken in." Until I had grown to be quite a youth this single garment was all that I wore.

1. **The pain and discomfort of clothing made for slaves is**
   **A** a summary of the passage
   **B** a paraphrase of the passage
   **C** the main idea of the passage
   **D** a supporting detail in the passage

2. **Which sentence <u>best</u> paraphrases the main idea of the passage?**
   **F** New clothing was a luxury and a reward for slaves.
   **G** Clothing for slaves was simple, practical, and durable.
   **H** The comfort of slaves was not a factor in clothing choice.
   **J** The life of a slave was determined by which clothes he was given.

3. **Which supporting detail about Washington's wooden shoes would <u>most likely</u> be included in a summary of the passage?**
   **A** The shoe tops were made of rough leather.
   **B** The shoes made a fearful noise when he walked.
   **C** Someone wearing the shoes looked awkward and strange.
   **D** The wood sole did not give when the foot pressed against it.

4. **Which detail should be paraphrased and included in a summary of the passage?**
   **F** In the portion of Virginia where I lived it was common to use flax
   **G** That part of the flax from which our clothing was made was largely the refuse
   **H** I can scarcely imagine any torture . . . equal to . . . putting on a new flax shirt
   **J** Until I had grown to be quite a youth this single garment was all that I wore

5. **Read this sentence from the text.**

   **That part of the flax from which our clothing was made was largely the refuse, which of course was the cheapest and roughest part.**

   **What does the word <u>refuse</u> mean as it is used in this passage?**
   **A** decline
   **B** fabric
   **C** recycle
   **D** waste

---

 **Test-Taking Tip**

Many reading tests include passages followed by questions. One helpful strategy for planning your time is to take the total time allotted and divide it by the number of passages. This tells you how much time to spend on each section of the test.

---

## Summarizing a Text

To create an effective summary, paraphrase the main idea and the most important supporting details. These concise statements will tell what the passage is about. Often related details can be grouped into a single statement.

**Directions:** Read the text. Then do Numbers 6–11.

# From "Travel Alert"

*by the United States Department of State*

**Travel Alert**

U.S. DEPARTMENT OF STATE
Bureau of Consular Affairs

**Hurricane Season**

May 30, 2013

1   The Department of State alerts U.S. citizens to the upcoming hurricane season in the Atlantic, the Caribbean, and the Gulf of Mexico. Hurricane season in the Atlantic begins June 1 and ends November 30.

2   The National Oceanic and Atmospheric Administration's (NOAA) Climate Prediction Center . . . expects to see an active or extremely active season in the Atlantic Basin this year. [There is] a 70 percent chance of 13 to 20 named storms, of which seven to eleven are predicted to strengthen to a hurricane. . . . Of those, three to six are expected to become major hurricanes. . . . NOAA recommends that those in hurricane-prone regions begin preparations for the upcoming season now.

3   During and after some previous storms, U.S. citizens traveling abroad encountered dangerous and often uncomfortable conditions. [These conditions] lasted for several days while awaiting transportation back to the United States. In the past, many U.S. citizens were forced to delay travel . . . due to infrastructure damage to airports and limited flight availability. Roads were also washed out or obstructed by debris. [This damage adversely affected] access to airports and land routes out of affected areas. Reports of looting and sporadic violence in the aftermath of natural disasters have occurred. Security personnel may not always be readily available to assist. In the event of a hurricane, travelers should be aware that they may not be able to depart the area for 24–48 hours or longer.

4   If you travel to these areas during hurricane season, we recommend you obtain travel insurance to cover unexpected expenses during an emergency. [You may be in a situation that] requires an evacuation from an overseas location. [If so,] the U.S. Department of State will work with commercial airlines to ensure that U.S. citizens are repatriated as safely and efficiently as possible. Commercial airlines are the Department's primary source of transportation in an evacuation. [O]ther means of transport are utilized only as a last resort. The U.S. Department of State will not provide no-cost transportation, but does have the authority to provide repatriation loans to those in financial need.

5   If you live in or are traveling to storm-prone regions, prepare for hurricanes and tropical storms by organizing a kit in a waterproof container that includes a supply of bottled water, non-perishable food items, a battery-powered or hand-crank radio, any medications taken regularly, and vital documents. . . . Emergency shelters often provide only very basic resources and may have limited medical and food supplies. NOAA and the Federal Emergency Management Agency (FEMA) have additional tips on their websites.

6. **Read these sentences.**

   Hurricane season in the Atlantic runs through the summer and part of the fall. The area affected includes the Atlantic, the Caribbean, and the Gulf of Mexico. US citizens should read the following advice from the Department of State.

   **The statement above is**

   **F** a critique of the first paragraph

   **G** a paraphrase of the first paragraph

   **H** a direct quotation from the first paragraph

   **J** a supporting detail from the first paragraph

7. **Which sentence best paraphrases the main idea of the passage?**

   **A** People should use caution when traveling to other countries.

   **B** NOAA and FEMA are good sources of hurricane information.

   **C** As hurricane season approaches, people should make preparations.

   **D** The upcoming Atlantic hurricane season will be active and destructive.

8. **Which supporting detail is most important to include in the summary?**

   **F** [There is] a 70 percent chance of 13 to 20 storms

   **G** Of those, three to six are expected to become major hurricanes

   **H** [These conditions] lasted for several days while awaiting transportation back to the United States.

   **J** We recommend you obtain travel insurance to cover unexpected expenses during an emergency.

9. **Which sentence best summarizes the details in the third paragraph?**

   **A** Risks to travelers include delays, unsafe travel conditions, and risks to personal safety.

   **B** Drivers should be cautious during hurricane season as roadways may be washed away or have obstacles.

   **C** United States citizens often experience hardships such as looting and violence when traveling to other countries.

   **D** Security personnel may be too busy with other issues to help United States citizens traveling in hurricane-prone areas.

10. **Which text feature identifies important information that should be included in a summary of this passage?**

    F   date

    G   italicized text

    H   paragraph breaks

    J   boldfaced headings

11. **The following sentences paraphrase the passage's main idea and supporting details. Read the sentences, and then consider which combination of statements would be the best to use in a summary of the travel alert.**

    i.   It is likely that 13 to 20 named storms will occur this season.

    ii.  Travelers should consider bringing a well-stocked emergency kit.

    iii. Hurricane season affects certain regions from June through November.

    iv.  During hurricane season, travelers should be prepared for emergencies.

    v.   The NOAA does not recommend travel to other countries during hurricane season.

    vi.  Travelers should be prepared for unsafe and uncomfortable conditions after a hurricane.

    vii. Purchasing traveler's insurance can help travelers with the unexpected expense of emergency evacuation.

    A   i, ii, iv, v, vi

    B   i, iii, iv, v, vii

    C   ii, iii, iv, vi, vii

    D   ii, iv, v, vi, vii

 **Test-Taking Tip**

When reading test passages, it is tempting to read the questions and then skim the passage only to find the answers. Unfortunately, when you do not read the entire passage, you may miss important themes or details. The gaps can cause confusion, especially with questions that ask you to perform higher-level thinking skills such as summarizing or synthesizing information. Always take the time to read the passage thoroughly. Later you can skim the passage to find the details needed to answer questions.

## Writing Practice

When you tell a friend about a book or movie, you are providing a summary. Your summary might explain what conflicts the characters face, how a conflict is resolved, or why certain events are important. A summary that includes only the most important details will be precise and effective.

**Directions:** Write a summary of the excerpt from *Up From Slavery* on page 23. Begin by paraphrasing the main idea. Then select and briefly describe the most significant and relevant details that will help the reader understand important aspects of the passage. Conclude by explaining whether you think the passage is effective in conveying ideas and why (or why not).

_____

_____

_____

_____

_____

_____

_____

_____

_____

_____

_____

_____

_____

_____

_____

_____

_____

_____

This lesson will help you practice identifying a theme in two passages. Use it with Core Lesson 1.5 *Identify a Theme* to reinforce and apply your knowledge.

| **Key Concept** | **Core Skills** |
|---|---|
| The theme is the underlying meaning of a story. An author reveals the theme in a work of fiction through characters, setting, language, and other literary elements. | • Synthesize Details That Relate to Theme<br>• Understand the Relationships among Ideas |

## Using Fictional Elements to Determine Theme

The theme is the central message of a text, and it may express a belief or opinion about life. The theme, however, is not always stated; it may be implied. The author may reveal the theme through narrators' or characters' comments or actions.

**Directions:** Read the text. Then do Numbers 1–4.

### From "Legend of Tu-Tok-A-Nu'-La (El Capitan)" from *Myths and Legends of California and the Old Southwest*
*edited by Katherine Berry Judson*

Here were once two little boys living in the valley who went down to the river to swim. After paddling and splashing about to their hearts' content, they went on shore and crept up on a huge boulder which stood beside the water. They lay down in the warm sunshine to dry themselves, but fell asleep. They slept so soundly that they knew nothing, though the great boulder grew day by day, and rose night by night, until it lifted them up beyond the sight of their tribe, who looked for them everywhere.

The rock grew until the boys were lifted high into the heaven, even far up above the blue sky, until they scraped their faces against the moon. And still, year after year, among the clouds they slept.

Then there was held a great council of all the animals to bring the boys down from the top of the great rock. Every animal leaped as high as he could up the face of the rocky wall. Mouse could only jump as high as one's hand; Rat, twice as high. Then Raccoon tried; he could jump a little farther. One after another of the animals tried, and Grizzly Bear made a great leap far up the wall, but fell back. Last of all Lion tried, and he jumped farther than any other animal, but fell down upon his back. Then came tiny Measuring-Worm, [who] began to creep up the rock. Soon he reached as high as Raccoon had jumped, then as high as Bear, then as high as Lion's leap, and by and by he was out of sight, climbing up the face of the rock. For one whole snow, Measuring-Worm climbed the rock, and at last he reached the top. Then he wakened the boys, and came down the same way he went up, and brought them down safely to the ground. Therefore the rock is called Tutokanula, the measuring worm. But white men call it El Capitan.

1.  **The actions of Measuring-Worm express the story's central message, or**

    **A** theme

    **B** main idea

    **C** perspective

    **D** topic sentence

2.  **Which sentence best states the theme of the passage?**

    **F**  The strongest person will survive in the end.

    **G**  Never judge someone by the way he or she looks.

    **H**  When you work together, you can solve a problem.

    **J**  By making a continued effort, you will finish the job.

3.  **Which detail from the passage helps you understand the theme?**

    **A**  And still, year after year, among the clouds they slept.

    **B**  Then there was held a great council of all the animals to bring the boys down from the top of the great rock.

    **C**  Every animal leaped as high as he could up the face of the rocky wall.

    **D**  For one whole snow, Measuring-Worm climbed the rock, and at last he reached the top.

4.  **Read this sentence from the text.**

    **Then came tiny Measuring-Worm, [who] began to creep up the rock.**

    **Which definition fits the word creep as it is used in this sentence?**

    **F**  moving slowly, low to the ground

    **G**  a hateful, mean or unpleasant person

    **H**  spreading out or growing on a surface

    **J**  a feeling of things crawling on your body

## Synthesizing Multiple Main Ideas to Determine Theme

To determine the theme of a text, synthesize information from fictional elements such as setting, plot, characterization, point of view, language, and conflict. As you read, also think about the main idea of each paragraph and synthesize these to state the theme.

**Directions:** Read the text. Then do Numbers 5–8.

# From "The Ingenious Patriot" *from Fantastic Fables*

*by Ambrose Bierce*

Having obtained an audience of the King, an Ingenious Patriot pulled a paper from his pocket, saying:

"May it please your Majesty, I have here a formula for constructing armour-plating which no gun can pierce. If these plates are adopted in the Royal Navy, our warships will be invulnerable, and therefore invincible. Here, also, are reports of your Majesty's Ministers, attesting the value of the invention. I will part with my right in it for a million tumtums."

After examining the papers, the King put them away and promised him an order on the Lord High Treasurer of the Extortion Department for a million tumtums.

"And here," said the Ingenious Patriot, pulling another paper from another pocket, "are the working plans of a gun that I have invented, which will pierce that armour. Your Majesty's Royal Brother, the Emperor of Bang, is anxious to purchase it, but loyalty to your Majesty's throne and person constrains me to offer it first to your Majesty. The price is one million tumtums."

*(Continued on next page)*

Having received the promise of another check, he thrust his hand into still another pocket, remarking:

"The price of the irresistible gun would have been much greater, your Majesty, but for the fact that its missiles can be so effectively averted by my peculiar method of treating the armour plates with a new—"

The King signed to the Great Head Factotum to approach.

"Search this man," he said, "and report how many pockets he has."

"Forty-three, Sire," said the Great Head Factotum, completing the scrutiny.

"May it please your Majesty," cried the Ingenious Patriot, in terror, "one of them contains tobacco."

"Hold him up by the ankles and shake him," said the King; "then give him a check for forty-two million tumtums and put him to death. Let a decree issue declaring ingenuity a capital offence."

5. **How can the point of view help you understand the theme?**
   A Viewing events from the perspective of the Great Head Factotum, you learn a lesson about money.
   B Viewing events from the patriot's perspective, you learn the dangers of greed with those in authority.
   C Viewing events from the king's perspective, you understand how difficult it is to protect one's kingdom.
   D Viewing events from the narrator's perspective, you understand the lessons the king and the patriot learned.

6. **How is the author's characterization of the main character as a patriot helpful in understanding the theme?**
   F The character is penalized for his ingenuity and sales tactics.
   G The character calls himself loyal, but his actions show otherwise.
   H The character acts with cunning, and enriches himself by doing so.
   J The character presents himself as a trusted and wise adviser to the king.

7. **Which of the following sentences is the best statement of the passage's theme?**
   A Weapons are dangerous.
   B Rulers are not always fair.
   C You shouldn't always listen to wise advice.
   D You can't always trust what a person says.

8. **How can readers determine the theme of the story?**
   F by stating information from the characterization of the king and the patriot, the language used in the dialog, and the outcome of the interaction between the characters
   G by quoting information from the characterization of the king and the patriot, the language used in the dialog, and the outcome of the interaction between the characters
   H by synthesizing information from the characterization of the king and the patriot, the language used in the dialog, and the outcome of the interaction between the characters
   J by summarizing information from the characterization of the king and the patriot, the language used in the dialog, and the outcome of the interaction between the characters

**Test-Taking Tip**

Some test answers can be found directly in a passage. For others, such as identifying theme and implied main ideas, you might need to synthesize information from several places. When you synthesize, make a list of important ideas. Mark out any that are not relevant. Then look for ways that the ideas are connected.

## Writing Practice

Authors of literary texts can convey the theme of their stories in many different ways. For example, fables, myths, and legends often communicate a theme through their characters. Often, readers must synthesize information from various literary elements in order to determine the theme.

**Directions:** Write an explanatory text that examines and analyzes how to synthesize three or more literary elements to determine the theme of "Legend of Tu-Tok-A-Nu'-La (El Capitan)" on page 29. These elements might be characterization, setting, plot, language, and point of view. Include a summary of the story, a statement of the theme, and effectively selected details from the story to support your analysis.

This lesson will help you practice determining the sequence of events in two types of texts. Use it with Core Lesson 2.1 *Sequence Events* to reinforce and apply your knowledge.

## Key Concept

The sequence of events is the order in which the events in a text occur.

## Core Skills

- Sequence Information
- Use Text Features

## Sequence of Time

To fully comprehend narrative passages and procedural texts, readers need to understand the order of events or steps. When reading a passage, use transitions and text features to help determine the sequence of events.

**Directions:** Read the text. Then do Numbers 1–5.

# Athletic Shoes

Picking a pair of athletic shoes used to be easy. When only a few brands and styles of shoes existed, you could just choose the most comfortable pair. But today, athletic shoes are a multibillion-dollar business. With thousands of different styles, colors, and features, picking a pair of athletic shoes can be complicated. Nevertheless, there are ways to find the ideal pair of shoes.

First, you should choose different shoes for working out than for everyday use. For everyday shoes, comfort and appearance are the most important selection criteria. For exercising, finding the right shoe involves several factors. Consider the type of activities you will engage in. If you mainly participate in a specific sport or activity, such as running, walking, or playing tennis, you will want to get shoes designed specifically for that activity. Running shoes, for example, contain extra padding to make running easier on your feet. Tennis shoes contain extra padding to cushion the toes. Walking shoes are specially designed to help you walk quickly and effortlessly. If you participate in many sports, a pair of cross-training shoes is a good idea. These shoes have enough padding for runners, but they also meet the needs of other athletes.

After you have decided which kind of shoe you would like, begin to look at individual pairs of shoes. When you try on shoes, make sure you are wearing the same kind of socks that you will be wearing when you work out. Also make sure you do more than just look at the shoes in a mirror; take a short walk around the shoe department to determine how they feel. Make sure they fit snugly but are not too tight. The tip of the shoe should be roomy enough for you to wiggle your toes. If your feet are jammed in, you run the risk of injuring yourself.

Finally, look for style and special features. For example, if you run early in the morning or late at night, you should select shoes with reflective material so drivers can see you in the dark. If you are interested in measuring the distance that you run or walk, consider shoes with a built-in pedometer. If you have trouble with your feet, shoes filled with air or gel provide extra cushioning that could help.

After you buy your shoes, make sure you break them in before your first workout. As you continue to wear them, watch for signs of wear and tear. Worn-out shoes can be just as harmful to your feet as improper footwear.

1. **According to the passage, what was easy to do before so many brands and styles of athletic shoes existed?**

   **A** buy the top-selling brand

   **B** purchase a pair of athletic shoes

   **C** use one pair of shoes to cross-train

   **D** walk around the store with the shoes on

2. **Which transition word in the passage tells you that style and special features should be the last things to consider before purchasing shoes?**

   **F** after

   **G** finally

   **H** next

   **J** then

3. **Read this sentence from the text.**

   **When you try on shoes, make sure you are wearing the same kind of socks that you will be wearing when you work out.**

   **Which phrase would best replace "When you try on shoes," without changing the meaning of the sentence?**

   **A** Until you try on shoes

   **B** After you have tried on shoes

   **C** Subsequent to trying on shoes

   **D** While you are trying on shoes

4. **Read this sentence from the text.**

   **Worn-out shoes can be just as harmful to your feet as improper footwear.**

   **What does the word improper mean as it is used in this sentence?**

   **F** not in good taste

   **G** not current or trendy

   **H** not well suited to one's needs

   **J** not following cultural expectations

5. **According to the passage, which step should come first in finding the right athletic shoes?**

   **A** Break in your shoes.

   **B** Try on different shoes.

   **C** Decide what kind of shoes you need.

   **D** Consider additional features you want.

## Sequence in a Process

Transition words make it easy to understand the order of a procedure or a process. In some cases, text features such as headings can also help the reader understand the order of events or actions.

**Directions:** Read the text. Then do Numbers 6–9.

# From *Natural Gas Basics*

*by the United States Energy Information Administration*

**How Was Natural Gas Formed?**

The main ingredient in natural gas is methane, a gas (or compound) composed of one carbon atom and four hydrogen atoms. Millions of years ago, the remains of plants and animals (diatoms) decayed and built up in thick layers. This decayed matter from plants and animals is called organic material—it was once alive. . . . Pressure and heat changed some of this organic material into coal, some into oil (petroleum), and some into natural gas—tiny bubbles of odorless gas.

In some places, gas escapes from small gaps in the rocks into the air; then, if there is enough activation energy from lightning or a fire, it burns. When people first saw the flames, they experimented with them and learned they could use them for heat and light.

**How Do We Get Natural Gas?**

The search for natural gas begins with geologists, who study the structure and processes of the Earth. They locate the types of rock that are likely to contain gas and oil deposits.

Today, geologists' tools include seismic surveys that are used to find the right places to drill wells. Seismic surveys use echoes from a vibration source at the Earth's surface (usually a vibrating pad under a truck built for this purpose) to collect information about the rocks beneath. Sometimes it is necessary to use small amounts of dynamite to provide the vibration that is needed.

Scientists and engineers explore a chosen area by studying rock samples from the earth and taking measurements. If the site seems promising, drilling begins. Some of these areas are on land, but many are offshore, deep in the ocean. Once the gas is found, it flows up through the well to the surface of the ground and into large pipelines.

Some of the gases that are produced along with methane, such as butane and propane (also known as "by-products"), are separated and cleaned at a gas processing plant. The by-products, once removed, are used in a number of ways. For example, propane can be used for cooking on gas grills.

Dry natural gas is also known as consumer-grade natural gas. In addition to natural gas production, the United States gas supply is augmented by imports, withdrawals from storage, and by supplemental gaseous fuels.

Most of the natural gas consumed in the United States is produced in the United States. Some is imported from Canada and shipped to the United States in pipelines. A small amount of natural gas is shipped to the United States as liquefied natural gas (LNG).

We can also use machines called "digesters" that turn today's organic material (plants, animal wastes, etc.) into natural gas. This process replaces waiting for millions of years for the gas to form naturally.

6. The sequence of events noted in the section "How Was Natural Gas Formed?" describes a

   F   feature
   G   flashback
   H   process
   J   transition

7. Which description best explains how this text is arranged?

   A   two processes described in order of importance
   B   two processes described with interrupting flashbacks
   C   two processes described, each in chronological order
   D   two processes described, each in reverse chronological order

8. Which text feature helps indicate that the process of forming natural gas comes before the process of obtaining it?

   F   the title
   G   visual graphics
   H   underlined phrases
   J   boldfaced headings

9. On the basis of information in the section "How Do We Get Natural Gas?," which transition phrase would accurately complete the following sentence?

   **Scientists study samples and take measurements**

   A   after taking a seismic survey
   B   until taking a seismic survey
   C   while taking a seismic survey
   D   before taking a seismic survey

## Language Practice

Colons and semicolons are punctuation marks used to make complex sentences easier for the reader to understand. A colon is often used after a complete sentence introducing a list or quotation. A semicolon often separates two complete sentences; it indicates that the two sentences are closely related. The semicolon may be followed by a linking adverb to clarify the sentences' relationship. In this case, the linking adverb is followed by a comma if it is at the beginning of the second sentence and surrounded by commas if it is in the middle.

The best way to see the country is to travel on back roads narrow roads where two cars can barely pass one another, single-lane roads with turn-outs for passing, or dirt tracks. Once my friend and I were navigating one of those bumpy dirt tracks in our rented SUV when we rounded a bend and came nose to nose with a wooden gate. It was closed and fastened shut with a chain. On the gate was a sign "Don't let out the bull! Close gate after driving through!" I was taking my turn behind the wheel that meant it was up to Mary to open and close the gate. It took her at least a minute to wrestle the heavy chain from the gate, but she finally succeeded and swung the gate wide. I rolled the car forward, pulled on the handbrake, and leaned over to push open the passenger door. That's when I saw the bull. He had just seen us and was beginning to move in our direction. Mary had the gate closed however the chain was not cooperating. I looked back across the field. The bull was getting closer, and he was picking up speed.

10. **Which version of the first underlined sentence correctly uses commas, colons, and/or semicolons?**

    F   The best way to see the country is to travel on back roads; narrow roads where two cars can barely pass one another, single-lane roads with turn-outs for passing, or dirt tracks.

    G   The best way to see the country is to travel on back roads, narrow roads where two cars can barely pass one another; single-lane roads with turn-outs for passing; or dirt tracks.

    H   The best way to see the country is: to travel on back roads, narrow roads where two cars can barely pass one another, single-lane roads with turn-outs for passing, or dirt tracks.

    J   The best way to see the country is to travel on back roads: narrow roads where two cars can barely pass one another, single-lane roads with turn-outs for passing, or dirt tracks.

11. **Which version of the second underlined sentence correctly uses commas, colons, and/or semicolons?**

    A   On the gate was a sign: "Don't let out the bull! Close gate after driving through!"

    B   On the gate was: a sign, "Don't let out the bull! Close gate after driving through!"

    C   On the gate was a sign; "Don't let out the bull! Close gate after driving through!"

    D   On the gate, was a sign; "Don't let out the bull! Close gate after driving through!"

12. **Which version of the third underlined sentence correctly uses commas, colons, and/ or semicolons?**

    F   I was taking my turn behind the wheel. That meant: it was up to Mary to open and close the gate.

    G   I was taking my turn behind the wheel that meant it was up to Mary: to open and close the gate.

    H   I was taking my turn behind the wheel; that meant it was up to Mary to open and close the gate.

    J   I was taking my turn behind the wheel that meant it was up to Mary; to open and close the gate.

13. **Which version of the fourth underlined sentence correctly uses commas, colons, and/ or semicolons?**

    A   Mary had the gate closed: however, the chain was not cooperating.

    B   Mary had the gate closed, however: the chain was not cooperating.

    C   Mary had the gate closed; however, the chain was not cooperating.

    D   Mary had the gate closed, however; the chain was not cooperating.

### ✔ Test-Taking Tip

When you read a passage with headings on a test, take note of section headings that organize the passage. These headings can also help you find the correct answer to a test question. Later, when you read the questions, notice whether a question tells you where to look in the passage for an answer. Going straight to that section will help you find the information quickly.

## Writing Practice

Sometimes when telling stories about a past event, events are described out of order. When you do this, it is important to use signal words and text features like headings to indicate that you are breaking from chronological order.

**Directions:** Write an informative text in which you effectively select details and accurately recount, in sequence, events described in the following article about the sinking of the Titanic. Use appropriate and varied transitions to link the sections of the text by including signal words and text features that make the sequence of events clear.

# From "Biggest Liner Plunges to the Bottom at 2:20 A.M. Rescuers There Too Late"

*from the New York Times*

CAPE RACE, N.F., April 15.—The White Star liner *Olympic* reports by wireless this evening that the Cunarder *Carpathia* reached, at daybreak this morning, the position from which wireless calls for help were sent out last night. [The *Titanic* sent these calls] after her collision with an iceberg. The *Carpathia* found only the lifeboats and the wreckage of what had been the biggest steamship afloat.

The *Titanic* had foundered at about 2:20 A.M., in latitude 41:16 north and longitude 50:14 west. This is about 30 minutes of latitude, or about 34 miles, due south of the position at which she struck the iceberg. All her boats are accounted for and about 655 souls have been saved of the crew and passengers. [Most] of the latter [are] presumably women and children.

There were about 2,100 persons aboard the *Titanic*.

The Leyland liner *California* is remaining and searching the position of the disaster, while the *Carpathia* is returning to New York with the survivors.

It can be positively stated that up to 11 o'clock tonight, nothing whatever had been received at or heard by the Marconi station here to the effect that the *Parisian*, *Virginian* or any other ships had picked up any survivors, other than those picked up by the *Carpathia*.

**First News of the Disaster**

The first news of the disaster to the *Titanic* was received by the Marconi wireless station here at 10:25 o'clock last night (as told in yesterday's New York Times). The Titanic was first heard giving the distress signal "C.Q.D.," which was answered by a number of ships, including the *Carpathia*, the *Baltic* and the *Olympic*. The Titanic said she had struck an iceberg and was in immediate need of assistance, giving her position as latitude 41:46 north and longitude 50:14 west.

At 10:55 o'clock the *Titanic* reported she was sinking by the head. [At] 11:25 o'clock the station here established communication with the Allan liner *Virginian*, from Halifax for Liverpool, and notified her of the Titanic's urgent need of assistance and gave her the *Titanic*'s position.

*(Continued on next page)*

The *Virginian* advised the Marconi station almost immediately that she was proceeding toward the scene of the disaster.

At 11:36 o'clock the *Titanic* informed the *Olympic* that they were putting the women off in boats and instructed the *Olympic* to have her boats ready to transfer the passengers.

The *Titanic*, during all this time, continued to give distress signals and to announce her position.

The wireless operator seemed absolutely cool and clear-headed. [His] sending throughout [was] steady and perfectly formed, and the judgment used by him was of the best.

The last signals heard from the *Titanic* were received at 12:27 A.M., when the *Virginian* reported having heard a few blurred signals which ended abruptly.

_____

_____

_____

_____

_____

_____

_____

_____

_____

_____

_____

_____

_____

_____

_____

This lesson will help you practice inferring relationships within two literary texts. Use it with Core Lesson 2.2 *Infer Relationships between Events, People, and Ideas* to reinforce and apply your knowledge.

### Key Concept

Making an inference is determining the most likely explanation for the given information.

### Core Skills

- Make Inferences
- Cite Evidence

## Inferring a Writer's Meaning

To make inferences about a text, use a combination of explicit details and implied information as clues. Then combine this information with your personal knowledge to draw conclusions about the relationships among characters, events, setting, and ideas in a text.

**Directions:** Read the text. Then do Numbers 1–5.

## From "Dick Baker's Cat"

*by Mark Twain*

One of my comrades . . . was one of the gentlest spirits that ever bore its patient cross in a weary exile: grave and simple Dick Baker, pocket-miner of Dead-Horse Gulch. He was forty-six, grey as a rat, earnest, thoughtful, slenderly educated, slouchily dressed and clay-soiled, but his heart was finer metal than any gold his shovel ever brought to light—than any, indeed, that ever was mined or minted.

Whenever he was out of luck and a little downhearted, he would fall to mourning over the loss of a wonderful cat he used to own. . . . [H]e always spoke of the strange sagacity of that cat with the air of a man who believed in his secret heart that there was something human about it— maybe even supernatural.

I heard him talking about this animal once. He said:

"Gentlemen, I used to have a cat here, by the name of Tom Quartz. . . . I had him here eight year—and he was the remarkablest cat *I* ever see. He was a large grey one of the Tom specie, an' he had more hard, natchral sense than any man in this camp. . . . He never ketched a rat in his life—'peared to be above it. He never cared for nothing but mining. He knowed more about mining . . . than any man *I* ever, ever see. You couldn't tell *him* noth'n 'bout placer-diggin's. . . . [A]s for pocket-mining, why he was just born for it. He would dig out after me an' Jim when we went over the hills prospect'n', and he would trot along behind us for as much as five mile. . . . [I]f the ground suited him, he would lay low 'n' keep dark till the first pan was washed. . . . [T]hen he would sidle up 'n' take a look, an' if there was about six or seven grains of gold *he* was satisfied. . . . [T]hen he would lay down on our coats and snore like a steamboat till we'd struck the pocket, an' then get up 'n' superintend. He was nearly lightnin' on superintending.

*(Continued on next page)*

"Well, by an' by, up comes this yer quartz excitement. Everybody was into it—everybody was pick'n' 'n' blast'n' instead of shovelin' dirt on the hillside—everybody was putt'n' down a shaft instead of scrapin' the surface. Noth'n' would do Jim, but *we* must tackle the ledges, too, 'n' so we did. We commenced putt'n' down a shaft. . . . Tom Quartz he begin to wonder what in the Dickens it was all about. *He* hadn't ever seen any mining like that before, 'n' he was all upset, as you may say—he couldn't come to a right understanding of it no way. . . . But that cat, you know, was *always* agin new-fangled arrangements. . . . *You* know how it is with old habits. But by an' by Tom Quartz begin to git sort of reconciled a little, though he never *could* altogether understand that eternal sinkin' of a shaft an' never pannin' out anything. At last he got to comin' down in the shaft, hisself, to try to cipher it out. An' when he'd git the blues . . . knowin' as he did, that the bills was runnin' up all the time an' we warn't makin' a cent—he would curl up on a gunny-sack in the corner an' go to sleep. Well, one day when the shaft was down about eight foot, the rock got so hard that we had to put in a blast—the first blast'n' we'd ever done since Tom Quartz was born. An' then we lit the fuse 'n' clumb out 'n' got off 'bout fifty yards—'n' forgot 'n' left Tom Quartz sound asleep on the gunny-sack. In 'bout a minute we seen a puff of smoke bust up out of the hole. . . . [E]verything let go with an awful crash. . . . [A]bout four million ton of rocks 'n' dirt 'n' smoke 'n' splinters shot up 'bout a mile an' a half into the air. . . .

[B]y George, right in the dead centre of it was old Tom Quartz a-goin' end over end, an' a-snortin' an' a-sneez'n, an' a-clawin' an' a-reach'n' for things like all possessed. . . . An' that was the last we see of *him* for about two minutes 'n' a half . . . [T]hen all of a sudden it begin to rain rocks and rubbage an' directly he come down ker-whoop about ten foot off f'm where we stood. Well, I reckon he was p'raps the orneriest-lookin' beast you ever see. One ear was sot back on his neck, 'n' his tail was stove up, 'n' his eye-winkers was singed off. . . . [H]e was all blacked up with powder an' smoke, an' all sloppy with mud 'n' slush f'm one end to the other. . . . He took a sort of a disgusted look at hisself, 'n' then he looked at us. . . . [T]hen he turned on his heel 'n' marched off home without ever saying another word.

"That was jest his style. . . . [A]fter that you never see a cat so prejudiced agin quartz-mining as what he was. . . .

I said, "Well, Mr. Baker, his prejudice against quartz-mining *was* remarkable, considering how he came by it. Couldn't you ever cure him of it?"

"*Cure him!* No! When Tom Quartz was sot once, he was *always* sot."

1. **Read this excerpt from the text.**

   **One of my comrades . . . was one of the gentlest spirits that ever bore its patient cross in a weary exile: grave and simple Dick Baker, pocket-miner of Dead-Horse Gulch. He was forty-six, grey as a rat, earnest, thoughtful, slenderly educated, slouchily dressed and clay-soiled, but his heart was finer metal than any gold his shovel ever brought to light—than any, indeed, that ever was mined or minted.**

   **On the basis of this excerpt, the reader can infer that the narrator considers Dick Baker to be**

   **A** clever but ultimately cruel

   **B** simple and uneducated but kind

   **C** well educated and a sharp dresser

   **D** good at mining but bad with money

2. **The narrator explicitly states that Dick Baker believes his cat has near-human intelligence. What does the narrator imply about his own personal opinion of the cat's ability?**

   F   Tom Quartz is smarter than Jim.

   G   The cat has amazing intelligence.

   H   Dogs are more intelligent than cats.

   J   The cat's near-human intelligence is doubtful.

3. **Read this excerpt from the text.**

   > [I]f the ground suited him, he would lay low 'n' keep dark till the first pan was washed. . . . [T]hen he would sidle up 'n' take a look, an' if there was about six or seven grains of gold *he* was satisfied. . . . [T]hen he would lay down on our coats and snore like a steamboat till we'd struck the pocket, an' then get up 'n' superintend. He was nearly lightnin' on superintending.

   **On the basis of the excerpt, the cat's behavior would be best described as**

   A   typical of a trained circus animal but not of a pet cat

   B   impressive for a cat, but regarded by its owner as unremarkable

   C   normal for most cats, but interpreted by the owner as humanlike

   D   so unbelievable that it would seem supernatural to most observers

4. **Read this excerpt from the text.**

   > Well, by an' by, up comes this yer quartz excitement. Everybody was into it—everybody was pick'n' 'n' blast'n' instead of shovelin' dirt on the hillside. . . . Tom Quartz he begin to wonder what in the Dickens it was all about. *He* hadn't ever seen any mining like that before, 'n' he was all upset, as you may say. . . . But that cat, you know, was *always* agin new-fangled arrangements. . . . But by an' by Tom Quartz begin to git sort of reconciled a little, though he never *could* altogether understand that eternal sinkin' of a shaft an' never pannin' out anything. . . . An' when he'd git the blues . . . knowin' as he did, that the bills was runnin' up all the time an' we warn't makin' a cent—he would curl up on a gunny-sack in the corner an' go to sleep.

   **Based on this description and the choice of words, what you can infer about the cat?**

   F   The cat does not think quartz is salable.

   G   The cat hopes to find a large supply of quartz.

   H   The cat thinks underground mining is not worthwhile.

   J   The cat prefers digging deep underground to searching the topsoil.

5. **From the description of what happens to Tom Quartz after Dick lights the fuse, you can infer that Dick feels the event was**

   A   amusing

   B   devastating

   C   frightening

   D   pleasing

# Citing Evidence

When making inferences about a text, a reader must look for evidence in the text. Evidence can include opinions, examples, and facts.

**Directions:** Read the text. Then do Numbers 6–9.

## From "An Open Door"

*by Anna Katharine Green*

1    It was a night to drive any man indoors. Not only was the darkness impenetrable, but the raw mist enveloping hill and valley made the open road anything but desirable to a belated wayfarer like myself.

2    Being young, untrammelled, and naturally indifferent to danger, I was not averse to adventure; and having my fortune to make, was always on the lookout for El Dorado, which to ardent souls lies ever beyond the next turning. Consequently, when I saw a light shimmering through the mist at my right, I resolved to make for it and the shelter it so opportunely offered.

3    But I did not realise then, as I do now, that shelter does not necessarily imply refuge, or I might not have undertaken this adventure with so light a heart. Yet who knows? The impulses of an unfettered spirit lean toward daring, and youth, as I have said, seeks the strange, the unknown, and sometimes the terrible.

4    My path towards this light was by no means an easy one. After confused wanderings through tangled hedges, and a struggle with obstacles of whose nature I received the most curious impression in the surrounding murk . . . I arrived in front of a long, low building, which, to my astonishment, I found standing with doors and windows open to the pervading mist, save for one square casement, through which the light shone from a row of candles placed on a long mahogany table.

5    The quiet and seeming emptiness of this odd and picturesque building made me pause. I am not much affected by visible danger, but this silent room, with its air of sinister expectancy, struck me most unpleasantly. . . . I was about to reconsider my first impulse and withdraw again to the road, when a second look thrown back upon the comfortable interior I was leaving convinced me of my folly, and sent me straight toward the door which stood so invitingly open.

6    But half-way up the path my progress was again stayed by the sight of a man issuing from the house I had so rashly looked upon as devoid of all human presence. He seemed in haste, and at the moment my eye first fell on him was engaged in replacing his watch in his pocket.

7    But he did not shut the door behind him, which I thought odd, especially as his final glance had been a backward one, and seemed to take in all the appointments of the place he was so hurriedly leaving.

8    As we met he raised his hat. This likewise struck me as peculiar, for the deference he displayed was more marked than that usually bestowed on strangers. . . . [H]is lack of surprise at an encounter more or less startling in such a mist, was calculated to puzzle an ordinary man like myself. Indeed, he was so little impressed by my presence there that he was for passing me without a word or any other hint of good-fellowship. . . . But this did not suit me. I was hungry, cold, and eager for creature comforts. . . . [T]he house before me gave forth, not only heat, but a savoury odour which in itself was an invitation hard to ignore. I therefore accosted the man.

*(Continued on next page)*

9   "Will bed and supper be provided for me here?" I asked. "I am tired out with a long tramp over the hills, and hungry enough to pay anything in reason—"

10   I stopped, for the man had disappeared. He had not paused at my appeal, and the mist had swallowed him. But at the break in my sentence his voice came back in good-natured tones, and I heard:

11   "Supper will be ready at nine, and there are beds for all. Enter, sir; you are the first to arrive, but the others cannot be far behind."

12   A queer greeting certainly. But when I strove to question him as to its meaning, his voice returned to me from such a distance that I doubted if my words had reached him any more than his answer had reached me.

13   "Well," thought I, "it isn't as if a lodging had been denied me. He invited me to enter, and enter I will."

14   The house, to which I now naturally directed a glance of much more careful scrutiny than before, was no ordinary farm-building, but a rambling old mansion. . . . Though furnished, warmed, and lighted with candles, . . . it had about it an air of disuse which made me feel myself an intruder, in spite of the welcome I had received. But I was not in a position to stand upon ceremony. . . . [E]re long I found myself inside the great room and before the blazing logs whose glow had lighted up the doorway and added its own attraction to the other allurements of the inviting place.

15   Though the open door made a draught which was anything but pleasant, I did not feel like closing it, and was astonished to observe the effect of the mist through the square thus left open to the night. It was not an agreeable one, and, instinctively turning my back upon that quarter of the room, I let my eyes roam over the wainscoted walls and the odd pieces of furniture which gave such an air of old-fashioned richness to the place. . . . But the solitude of the place . . . struck cold to my heart, and I missed the cheer rightfully belonging to such attractive surroundings.

**6.**   **In the first paragraph, the phrases "darkness impenetrable" and "raw mist enveloping hill and valley" are**

  **F**  inferences made by the reader about the story's setting

  **G**  examples explaining why it is not a good night to be outdoors

  **H**  facts about weather conditions in the region where the author lives

  **J**  opinions expressed by the narrator about current weather conditions

**7.**   **Read this sentence from the passage.**

> **The impulses of an unfettered spirit lean toward daring, and youth, as I have said, seeks the strange, the unknown, and sometimes the terrible.**

  **What does the word <u>unfettered</u> mean as it is used in this sentence?**

  **A**  unforgiving

  **B**  unguarded

  **C**  unnatural

  **D**  unrestrained

8. **Read this excerpt from the passage.**

> The house, to which I now naturally directed a glance of much more careful scrutiny than before, was no ordinary farm-building, but a rambling old mansion. . . . Though furnished, warmed, and lighted with candles, . . . it had about it an air of disuse which made me feel myself an intruder, in spite of the welcome I had received. But I was not in a position to stand upon ceremony. . . . [E]re long I found myself inside the great room and before the blazing logs whose glow had lighted up the doorway and added its own attraction to the other allurements of the inviting place.

**Which part of this paragraph could you cite to support the inference that the narrator feels uneasy in this setting?**

**F** The house . . . was no ordinary farm-building, but a rambling old mansion . . .

**G** Though furnished, warmed, and lighted with candles, . . . it had about it an air of disuse . . .

**H** . . . which made me feel myself an intruder, in spite of the welcome I had received.

**J** I found myself . . . before the blazing logs whose glow had . . . added its own attraction . . .

9. **Which sentence is a valid inference that a reader might make after reading the passage?**

**A** No one has ever lived in the house.

**B** The man leaving the house is the butler.

**C** Other people have been invited to the house.

**D** The narrator decides to leave the house immediately.

---

## ✓ Test-Taking Tip

Use your prior knowledge when making inferences about a passage on a test. Before reading the passage, read the title, study illustrations or graphics that accompany the text, and skim the passage for words that are highlighted or repeated. Then use what you already know about these words and ideas to predict which topics are likely to be discussed in the passage. While you read, combine details in the text with what you already know to make inferences that will help you understand what you are reading.

## Writing Practice

When writing, authors do not explain everything they want readers to know. Many details are implicit; readers must make inferences to understand the meaning of the text.

**Directions:** Write an explanatory text summarizing the excerpt from "An Open Door" on pages 43 and 44. In your summary, clarify the relationships among the setting, characters, and plot using concrete details and examples. Use these connections to analyze the content and to make inferences about the story.

_____

_____

_____

_____

_____

_____

_____

_____

_____

_____

_____

_____

_____

_____

_____

_____

_____

_____

This lesson will help you practice analyzing relationships among text elements in two literary passages. Use it with Core Lesson 2.3 *Analyze Relationships between Ideas* to reinforce and apply your knowledge.

## Key Concept

Relationships exist between different text elements—between characters, between characters and setting, between plot and setting, or between ideas.

## Core Skills

- Identify Literary Elements
- Analyze the Relationship between Plot and Setting

## Identifying Literary Elements

Literary texts, especially stories, contain certain key elements that help build the narrative, or the story that is being told. The key elements include plot, setting, theme, and character. Writers use characterization to describe their characters through details such as dialogue, actions, and descriptions.

**Directions:** Read the text. Then do Numbers 1–4.

## From *A Christmas Carol: A Ghost Story of Christmas*
### *by Charles Dickens*

Once upon a time—of all the good days in the year, on Christmas Eve—old Scrooge sat busy in his counting-house. It was cold, bleak, biting weather: foggy withal: and he could hear the people in the court outside, go wheezing up and down, beating their hands upon their breasts, and stamping their feet upon the pavement stones to warm them. The city clocks had only just gone three, but it was quite dark already—it had not been light all day—and candles were flaring in the windows of the neighbouring offices, like ruddy smears upon the palpable brown air. The fog came pouring in at every chink and keyhole, and was so dense without, that although the court was of the narrowest, the houses opposite were mere phantoms. To see the dingy cloud come drooping down, obscuring everything, one might have thought that Nature lived hard by, and was brewing on a large scale.

The door of Scrooge's counting-house was open that he might keep his eye upon his clerk, who in a dismal little cell beyond, a sort of tank, was copying letters. Scrooge had a very small fire, but the clerk's fire was so very much smaller that it looked like one coal. But he couldn't replenish it, for Scrooge kept the coal-box in his own room; and so surely as the clerk came in with the shovel, the master predicted that it would be necessary for them to part. Wherefore the clerk put on his white comforter, and tried to warm himself at the candle; in which effort, not being a man of a strong imagination, he failed.

"A merry Christmas, uncle! God save you!" cried a cheerful voice. It was the voice of Scrooge's nephew, who came upon him so quickly that this was the first intimation he had of his approach.

"Bah!" said Scrooge, "Humbug!"

He had so heated himself with rapid walking in the fog and frost, this nephew of Scrooge's, that he was all in a glow; his face was ruddy and handsome; his eyes sparkled, and his breath smoked again.

*(Continued on next page)*

"Christmas a humbug, uncle!" said Scrooge's nephew. "You don't mean that, I am sure?"

"I do," said Scrooge. "Merry Christmas! What right have you to be merry? What reason have you to be merry? You're poor enough."

"Come, then," returned the nephew gaily. "What right have you to be dismal? What reason have you to be morose? You're rich enough."

Scrooge having no better answer ready on the spur of the moment, said, "Bah!" again; and followed it up with "Humbug."

1. **Which detail from the passage describes the story's main character, Scrooge?**
   **A** He felt very cold.
   **B** He was in a bad mood.
   **C** He had a cheerful voice.
   **D** He did not have much money.

2. **The phrases "cold, bleak, biting weather: foggy withal" and "it had not been light all day" are details about the story's**
   **F** characters
   **G** narrative
   **H** setting
   **J** theme

3. **Which event is not part of the plot in this passage?**
   **A** Scrooge says, "Bah! Humbug!"
   **B** Scrooge walks through the fog.
   **C** Scrooge's nephew comes to visit his uncle.
   **D** Scrooge's clerk tries to warm himself with heat from a candle.

4. **Which quotation from the passage is an example of characterization?**
   **F** The city clocks had only just gone three . . .
   **G** candles were flaring in the windows of the neighbouring offices . . .
   **H** see the dingy cloud come drooping down . . .
   **J** his face was ruddy and handsome; his eyes sparkled . . .

## Analyzing Relationships in Text

When you read a text, the various relationships between the setting, characters, and events in the plot can help you understand or infer the story's theme.

**Directions:** Read the text. Then do Numbers 5–10.

# From *Room Number 3 and Other Detective Stories*
### by Anna Katharine Greene

"What door is that? You've opened all the others; why do you pass that one by?"

"Oh, that! That's only Number 3. A mere closet, gentlemen," responded the landlord in a pleasant voice. "To be sure, we sometimes use it as a sleeping-room when we are hard pushed. Jake, the clerk you saw below, used it last night. But it's not on our regular list. Do you want a peep at it?"

"Most assuredly. As you know, it's our duty to see every room in this house, whether it is on your regular list or not."

"All right. I haven't the key of this one with me. But—yes, I have. There, gentlemen!" he cried, unlocking the door and holding it open for them to look inside. "You see it no more answers the young lady's description than the others do. And I haven't another to show you. You have seen all those in front, and this is the last one in the rear. You'll have to believe our story. The old lady never put foot in this tavern."

The two men he addressed peered into the shadowy recesses before them, and one of them, a tall and uncommonly good-looking young man of stalwart build and unusually earnest manner, stepped softly inside. He was a gentleman farmer living near, recently appointed deputy sheriff on account of a recent outbreak of horse-stealing in the neighbourhood.

"I observe," he remarked, after a hurried glance about him, "that the paper on these walls is not at all like that she describes. She was very particular about the paper; said that it was of a muddy pink colour and had big scrolls on it which seemed to move and crawl about in whirls as you looked at it. This paper is blue and striped. Otherwise—"

"Let's go below," suggested his companion, who, from the deference with which his most casual word was received, was evidently a man of some authority. "It's cold here, and there are several new questions I should like to put to the young lady. Mr. Quimby,"—this to the landlord, "I've no doubt you are right, but we'll give this poor girl another chance. I believe in giving every one the utmost chance possible."

"My reputation is in your hands, Coroner Golden," was the quiet reply. Then, as they both turned, "my reputation against the word of an obviously demented girl."

The words made their own echo. As the third man moved to follow the other two into the hall, he seemed to catch this echo, for he involuntarily cast another look behind him as if expectant of some contradiction reaching him from the bare and melancholy walls he was leaving. But no such contradiction came. Instead, he appeared to read confirmation there of the landlord's plain and unembittered statement. The dull blue paper with its old-fashioned and uninteresting stripes seemed to have disfigured the walls for years. It was not only grimy with age, but showed here and there huge discoloured spots, especially around the stovepipe-hole high up on the left-hand side. Certainly he was a dreamer to doubt such plain evidences as these. Yet—

*(Continued on next page)*

Here his eye encountered Quimby's, and pulling himself up short, he hastily fell into the wake of his comrade now hastening down the narrow passage to the wider hall in front. Had it occurred to him to turn again before rounding the corner—but no, I doubt if he would have learned anything even then. The closing of a door by a careful hand—the slipping up behind him of an eager and noiseless step—what is there in these to re-awaken curiosity and fix suspicion? Nothing, when the man concerned is Jacob Quimby; nothing. Better that he failed to look back; it left his judgment freer for the question confronting him in the room below.

Three Forks Tavern has been long forgotten, but at the time of which I write it was a well-known but little-frequented house, situated just back of the highway on the verge of the forest lying between the two towns of Chester and Danton in southern Ohio. It was of ancient build, and had all the picturesqueness of age and the English traditions of its original builder. Though so near two thriving towns, it retained its own quality of apparent remoteness from city life and city ways. This in a measure was made possible by the nearness of the woods which almost enveloped it; but the character of the man who ran it had still more to do with it, his sympathies being entirely with the old, and not at all with the new. . . . This, while it appealed to a certain class of summer boarders, did not so much meet the wants of the casual traveller, so that while the house might from some reason or other be overfilled one night, it was just as likely to be almost empty the next. . . . The building itself was of wooden construction, high in front and low in the rear, with gables toward the highway, projecting here and there above a strip of rude old-fashioned carving. These gables were new, that is, they were only a century old; the portion now called the extension, in the passages of which we first found the men we have introduced to you, was the original house.

5. **Which statement best describes the relationship between the setting and plot of this passage?**
   A   Three men walk down a hallway of an old tavern.
   B   A man questions the sanity of a young woman involved in a crime.
   C   A conversation between three men reveals information about a crime.
   D   A man makes observations about a room possibly involved in a crime.

6. **Which statement describes the relationship between the characters and events in this passage?**
   F   A tavern owner cooperates with the investigation by a coroner and a deputy sheriff.
   G   A coroner convinces a suspicious deputy sheriff to investigate a local tavern owner.
   H   A demented young woman tells a deputy sheriff that a tavern owner committed a crime.
   J   A coroner and a deputy sheriff discover that a tavern owner is the prime suspect in a crime.

7. **Read this excerpt from the text.**

   **It was of ancient build, and had all the picturesquesness of age and the English traditions of its original builder. Though so near two thriving towns, it retained its own quality of apparent remoteness from city life and city ways. This in a measure was made possible by the nearness of the woods which almost enveloped it; but the character of the man who ran it had still more to do with it, his sympathies being entirely with the old, and not at all with the new. . . .**

   **Which phrase best describes the relationship between Three Forks Tavern and its owner?**
   A   The owner is indifferent to the tavern.
   B   The tavern has an impact on the owner's mood.
   C   The owner wants to keep the tavern from changing.
   D   The tavern is important in changing the owner's life.

**8.** A key detail that ties the story's plot to its setting is

   **F** the gable on the building

   **G** the striped blue wallpaper in Room 3

   **H** the fact that Room 3 is where Jake slept

   **J** the closeness of the tavern to Danton, Ohio

**9.** Read this sentence from the story.

> Though so near two thriving towns, it retained its own quality of apparent remoteness from city life and city ways.

What does the word <u>retained</u> mean as it is used in this sentence?

   **A** employed

   **B** preserved

   **C** remembered

   **D** restrained

**10.** Read this excerpt from the story.

> Had it occurred to him to turn again before rounding the corner—but no, I doubt if he would have learned anything even then. The closing of a door by a careful hand—the slipping up behind him of an eager and noiseless step—what is there in these to re-awaken curiosity and fix suspicion? Nothing, when the man concerned is Jacob Quimby; nothing.

The deputy sheriff's thoughts about Jacob Quimby could be evidence to support which of these themes?

   **F** the importance of considering other people's points of view

   **G** the importance of considering everyone to be a suspect at first

   **H** the importance of intuition and careful observations in judgments

   **J** the importance of being truthful and transparent about one's objectives

---

### ✔ Test-Taking Tip

Understanding what a question is asking is an important part of taking a test. Unfortunately, not all questions are simple and easy to understand. When you come across a long or complex question, especially one referring to a passage, read it carefully. Then try breaking the question into parts. For example: Does part of the question tell you where to look for the answer? What is the question asking you about the passage you read? What is the question asking or telling you about the answer options? Does the question throw in a "twist," such as asking which answer does <u>not</u> relate to the text?

## Writing Practice

Setting, character, and events often play interconnected roles in narratives. Events may be affected both by the environment and the characters involved. Characters and events may be mutually dependent as well.

**Directions:** Reread the excerpt from *A Christmas Carol* on pages 47 and 48. Then write an explanatory text that clarifies and analyzes how different elements of the story relate to each other. What is the relationship between the setting and the plot, between the setting and the characters, and between the characters and the events? How would these relationships change if any of the text elements were different? How would the excerpt's meaning change? Use details from the text to support your ideas. Convey information clearly and accurately through the effective selection, organization, and analysis of content.

_____

_____

_____

_____

_____

_____

_____

_____

_____

_____

_____

_____

_____

_____

_____

_____

This lesson will help you practice determining implicit relationships between ideas in two types of texts. Use it with Core Lesson 2.4 *Determine Implicit Relationships between Ideas* to reinforce and apply your knowledge.

## Key Concept

Just as ideas are sometimes implied by writers, so are the relationships between ideas. When this occurs, readers must find clues in the text to help them understand how the ideas connect.

## Core Skills

• Determine Implied Relationships between Ideas
• Predict Outcomes

## Interpreting Implied Relationships between Ideas

Authors sometimes present explicit ideas with implicit relationships among them. Readers often need to make inferences about these relationships for a full understanding of a text. Readers can use language structure, punctuation, and the proximity of words and ideas to support their inferences.

**Directions:** Read the text. Then do Numbers 1–4.

# Warm and Cold Air Masses

1   Humidity and temperature affect how an air mass or body of air interacts in the atmosphere. Air masses are created when a body of air takes on the characteristics from the land or water over which it forms. The central region of Canada usually creates cold and dry air masses. Air masses that form over the Gulf of Mexico are warm and have high humidity. The Pacific Northwest creates air masses that are cool but also humid. The air masses that begin over the southwestern region of the United States are often dry but warm. Meteorologists track these air masses to help them make weather forecasts. The air masses that move across the United States from west to east help meteorologists predict the weather.

2   Cold air masses tend to be unstable and turbulent and move faster than warm air masses. When a cold air mass comes into contact with a warm air mass, it forces the warmer air upwards. This forces any moisture in that air to condense quickly. The clouds that are formed by quick vertical air movements are cumulus clouds—puffy, cotton-like clouds. If the air is holding a great deal of moisture, the instant vertical draft creates a cumulonimbus or thunderhead. These are the storm clouds that drop a heavy load of precipitation quickly. Very often the quick rush of moist air will create a separation of electric charges within the cloud. This is how lightning is created. The release of the charged particles through the air superheats the individual air particles. They expand so fast that small sonic booms, or thunder, are heard.

3   Warm air masses are usually stable, and the wind that accompanies them is steady. Clouds that are formed by warm air masses are stratus clouds—low-lying, level clouds that in warm weather bring precipitation in the form of drizzle. As the warm air continues over the cooler air mass, the cloud formation becomes higher and thinner. The highest wispy clouds are cirrus clouds and do not contain enough moisture to bring precipitation.

*(Continued on next page)*

**Air Masses Cause Fronts**

4    A front occurs when two air masses collide and a boundary between the two masses forms. The weather for the land below is affected. Fronts may be either weak or strong. Strong fronts generally bring precipitation. When cold air acts like a plow and pushes warm air back, a cold front forms. If the cold air retreats, and the warm air pushes it away, a warm front occurs. Sometimes, the boundary between the two air masses does not move, and the front becomes stationary. Stationary fronts bring conditions similar to those brought by warm fronts. The precipitation that results, however, is usually milder and lasts longer.

5    More commonly, these collisions of fronts take place at the change of seasons. In the central part of the United States, spring means collisions of the newly arriving warm, moist air from the Gulf of Mexico with the retreating dry and cold air from central Canada. This annual springtime tradition generates the conditions that cause tornadoes. Tornadoes are the result of a very isolated strong updraft of warm, moist air. The rotation of the planet puts the circulation pattern of a counterclockwise spin into the updraft. (This is known as the Coriolis Effect and is demonstrated by all wind and water currents in both hemispheres. It is the reason the trade vessels in the Atlantic Ocean coming from Europe to North America must travel south to the equator instead of straight across the Atlantic.) Tornadoes may have wind speeds of up to 300 miles per hour, and they travel across the ground at around 30 miles per hour. Most tornadoes are produced in a region known as Tornado Alley: an area starting in the northern sections of Texas, through Oklahoma, Kansas, Missouri, and parts of Iowa and Illinois.

6    Hurricanes are also seasonal storms. As the energy from the sun leaves the northern hemisphere in the late summer, the oceans near the equator develop air mass and water-current low pressure systems. Hurricane season is August through October, when the conditions are right for the start of these large circulation patterns that are fueled by the warm ocean waters near the equator.

1.  **The word patterns at the beginning of paragraphs 2 and 3 make it clear that the author is**

    A   explaining how warm air masses slowly become cold air masses

    B   explaining how cold air masses slowly become warm air masses

    C   comparing similar characteristics of warm and cold air masses

    D   contrasting different characteristics of warm and cold air masses

2.  **In paragraph 1, what information is implied by explicit details about air masses?**

    F   Air masses in the Southwest are dry.

    G   Humidity affects how air masses interact.

    H   Air masses over the Gulf of Mexico are warm.

    J   The weather in central Canada is cold and dry.

3.  **Based on the details describing cold and warm air masses in paragraphs 2 and 3, a reader could infer that**

    A   cold air masses cause heavier rain than warm air masses

    B   the winds in warm air masses are gustier than in cold air masses

    C   rain only occurs when cold air masses come in contact with warm air masses

    D   puffy, cotton-like clouds form when warm air masses and cold air masses meet

4. **Based on the details in the text about storms, readers can logically infer that**

   F  tornadoes happen most often over water

   G  the Coriolis Effect causes hurricanes to have a clockwise spin

   H  tornadoes occur most often in northwestern states, like Oregon

   J  the Coriolis Effect causes hurricanes to have a counterclockwise spin

## Citing Evidence of Implied Relationships

When inferring the relationship between ideas, a reader must support inferences with evidence supporting the implied relationship. Based on this evidence, the reader can predict outcomes within the text or predict how this evidence may apply to other texts or to situations outside of one particular text.

**Directions:** Read the text. Then do Numbers 5–9.

# Supreme Court Decision on Repealing the Defense of Marriage Act (DOMA)

*Under the 1996 Defense of Marriage Act (DOMA), a state was not required to recognize the rights of same-sex couples who were married outside that state. However, in 2013, the United States Supreme Court agreed with the ruling of a lower court that DOMA's ban on federal benefits for same-sex couples is unconstitutional.*

DOMA's principal effect is to identify a subset of state-sanctioned marriages and make them unequal. The principal purpose is to impose inequality, not for other reasons like governmental efficiency. Responsibilities, as well as rights, enhance the dignity and integrity of the person. And DOMA contrives to deprive some couples married under the laws of their state, but not other couples, of both rights and responsibilities. By creating two contradictory marriage regimes within the same state, DOMA forces same-sex couples to live as married for the purpose of state law but unmarried for the purpose of federal law. [This diminishes] the stability and predictability of basic personal relations the state has found it proper to acknowledge and protect. By this dynamic DOMA undermines both the public and private significance of state-sanctioned same-sex marriages. . . . [It] tells those couples, and all the world, that their otherwise valid marriages are unworthy of federal recognition. This places same-sex couples in an unstable position of being in a second-tier marriage. The differentiation demeans the couple, whose moral and sexual choices the Constitution protects . . . and whose relationship the state has sought to dignify. And it humiliates tens of thousands of children now being raised by same-sex couples. The law in question makes it even more difficult for the children to understand the integrity and closeness of their own family and its concord with other families in their community and in their daily lives.

Under DOMA, same-sex married couples have their lives burdened . . . in visible and public ways. By its great reach, DOMA touches many aspects of married and family life, from the mundane to the profound. It prevents same-sex married couples from obtaining government healthcare benefits they would otherwise receive. . . . It deprives them of the Bankruptcy Code's special protections for domestic-support obligations. . . . It forces them to follow a complicated procedure to file their state and federal taxes jointly. . . . It prohibits them from being buried together in veterans' cemeteries. . . .

DOMA also brings financial harm to children of same-sex couples. It raises the cost of health care for families by taxing health benefits provided by employers to their workers' same-sex spouses. . . . And it denies or reduces benefits allowed to families upon the loss of a spouse and parent. . . .

*(Continued on next page)*

DOMA divests married same-sex couples of the duties and responsibilities that are an essential part of married life and that they in most cases would be honored to accept were DOMA not in force. For instance, because it is expected that spouses will support each other as they pursue educational opportunities, federal law takes into consideration a spouse's income in calculating a student's federal financial aid eligibility. . . . Same-sex married couples are exempt from this requirement. The same is true with respect to federal ethics rules. Federal executive and agency officials are prohibited from "participat[ing] personally and substantially" in matters as to which they or their spouses have a financial interest. . . . A similar statute prohibits senators, Senate employees, and their spouses from accepting high-value gifts from certain sources . . . , and another mandates detailed financial disclosures by numerous high-ranking officials and their spouses. . . . Under DOMA, however, these government-integrity rules do not apply to same-sex spouses. . . .

The class to which DOMA directs its restrictions and restraints are those persons who are joined in same-sex marriages made lawful by the state. DOMA singles out a class of persons deemed by a state entitled to recognition and protection to enhance their own liberty. It imposes a disability on the class by refusing to acknowledge a status the state finds to be dignified and proper. DOMA instructs all federal officials, and indeed all persons with whom same-sex couples interact, including their own children, that their marriage is less worthy than the marriages of others. The federal statute is invalid, for no legitimate purpose overcomes the purpose and effect to disparage and to injure those whom the state, by its marriage laws, sought to protect in personhood and dignity. By seeking to displace this protection and treating those persons as living in marriages less respected than others, the federal statute is in violation of the Fifth Amendment. This opinion and its holding are confined to those lawful marriages.

The judgment of the Court of Appeals for the Second Circuit is affirmed.

It is so ordered.

5. **Read this sentence from the text.**

   > **Under DOMA, however, these government-integrity rules do not apply to same-sex spouses. . . .**

   **This sentence is evidence to support which of the following predicted outcomes?**

   **A** The Supreme Court will uphold DOMA.

   **B** The Supreme Court will overturn DOMA.

   **C** The Supreme Court will uphold government-integrity rules.

   **D** The Supreme Court will overturn government-integrity rules.

6. **Which of these details helps the reader infer that the Supreme Court based its final decision on existing legislation?**

   **F** DOMA singles out a class of persons deemed by a state entitled to recognition and protection . . .

   **G** [DOMA] imposes a disability . . . by refusing to acknowledge a status the state finds to be dignified and proper . . .

   **H** [DOMA] is invalid, [and in displacing state] protection, [is] in violation of the Fifth Amendment.

   **J** [The Court's] opinion and its holding are confined to those lawful marriages [protected by the state].

7.  **Read this excerpt from the text.**

> Responsibilities, as well as rights, enhance the dignity and integrity of the person. And DOMA contrives to deprive some couples married under the laws of their state, but not other couples, of both rights and responsibilities.

**On the basis of the proximity of the two statements, what conclusion can readers infer?**

**A**  DOMA diminishes the dignity and integrity of all couples.

**B**  DOMA diminishes the dignity and integrity of some couples.

**C**  DOMA diminishes the rights and responsibilities of all couples.

**D**  DOMA diminishes the dignity and integrity of opposite-sex couples.

8.  **Based on the Supreme Court's decision about DOMA, what type of statutes might you predict would also be overturned by the same court?**

**F**  those that deny underage couples with parental consent the right to marry

**G**  those that deny citizens the types of responsibilities that enhance integrity

**H**  those that enable the federal government to deny rights already recognized by the state

**J**  those that impact the financial disclosures of high-ranking federal officials and their spouses

9.  **Read this sentence from the text.**

> The law in question makes it even more difficult for the children to understand the integrity and closeness of their own family and its concord with other families in their community and in their daily lives.

**Which definition fits the word <u>concord</u> as it is used in this sentence?**

**A**  serenity

**B**  sympathy

**C**  tranquility

**D**  unity

 **Test-Taking Tip**

When you answer questions about a reading passage on a test, go back to the passage to find the answers. Before looking for the answers in the passage, read the questions carefully to see whether some of the context in the questions or in the answer options can help you find the answers when you reread.

## Writing Practice

To reveal their ideas without stating them, authors use certain text structures and patterns. For example, a product reviewer might contrast two items to highlight the one he or she prefers. Readers can infer that the reviewer prefers the item he or she described in favorable terms over the one he or she criticized.

**Directions:** Examine the text structure of the following passage. Then write an explanatory text analyzing the passage. Include a summary of the passage, and use your prior knowledge to explain the implicit relationships among the text's ideas. Effectively select and cite details in the text to support your inferences, and explain how these details helped you make those inferences.

# From "Herschel Telescope Detects Water on Dwarf Planet"
### by NASA

Scientists using the Herschel space observatory have made the first definitive detection of water vapor on the . . . [dwarf planet] Ceres.

Plumes of water vapor are thought to shoot up periodically from Ceres when portions of its icy surface warm slightly. . . .

Herschel is a European Space Agency (ESA) mission with important NASA contributions.

"This is the first time water vapor has been unequivocally detected on Ceres or any other object in the asteroid belt. [It is] proof that Ceres has an icy surface and an atmosphere," said Michael Küppers of ESA in Spain. . . .

The results come at the right time for NASA's Dawn mission, which is on its way to Ceres. . . . Dawn is scheduled to arrive at Ceres in the spring of 2015, where it will take the closest look ever at its surface.

"We . . . don't have to wait long before getting more context on this intriguing result, right from the source itself," said Carol Raymond, the deputy principal investigator for Dawn. . . . "Dawn will map the geology and chemistry of the surface in high resolution, revealing the processes that drive the outgassing activity."

For the last century, Ceres was known as the largest asteroid in our solar system. But in 2006, the International Astronomical Union . . . reclassified Ceres as a dwarf planet because of its large size. It is roughly 590 miles (950 kilometers) in diameter. When it first was spotted in 1801, astronomers thought it was a planet orbiting between Mars and Jupiter. Later, other cosmic bodies with similar orbits were found, marking the discovery of our solar system's main belt of asteroids.

Scientists believe Ceres contains rock in its interior with a thick mantle of ice. . . . [If] melted, . . . [the ice might] amount to more fresh water than is present on all of Earth. The materials making up Ceres likely date from the first few million years of our solar system's existence and accumulated before the planets formed.

Until now, ice had been theorized to exist on Ceres but had not been detected conclusively. It took Herschel's far-infrared vision to see, finally, a clear spectral signature of the water vapor. But Herschel did not see water vapor every time it looked. While the telescope spied water vapor four different times, on one occasion there was no signature.

Here is what scientists think is happening: when Ceres swings through the part of its orbit that is closer to the sun, a portion of its icy surface becomes warm enough to cause water vapor to escape in plumes at a rate of about 6 kilograms (13 pounds) per second. When Ceres is in the colder part of its orbit, no water escapes.

*(Continued on next page)*

The strength of the signal also varied over hours, weeks and months, because of the water vapor plumes rotating in and out of Herschel's views as the object spun on its axis. This enabled the scientists to localize the source of water to two darker spots on the surface of Ceres, previously seen by NASA's Hubble Space Telescope and ground-based telescopes. The dark spots might be more likely to outgas because dark material warms faster than light material. When the Dawn spacecraft arrives at Ceres, it will be able to investigate these features.

This lesson will help you practice analyzing details to understand two types of complex texts. Use it with Core Lesson 2.5 *Analyze the Role of Details in Complex Texts* to reinforce and apply your knowledge.

## Key Concept

The details in complex informational and literary texts provide clues to the main ideas, significance of events, and relationships implied by the author.

## Core Skills

- Comprehend Complex Texts
- Use Details to Analyze Complex Texts

## Examining Complex Literary Texts

Complex literary texts often contain challenging words, abstract ideas, or implicit purposes. In addition, the subject might be unfamiliar, the text might have more than one theme, and the text structure might be unusual. To understand complex literary texts, readers should scan the text to pick up clues from the title and key details, combine these clues with their own knowledge, and draw from their own life experiences.

**Directions:** Read the text. Then do Numbers 1–4.

## From "The Black Cat"

*by Edgar Allan Poe*

1    For the most wild, yet most homely narrative which I am about to pen, I neither expect nor solicit belief. Mad indeed would I be to expect it in a case where my very senses reject their own evidence. Yet mad am I not—and very surely do I not dream. But tomorrow I die, and today I would unburthen my soul. My immediate purpose is to place before the world plainly, succinctly, and without comment, a series of mere household events. In their consequences these events have terrified—have tortured—have destroyed me. Yet I will not attempt to expound them. To me they presented little but horror—to many they will seem less terrible than *baroques*. Hereafter, perhaps, some intellect may be found which will reduce my phantasm to the commonplace—some intellect more calm, more logical, and far less excitable than my own, which will perceive, in the circumstances I detail with awe, nothing more than an ordinary succession of very natural causes and effects.

2    From my infancy I was noted for the docility and humanity of my disposition. My tenderness of heart was even so conspicuous as to make me the jest of my companions. I was especially fond of animals, and was indulged by my parents with a great variety of pets. With these I spent most of my time, and never was so happy as when feeding and caressing them. This peculiarity of character grew with my growth, and in my manhood I derived from it one of my principal sources of pleasure. To those who have cherished an affection for a faithful and sagacious dog, I need hardly be at the trouble of explaining the nature or the intensity of the gratification thus derivable. There is something in the unselfish and self-sacrificing love of a brute which goes directly to the heart of him who has had frequent occasion to test the paltry friendship and gossamer fidelity of mere *Man*.

3    I married early, and was happy to find in my wife a disposition not uncongenial with my own. Observing my partiality for domestic pets, she lost no opportunity of procuring those of the most agreeable kind. We had birds, gold-fish, a fine dog, rabbits, a small monkey, and *a cat*.

*(Continued on next page)*

4    This latter was a remarkably large and beautiful animal, entirely black, and sagacious to
an astonishing degree. In speaking of his intelligence, my wife, who at heart was not a little
tinctured with superstition, made frequent allusion to the ancient popular notion which regarded
all black cats as witches in disguise. Not that she was ever *serious* upon this point, and I mention
the matter at all for no better reason than that it happens just now to be remembered.

1. **By scanning the title and the first sentence of each paragraph, the reader can tell
   that the narrator is discussing**
   A   his life and his cat
   B   cats and superstitions
   C   his childhood and relatives
   D   marriage and fiction writing

2. **Which sentence best summarizes paragraph 1?**
   F   The narrator says that perhaps readers will be persuaded to agree with the events he is
       about to describe.
   G   The narrator says that perhaps readers will be terrified yet entertained by the events he is
       about to describe.
   H   The narrator says that perhaps readers will determine a logical explanation for the events
       he is about to describe.
   J   The narrator says that perhaps readers will understand why he has written about the
       events he is about to describe.

3. **Which statement best summarizes the main idea of paragraph 3?**
   A   The narrator married someone who was agreeable.
   B   The narrator's wife had pets of all different kinds.
   C   The narrator married someone who shared his loved of animals.
   D   The narrator's wife allowed him to get fish, birds, a dog, and a cat.

4. **Read this sentence from the text.**

   **There is something in the unselfish and self-sacrificing love of a brute which
   goes directly to the heart of him who has had frequent occasion to test the paltry
   friendship and gossamer fidelity of mere *Man*.**

   **Which definition fits the word brute as it is used in this sentence?**
   F   animal
   G   monster
   H   savage
   J   thug

## Understanding Complex Informational Texts

Like complex literary texts, complex informational texts can be challenging when the reader
is not familiar with technical vocabulary and concepts. It is helpful to scan for recurring
words, make predictions and connections based on prior knowledge, and visualize as you read.
Paraphrase difficult words, concepts, and complex sentences; summarize the main points implied
by the details; and try to identify the author's main ideas. Then as you read the details, think
about how they relate to the main ideas.

**Directions:** Read the text. Then do Numbers 5–9.

# From the speech "Remarks by the President on College Affordability"

*by Barack Obama*

1    A higher education is the single best investment you can make in your future. And I'm proud of all the students who are making that investment. . . . And that's not just me saying it. Look, right now, the unemployment rate for Americans with at least a college degree is about one-third lower than the national average. The incomes of folks who have at least a college degree are more than twice those of Americans without a high school diploma. So more than ever before, some form of higher education is the surest path into the middle class.

2    But what I want to talk about today is what's become a barrier and a burden for too many American families—and that is the soaring cost of higher education. . . .

3    This is something that everybody knows you need—a college education. On the other hand, college has never been more expensive. Over the past three decades, the average tuition at a public four-year college has gone up by more than 250 percent—250 percent. Now, a typical family's income has only gone up 16 percent. So think about that—tuition has gone up 250 percent; income gone up 16 percent. That's a big gap. . . .

4    The average student who borrows for college now graduates owing more than $26,000. Some owe a lot more than that. And I've heard from a lot of these young people who are frustrated that they've done everything they're supposed to do—got good grades in high school, applied to college, did well in school—but now they come out, they've got this crushing debt that's crippling their sense of self-reliance and their dreams. It becomes hard to start a family and buy a home if you're servicing $1,000 worth of debt every month. It becomes harder to start a business if you are servicing $1,000 worth of debt every month, right? . . .

5    So at a time when a higher education has never been more important or more expensive, too many students are facing a choice that they should never have to make: Either they say no to college and pay the price for not getting a degree—and that's a price that lasts a lifetime—or you do what it takes to go to college, but then you run the risk that you won't be able to pay it off because you've got so much debt. . . .

6    So the bottom line is this—we've got a crisis in terms of college affordability and student debt. And over the past four years, what we've tried to do is to take some steps to make college more affordable. So we enacted historic reforms to the student loan system, so taxpayer dollars stop padding the pockets of big banks and instead help more kids afford college. . . .

7    Because what was happening was the old system, the student loan programs were going through banks; they didn't have any risk because the federal government guaranteed the loans, but they were still taking billions of dollars out of the program. We said, well, let's just give the loans directly to the students and we can put more money to helping students.

8    Then we set up a consumer watchdog. And that consumer watchdog is already helping students and families navigate the financial options that are out there to pay for college without getting ripped off by shady lenders. . . .

9    Then, we took action to cap loan repayments at 10 percent of monthly income for many borrowers who are trying to responsibly manage their federal student loan debt. . . . So overall, we've made college more affordable for millions of students and families through tax credits and grants and student loans that go farther than they did before. And then, just a few weeks ago, Democrats and Republicans worked together to keep student loan rates from doubling. . . .

*(Continued on next page)*

10   So that's all a good start, but it's not enough. The problem is, is that even if the federal government keeps on putting more and more money in the system, if the cost is going up by 250 percent, tax revenues aren't going up 250 percent—and so [at] some point, the government will run out of money, which means more and more costs are being loaded on to students and their families.

11   The system's current trajectory is not sustainable. And what that means is state legislatures are going to have to step up. They can't just keep cutting support for public colleges and universities. . . . That's just the truth. Colleges are not going to be able to just keep on increasing tuition year after year, and then passing it on to students and families and taxpayers. . . . Our economy can't afford the trillion dollars in outstanding student loan debt, much of which may not get repaid because students don't have the capacity to pay it. We can't price the middle class and everybody working to get into the middle class out of a college education. We're going to have to do things differently. We can't go about business as usual.

5.   **What is the main theme of the speech?**
     **A**  The cost of higher education is too high.
     **B**  The income of college graduates needs to increase.
     **C**  The importance of higher education is overestimated.
     **D**  The unemployment rate for college graduates is too high.

6.   **Which detail offers the strongest support for the idea that college tuition is no longer affordable to the average American?**
     **F**  Some college graduates owe more than $26,000 in loan debt.
     **G**  It is hard to start a family if you have to pay $1000 in debt each month.
     **H**  Federal tax revenues have not increased by 250 percent, but college costs have.
     **J**  Average tuition increased 250 percent while average income increased 16 percent.

7.   **Which mental picture could best help a reader visualize the main problem described in the text?**
     **A**  a person driving a fancy car
     **B**  a graduating class of students in caps and gowns
     **C**  a long line of people at the unemployment office
     **D**  a college graduate writing a check for $1000 to a bank each month

8.   **Which statement best summarizes the technical information in paragraphs 7, 8, and 9?**
     **F**  The government offered tax credits and grants to make college more affordable.
     **G**  The government took several steps to help and protect students who take out loans.
     **H**  The government took lending away from the banks to offer more money to students.
     **J**  The government's political parties worked together to keep loan rates from doubling.

9.   **On the basis of the first sentences of paragraphs 10 and 11, what is the author's conclusion?**
     **A**  The old system was not sustainable, so changes were made.
     **B**  Some changes were made to the old system, but more must be made.
     **C**  The changes made will redirect the trajectory of the current system.
     **D**  If the current system does not change, the government will run out of money.

## Language Practice

To simplify and add variety to writing, it is common to replace nouns with pronouns. Pronouns include *he, she, it, they, his, her, its,* and *their.* The noun that is replaced is referred to as the antecedent. It is important to use the correct pronoun to match the antecedent to which it refers.

**Directions:** Read the draft of an excerpt from an essay. Then do Numbers 10 through 13.

One cannot expect to be successful if they do not commit to the pursuit of success. Many people believe that talent comes naturally, but they are mistaken. Talent is a result of practice and persistence and of a constant engagement with the learning process. Each person might have gifts or genetic traits that make one more likely to master certain activities. But this does not mean that mastery is instantaneous, without cost or effort. Rather, those must be developed over time.

10. **Which version of the first underlined sentence uses a pronoun that matches its antecedent?**
    F   One cannot expect to be successful if it does not commit to the pursuit of success.
    G   One cannot expect to be successful if you do not commit to the pursuit of success.
    H   One cannot expect to be successful if they do not commit to the pursuit of success.
    J   One cannot expect to be successful if one does not commit to the pursuit of success.

11. **The correct pronoun is used in which version of the second underlined sentence?**
    A   Many people believe that talent comes naturally, but I am mistaken.
    B   Many people believe that talent comes naturally, but you are mistaken.
    C   Many people believe that talent comes naturally, but they are mistaken.
    D   Many people believe that talent comes naturally, but he or she is mistaken.

12. **In which version of the third underlined sentence do the pronoun and antecedent match?**
    F   Each person might have gifts or genetic traits that make them more likely to master certain skills.
    G   Each person might have gifts or genetic traits that make those more likely to master certain skills.
    H   Each person might have gifts or genetic traits that make you and me more likely to master certain skills.
    J   Each person might have gifts or genetic traits that make him or her more likely to master certain skills.

13. **Which version of the final underlined sentences contains a matching pronoun and antecedent?**
    A   But this does not mean that mastery is instantaneous, without cost or effort. Rather, it must be developed over time.
    B   But this does not mean that mastery is instantaneous, without cost or effort. Rather, they must be developed over time.
    C   But this does not mean that mastery is instantaneous, without cost or effort. Rather, those must be developed over time.
    D   But this does not mean that mastery is instantaneous, without cost or effort. Rather, he or she must be developed over time.

The essay portion of the test assesses numerous abilities. These include your organizational skills and stylistic choices, the effectiveness of your arguments, your use of evidence, and your grasp of standard English conventions. In other words, your score will take into account what you write and how you write it. Therefore, it's important to become comfortable with content and presentation.

## Writing Practice

To understand complex informational texts, it is necessary to combine key details with your own prior knowledge to determine the main idea. You may also need to use context clues to determine the meaning of technical words, make predictions and connections to your own life, and visualize.

**Directions:** Read the following passage. Then write an informative text in which you summarize the text. Include in your summary a paraphrase of the passage's main idea and a description of the most significant and relevant details. In a second paragraph, examine the complex ideas in the text and provide an analysis of how the details helped you determine the main idea and how the main idea developed over the course of the text through the details.

### From "Nutrient Pollution"

*by the Environmental Protection Agency*

. . . Nitrogen and phosphorus are nutrients that are natural parts of aquatic ecosystems. Nitrogen is also the most abundant element in the air we breathe. Nitrogen and phosphorus support the growth of algae and aquatic plants, which provide food and habitat for fish, shellfish and smaller organisms that live in water.

But when too much nitrogen and phosphorus enter the environment—usually from a wide range of human activities—the air and water can become polluted. Nutrient pollution has impacted many streams, rivers, lakes, bays and coastal waters for the past several decades. [The result has been] serious environmental and human health issues and [an impact on] the economy.

Too much nitrogen and phosphorus in the water causes algae to grow faster than ecosystems can handle. Significant increases in algae harm water quality, food resources, and habitats. [Algae growths also] decrease the oxygen that fish and other aquatic life need to survive. Large growths of algae are called algal blooms. . . . [They] can severely reduce or eliminate oxygen in the water, leading to illnesses in fish and the death of large numbers of fish. Some algal blooms are harmful to humans because they produce elevated toxins and bacterial growth. [In turn, these] can make people sick if they come into contact with polluted water, consume tainted fish or shellfish, or drink contaminated water.

Nutrient pollution in ground water—which millions of people in the United States use as their drinking water source—can be harmful, even at low levels. Infants are vulnerable to a nitrogen-based compound called nitrates in drinking water. Excess nitrogen in the atmosphere can produce pollutants such as ammonia and ozone, which can impair our ability to breathe, limit visibility, and alter plant growth. When excess nitrogen comes back to Earth from the atmosphere, it can harm the health of forests, soils, and waterways.

_____

_____

_____

_____

_____

_____

_____

_____

_____

_____

_____

_____

_____

_____

_____

_____

_____

_____

_____

This lesson will help you practice determining connotative and figurative meanings in two types of texts. Use it with Core Lesson 3.1 *Determine Connotative and Figurative Meanings* to reinforce and apply your knowledge.

## Key Concept

The connotative meaning of a word or phrase is the meaning suggested by the word. Figurative language includes words or phrases that imply more than their literal meaning.

## Core Skills

- Analyze and Evaluate Word Choice
- Interpret Words and Phrases

## Identifying Connotative and Figurative Meanings

Authors use connotative and figurative language to set the tone and mood of a text. The tone is the expression of an author's attitude about the subject. The mood is the emotion that the reader feels when reading the text. As you read, analyze the author's use of specific words and phrases to identify the text's tone and mood.

**Directions:** Read the text. Then do Numbers 1–6.

## The Pony Express

From 1860 to 1861, the young riders of the Pony Express galloped their way across the western United States into American history. When the Pony Express first began its operation, there was no quick way for people on the East Coast of the United States to communicate with people on the West Coast. Mail was delivered by steamship or stagecoach. The founders of the Pony Express came up with a better—and faster—method.

They created a mail service between St. Joseph, Missouri, and Sacramento, California, that consisted of riders, horses, and way stations. Most of the riders were young teenagers, often orphans. They were lightweight, hard-working, and brave enough to take on incredible risks. Each rider would mount a fresh horse and ride at breakneck speed to the next station, about ten to fifteen miles away. There the rider would mount another fresh horse and ride on from station to station until he had covered about 75 miles. Then a new rider would take over the mailbag and complete the next section of the Pony Express route.

At its busiest point of operation, the Pony Express had more than 80 riders, between 400 and 500 horses, and more than 100 stations. The riders were often heroic for their dedication to getting the mail through. They rode during the day and during the night. They crossed mountains and deserts and rough trails in all kinds of weather. They carried firearms to protect themselves from the many dangers they encountered while crossing the Wild West.

The Pony Express had a short but glorious history. It ended after 19 months of operation when the Pacific Telegraph line was completed in October 1861. Then the Pony Express and its riders ended their exciting chapter in American history.

1. **Which sentence from the passage contains an example of figurative language?**
   A ... the young riders of the Pony Express galloped their way ... into American history.
   B Most of the riders were young teenagers, often orphans.
   C Then a new rider would take over the mailbag and complete the next section of the ... route.
   D The riders were often heroic for their dedication to getting the mail through.

2.  **What is the mood of the passage?**

    F  concern

    G  excitement

    H  longing

    J  suspense

3.  **What is the tone in the passage?**

    A  complimentary

    B  indifferent

    C  suspicious

    D  sympathetic

4.  **Read this sentence from the text.**

    Then the Pony Express and its riders ended their exciting chapter in American history.

    **Which literary element is used in this sentence?**

    F  connotation

    G  metaphor

    H  personification

    J  simile

5.  **Read this sentence from the text.**

    Each rider would mount a fresh horse and ride at breakneck speed to the next station, about ten to fifteen miles away.

    **What is the connotative meaning of the word "breakneck" in this sentence?**

    A  cautious

    B  dangerous

    C  relaxed

    D  torturous

6.  **Read this excerpt from the text.**

    The Pony Express had a short but glorious history. It ended after 19 months of operation when the Pacific Telegraph line was completed in October 1861. Then the Pony Express and its riders ended their exciting chapter in American history.

    **What does the word** <u>glorious</u> **mean as it is used in this excerpt?**

    F  interesting

    G  troubled

    H  virtuous

    J  wonderful

# Understanding Connotative and Figurative Meanings in Literary Texts

Both connotative and figurative language add depth to literary texts. An author's descriptions and word choices indicate the author's attitude about the subject, and they also influence how the reader will feel toward the characters and about the events in the story. As you read, reflect on the author's reason for using certain words and phrases.

**Directions:** Read the text. Then do Numbers 7–11.

## From "Rip Van Winkle"

### *by Washington Irving*

1   Rip Van Winkle was one of those happy mortals of foolish, pleasant dispositions who take the world easy, eat white bread or brown (which ever can be got with least thought or trouble), and would rather starve on a penny than work for a pound. He would have whistled life away in perfect contentment but for his wife's continual harping about his idleness, his carelessness, and the ruin he was bringing on his family. Morning, noon, and night, her tongue was incessantly going. Every thing he said or did was sure to produce a torrent of criticism. Rip had but one way of replying to all lectures of the kind. He shrugged his shoulders, shook his head, cast up his eyes, but said nothing. This, however, always provoked a fresh volley from his wife. He was then forced to retreat to the outside of the house—the only side which, in truth, belongs to a henpecked husband.

2   Rip's sole domestic adherent was his dog Wolf, who was as much henpecked as his master. Dame Van Winkle regarded them as companions in idleness, looking upon Wolf with an evil eye as the cause of his master's so often going astray. True, he was as courageous an animal as ever scoured the woods—but what courage can withstand the terrors of a woman's tongue? The moment Wolf entered the house, his crest fell, his tail drooped to the ground, or curled between his legs. He sneaked about . . . , casting many a sidelong glance at Dame Van Winkle. At the least flourish of a broomstick or ladle, he flew to the door with a pre-emptive yelp.

3   Times grew worse and worse with Rip Van Winkle as years of matrimony rolled on. A tart temper never mellows with age, and a sharp tongue is the only edge tool that grows keener by constant use. For a long while he used to console himself by frequenting a kind of club of the sages, philosophers, and other idle men of the village. Sessions were held on a bench before a small inn. . . . Here they used to sit in the shade of a long lazy summer's day, talk listlessly over village gossip, or tell endless sleepy stories about nothing. . . .

4   The opinions of this band were completely controlled by Nicholas Vedder, a patriarch of the village and landlord of the inn. . . . It is true, he was rarely heard to speak, but smoked his pipe incessantly. His adherents, however (for every great man has his adherents), perfectly understood him and knew how to gather his opinions. When any thing that was read or related displeased him, he was observed to smoke his pipe vehemently and send forth short, frequent, and angry puffs. When pleased, he would inhale the smoke slowly and tranquilly, emitting it in light and placid clouds. Sometimes he would even deign to take the pipe from his mouth to let the fragrant vapour curl about his nose, gravely nodding his head in token of approval.

5   From even this strong hold the unlucky Rip was at length thwarted by his unruly wife, who would suddenly break in upon the tranquility of the meeting and call the members all to task. That honourable personage, Nicholas Vedder himself, was hardly safe from the daring tongue of this terrible shrew who charged him outright with encouraging her husband in habits of idleness.

*(Continued on next page)*

6   Poor Rip was at last reduced almost to despair. His only alternative to escape from the labour of the farm and the clamour of his wife was to take gun in hand and stroll away into the woods. Here he would sometimes seat himself at the foot of a tree and share the contents of his wallet with Wolf, with whom he sympathized as a fellow sufferer in persecution. "Poor Wolf," he would say, "thy mistress leads thee a dog's life of it; but never mind, my lad, while I live thou shalt never want a friend to stand by thee!" Wolf would wag his tail, look wistfully in his master's face, and if dogs can feel pity, I truly believe he reciprocated the sentiment with all his heart.

**7.  Based on the language used in the passage, how do you think the author wants readers to feel toward Rip Van Winkle?**

**A**  irritated

**B**  loyal

**C**  sympathetic

**D**  understanding

**8.  Read these sentences from the text.**

> **(Paragraph 2) Rip's sole domestic adherent was his dog Wolf, who was as much henpecked as his master.**

> **(Paragraph 4) His adherents, however (for every great man has his adherents), perfectly understood him and knew how to gather his opinions.**

**Which pair of words could replace "adherent" and "adherents"?**

**F**  pet/pets

**G**  friend/friends

**H**  enemy/enemies

**J**  student/students

**9.  How does the mood change between the fourth and fifth paragraphs?**

**A**  It changes from calm to frenzied.

**B**  It changes from riotous to peaceful.

**C**  It changes from humorous to serious.

**D**  It changes from unpleasant to pleasant.

**10.  Which word best describes Dame Van Winkle?**

**F**  domineering

**G**  flirtatious

**H**  meek

**J**  passive

**11.  Read this sentence from the text.**

> **He was then forced to retreat to the outside of the house—the only side which, in truth, belongs to a henpecked husband.**

**In this context, which definition fits henpecked?**

**A**  enjoying lovely solitude

**B**  taking pleasure in silence

**C**  suffering constant nagging

**D**  feeling spiritually fulfilled

## Language Practice

Homophones are words that sound the same but are spelled differently and have different meanings. Using the correct homophones is an important part of crafting a text that is clear and easy to understand.

**Directions** For Numbers 12 and 13, read the question and choose the best answer.

12. **Which sentence contains no misspelled words?**

   **F** Courtney and Malik were a grate pair with similar interests, accept when it came to food.

   **G** Courtney and Malik were a great pair with similar interests, except when it came to food.

   **H** Courtney and Malik were a great pear with similar interests, accept when it came to food.

   **J** Courtney and Malik were a grate pare with similar interests, except when it came to food.

13. **In which option are all the words spelled correctly?**

   **A** Unlike Malik, Courtney loved seafood, especially muscles. Malik ate mostly vegetables. His favorites were leaks and carats.

   **B** Unlike Malik, Courtney loved seafood, especially muscles. Malik ate mostly vegetables. His favorites were leeks and karats.

   **C** Unlike Malik, Courtney loved seafood, especially mussels. Malik ate mostly vegetables. His favorites were leaks and carrots.

   **D** Unlike Malik, Courtney loved seafood, especially mussels. Malik ate mostly vegetables. His favorites were leeks and carrots.

### ✔ Test-Taking Tip

If you can't identify the correct answer in an activity on a test, begin by eliminating answer choices that are clearly wrong. Sometimes, but not always, the correct choice is quite different from the other choices.

## Writing Practice

Connotative and figurative language brings depth to your writing. This descriptive language adds interest while guiding the reader to react to the text in a specific way. For example, "Jaime was silent" simply says that Jaime didn't make any noise. "Jaime was as quiet as a mouse" is more descriptive. It describes Jaime as quiet, but it also makes Jaime seem small and meek.

**Directions:** Write an explanatory text that clearly analyzes the use of connotative and figurative language in "Rip Van Winkle" on pages 69 and 70. What does Irving accomplish with his language? If he had made different word choices, how might they affect the story? Develop the topic thoroughly by selecting concrete details, quotations, or other examples from the text to support your analysis.

_____

_____

_____

_____

This lesson will help you practice analyzing tone in two types of texts. Use it with Core Lesson 3.2 *Analyze Tone* to reinforce and apply your knowledge.

## Key Concept

Tone is the expression of a writer's attitude through stylistic choices.

## Core Skills

- Analyze Word Choice
- Interpret Words and Phrases to Draw Conclusions

## Identifying Author's Tone in an Informational Text

The tone an author conveys in a text is much like the tone of your voice when you speak. In writing, authors convey tone through word choices and sentence structure. The tone of an informational text should fit the author's purpose for writing, the topic, and the genre.

**Directions:** Read the text. Then do Numbers 1–5.

# Letter of Complaint

Manager
Value Inn Hotel
122 Massachusetts Avenue
Washington, DC 20027

Dear Manager,

I am writing about a number of problems I had while staying at your hotel in May of this year. The headaches began at the front desk, where I had to wait in line for 10 minutes. When I finally reached the desk, the employee was unable to find my reservation even after I spelled my name several times and gave her my reservation number. She then said there were no more non-smoking rooms, even though I had reserved one weeks ago. She also informed me that only rooms on the twenty-second floor were available despite the fact that I had reserved a lower-floor room.

Naturally, I had trouble with my room key and had to return to the desk, where more customers were in line. The clerk who checked me in wasn't there, and the new clerk huffily told me to wait in line with the others. I waited 15 more minutes to get a key to my room. When I finally entered my room, it was nothing short of a disaster. I returned to the front desk for a third time. Imagine my surprise when the clerk offered me a non-smoking room on a lower floor!

Despite the better room, my troubles were far from over. Your website clearly said that Internet access was free, yet I had to pay $9.95 to access it. When I made my reservation, I was told that the pool was open. Once at the hotel, however, I learned that the pool was not scheduled to open until the following weekend, which was Memorial Day. As the cherry on top, the air conditioner in my room broke down during the night. I called the front desk, but the engineer was not successful in his attempt to repair it. Since there were no other rooms available (apparently not even those on the twenty-second floor), I had to sleep in a stuffy, uncomfortable room.

I complained to a desk clerk about all of these problems, but she said that there was nothing she could do to solve them. Because of the problems I experienced, I would like the cost of my stay refunded to me.

Sincerely,

Charles Walters

1. **How does the topic of this passage affect its tone?**

   **A** The topic, a compliment about a hotel stay, sets a neutral tone.

   **B** The topic, a complaint about a hotel stay, sets an angry, frustrated tone.

   **C** The topic, a complaint about a hotel stay, sets a tone of disappointment.

   **D** The topic, a compliment about a hotel stay, sets a tone of congratulations.

2. **Read this excerpt from the text.**

   > I am writing about a number of problems I had while staying at your hotel in May of this year. The headaches began at the front desk, where I had to wait in line for 10 minutes. When I finally reached the desk, the employee was unable to find my reservation even after I spelled my name several times and gave her my reservation number. She then said there were no more non-smoking rooms, even though I had reserved one weeks ago. She also informed me that only rooms on the twenty-second floor were available despite the fact that I had reserved a lower-floor room.

   **Which word from the excerpt conveys the tone of the passage?**

   **F** employee

   **G** headaches

   **H** informed

   **J** reservation

3. **Read this excerpt from the text.**

   > Naturally, I had trouble with my room key and had to return to the desk, where more customers were in line. The clerk who checked me in wasn't there, and the new clerk huffily told me to wait in line with the others. I waited 15 more minutes to get a key to my room. When I finally entered my room, it was nothing short of a disaster. I returned to the front desk for a third time. Imagine my surprise when the clerk offered me a non-smoking room on a lower floor!

   **Which sentence from the excerpt best expresses the tone of the passage?**

   **A** Naturally, I had trouble with my room key and had to return to the desk.

   **B** I waited 15 more minutes to get a key to my room.

   **C** I returned to the front desk for a third time.

   **D** Imagine my surprise when the clerk offered me a non-smoking room on a lower floor!

4. **How would the phrases "a number of problems" and "all of these problems" likely make the hotel manager feel when reading the letter?**

   **F** content

   **G** embarrassed

   **H** motivated

   **J** relieved

5. **Read this sentence from the passage.**

   > As the cherry on top, the air conditioner in my room broke that night.

   **Which aspect of this sentence would be changed by replacing "As the cherry on top" with "Thankfully"?**

   **A** meaning

   **B** mood

   **C** purpose

   **D** tone

## Analyzing Tone in a Literary Text

Tone plays an important role in literary writing. It can help build suspense in a mystery story or create a sense of urgency in an adventure story. When writers carefully craft the details of a story, the words and phrases they choose help express the tone.

**Directions:** Read the text. Then do Numbers 6–11.

# From "The Thief"

*by Anna Katherine Greene*

"And now, if you have all seen the coin and sufficiently admired it, you may pass it back. I make a point of never leaving it off the shelf for more than fifteen minutes."

The half dozen or more guests seated about the board of the genial speaker, glanced casually at each other as though expecting to see the object mentioned immediately produced.

But no coin appeared.

"I have other amusements waiting," suggested their host, with a smile in which even his wife could detect no signs of impatience. "Now let Robert put it back into the cabinet."

Robert was the butler.

Blank looks, negative gestures, but still no coin.

"Perhaps it is in somebody's lap," timidly ventured one of the younger women. "It doesn't seem to be on the table."

Immediately all the ladies began lifting their napkins and shaking out the gloves which lay under them, in an effort to relieve their own embarrassment and that of the gentlemen who had not even so simple a resource as this at their command.

"It can't be lost," protested Mr. Sedgwick, with an air of perfect confidence. "I saw it but a minute ago in somebody's hand. Darrow, you had it; what did you do with it?"

"Passed it along."

"Well, well, it must be under somebody's plate or doily." And he began to move about his own and such dishes as were within reach of his hand.

Each guest imitated him, lifting glasses and turning over spoons till Mr. Sedgwick himself bade them desist. "It's slipped to the floor," he nonchalantly concluded. "A toast to the ladies, and we will give Robert the chance of looking for it."

As they drank this toast, his apparently careless, but quietly astute, glance took in each countenance about him. The coin was very valuable and its loss would be keenly felt by him. Had it slipped from the table some one's eye would have perceived it, some hand would have followed it. Only a minute or two before, the attention of the whole party had been concentrated upon it. Darrow had held it up for all to see, while he discoursed upon its history. He would take Darrow aside at the first opportunity and ask him—But—it! how could he do that? These were his intimate friends. He knew them well, more than well, with one exception, and he—Well, he was the handsomest of the lot and the most debonair and agreeable. A little more gay than usual tonight, possibly a trifle too gay, considering that a man of Mr. Blake's social weight and business standing sat at the board; but not to be suspected, no, not to be suspected, even if he was the next man after Darrow and had betrayed something like confusion when the eyes of the whole table turned his way at the former's simple statement of "I passed it on." . . .

*(Continued on next page)*

"And now, some music!" he cheerfully cried, as with lingering glances and some further pokings about of the table furniture, the various guests left their places and followed him into the adjoining room.

But the ladies were too nervous and the gentlemen not sufficiently sure of their voices to undertake the entertainment of the rest at a moment of such acknowledged suspense; and notwithstanding the exertions of their host and his quiet but much discomfited wife, it soon became apparent that but one thought engrossed them all, and that any attempt at conversation must prove futile so long as the curtains between the two rooms remained open and they could see Robert on his hands and knees searching the floor and shoving aside the rugs.

Darrow, who was Mr. Sedgwick's brother-in-law and almost as much at home in the house as Sedgwick himself, made a move to draw these curtains, but something in his relative's face stopped him and he desisted with some laughing remark which did not attract enough attention, even, to elicit any response. . . .

"Robert will find it if it is there." Then, distressed at this involuntary disclosure of his thought, added in his whole-hearted way: "It's such a little thing, and the room is so big and a round object rolls unexpectedly far, you know. Well, have you got it?" he eagerly demanded, as the butler finally showed himself in the door.

"No, sir; and it's not in the dining-room. I have cleared the table and thoroughly searched the floor."

Mr. Sedgwick knew that he had. He had no doubts about Robert. Robert had been in his employ for years and had often handled his coins and, at his order, sometimes shown them.

"Very well," said he, "we'll not bother about it any more to-night; you may draw the curtains."

But here the clear, almost strident voice of the youngest man of the party interposed.

"Wait a minute," said he. "This especial coin is . . . unique in this country, and not only worth a great deal of money, but cannot be duplicated at any cost. . . . Gentlemen—I leave the ladies entirely out of this—I do not propose that he shall have further opportunity to associate me with this very natural doubt. I demand the privilege of emptying my pockets here and now, before any of us have left his presence. I am a connoisseur in coins myself and consequently find it imperative to take the initiative in this matter."

6. **What tone can a reader expect from a passage of this genre?**

   F  disbelief

   G  neutrality

   H  suspense

   J  wonder

7. **Read this excerpt from the passage.**

   > . . . it soon became apparent that but one thought engrossed them all, and that any attempt at conversation must prove futile so long as the curtains between the two rooms remained open . . .

   **What does the word <u>futile</u> mean as it is used in this excerpt?**

   A  annoying

   B  careless

   C  pointless

   D  useful

8. **Read this excerpt from the passage.**

> But no coin appeared.
>
> "I have other amusements waiting," suggested their host, with a smile in which even his wife could detect no signs of impatience. "Now let Robert put it back into the cabinet."
>
> Robert was the butler.
>
> Blank looks, negative gestures, but still no coin.

**The author uses short phrases and short sentences in this excerpt so the tone will**

  **F** remain lighthearted and fun

  **G** show the confusion of the guests

  **H** serve to cast a suspecting shadow on the butler

  **J** build the reader's interest in what happens next

9. **Which word best describes the tone of the story?**

  **A** frantic

  **B** friendly

  **C** intense

  **D** terrifying

10. **Read this excerpt from the text.**

> As they drank this toast, his apparently careless, but quietly astute, glance took in each countenance about him. The coin was very valuable and its loss would be keenly felt by him. Had it slipped from the table some one's eye would have perceived it, some hand would have followed it. Only a minute or two before, the attention of the whole party had been concentrated upon it. Darrow had held it up for all to see, while he discoursed upon its history. He would take Darrow aside at the first opportunity and ask him—But—it! how could he do that? . . . He knew them well, more than well, with one exception, and he—Well, he was the handsomest of the lot and the most debonair and agreeable. A little more gay than usual to-night, possibly a trifle too gay, considering that a man of Mr. Blake's social weight and business standing sat at the board; but not to be suspected, no, not to be suspected, even if he was the next man after Darrow and had betrayed something like confusion when the eyes of the whole table turned his way at the former's simple statement of "I passed it on." . . .

**How does this excerpt affect the tone of the passage?**

  **F** It misleads readers by naming Darrow as the culprit.

  **G** It builds tension by revealing Mr. Sedgwick's suspicions.

  **H** It distracts from the theft by focusing on a description of one guest.

  **J** It slows down the pace of the story by telling how Robert searches for the coin.

11. **Read this sentence from the passage.**

> "Perhaps it is in somebody's lap," timidly ventured one of the younger women. "It doesn't seem to be on the table."

**Which word could replace "timidly" in this sentence?**

  **A** boldly

  **B** hesitantly

  **C** loudly

  **D** proudly

**Test-Taking Tip**

Some test items ask about specific words, phrases, paragraphs, or sections of a passage. Before answering a question about a passage detail, always reread the related sentence or paragraph. As you reread, focus on what the question is about. For example, if the item is about the meaning of a word, think about how the word is used in the context of the passage.

## Writing Practice

Connotative words, figurative language, and sentence structure are the building blocks an author uses to express tone. Tone can vary greatly from one text to another, depending on the author's purpose for writing.

**Directions:** Write an explanatory text describing and contrasting the tone of the two passages in this lesson: the letter to the hotel manager on page 73 and "The Thief" on pages 75 and 76. Analyze the content in each text, and explain how different topics and genres, techniques such as word choice, and sentence structure contribute to the differences in tone.

_____

_____

_____

_____

_____

_____

_____

_____

_____

_____

_____

_____

_____

_____

This lesson will help you practice analyzing word choice in two speeches. Use it with Core Lesson 3.3 *Analyze Word Choice* to reinforce and apply your knowledge.

## Key Concept

To communicate accurately, authors make careful decisions about the words they use.

## Core Skills

- Analyze Word Choice
- Evaluate Word Choice

## Choosing the Right Word

An author's word choices determine the tone, mood, and impact of a text. Readers or listeners can gain a deeper understanding of what an author wants them to feel, think, and know by analyzing word choices and writing style.

**Directions:** Read the text. Then do Number 1–5.

# From "President Updates America on Operations Liberty Shield and Iraqi Freedom"

*by George W. Bush*

Right now men and women from every part of America, supported by a strong coalition, are fighting to disarm a dangerous regime and to liberate an oppressed people.

It has been 11 days since the major ground war began. In this short time, our troops have performed brilliantly, with skill and with bravery. . . . In 11 days, coalition forces have taken control of most of western and southern Iraq. In 11 days, we've seized key bridges, opened a northern front, achieved—nearly achieved—complete air superiority, and are delivering tons of humanitarian aid. By quick and decisive action, our troops are preventing Saddam Hussein from destroying the Iraqi people's oil fields. Our forces moved into Iraqi missile launch areas that threatened neighboring countries. Many dangers lie ahead, but day by day, we are moving closer to Baghdad. Day by day, we are moving closer to victory. . . .

Our victory will mean the end of a tyrant who rules by fear and torture. Our victory will remove a sponsor of terror, armed with weapons of terror. Our victory will uphold the just demands of the United Nations and the civilized world. And when victory comes, it will be shared by the long-suffering people of Iraq, who deserve freedom and dignity. . . .

The dictator's regime has ruled by fear and continues to use fear as a tool of domination to the end. Many Iraqis have been ordered to fight or die by Saddam's death squads. Others are pressed into service by threats against their children. Iraqi civilians attempting to flee to liberated areas have been shot and shelled from behind by Saddam's thugs. Schools and hospitals have been used to store military equipment. . . . Iraqis who show friendship toward coalition troops are murdered in cold blood by the regime's enforcers.

The people of Iraq have lived in this nightmare world for more than two decades. It is understandable that fear and distrust run deep. Yet, here in the city where America itself gained freedom, I give this pledge to the citizens of Iraq: We're coming with a mighty force to end the reign of your oppressors. We are coming to bring you food and medicine and a better life. And we are coming, and we will not stop, we will not relent until your country is free. . . .

*(Continued on next page)*

We know that our enemies are desperate; we know that they're dangerous. The dying regime in Iraq may try to bring terror to our shores. Other parts of the global terror network may view this as a moment to strike, thinking that we're distracted. They're wrong.

. . . The United States and allied troops are shattering the al Qaeda network. We're hunting them down, one at a time. We're finding them, we're interrogating them, and we're bringing them to justice. . . .

We will end the Iraqi regime, an ally of terrorist groups and a producer of weapons of mass destruction. . . . Shortly before we begin the liberation of Iraq, we launched Operation Liberty Shield, to implement additional measures to defend the American homeland against terrorist attacks.

This nationwide effort is focused on five specific areas. First, we are taking even greater security measures at our borders and ports. We have relocated hundreds of security personnel on our borders. We've added additional reconnaissance aircraft patrols at our borders. . . . Friends and immigrants will always be welcome in this land. Yet we will use all our power to keep out the terrorists and the criminals so they can't hurt our citizens. . . .

Second, we are strengthening protections throughout our national transportation system. We're enforcing temporary flight restrictions over some of our major cities. We've stepped up surveillance of hazardous material shipments within our country and taken measures to keep them away from places where large numbers of people gather. . . . We will do all in our power to make sure our skies and rails and roads are safe from terror.

Third, we've increased surveillance of suspected terrorists. Certain individual[s] with ties to Iraqi intelligence services have been ordered out of this country. We're interviewing Iraqi-born individuals on a voluntary basis for two reasons: to gain information on possible terrorist plans, and to make sure they've not experienced discrimination or hate crimes. . . . Iraqi Americans will be protected, and enemy agents will be stopped. . . .

Fourth, under Operation Liberty Shield, we are guarding our nation's most important infrastructure with greater vigilance. Under the direction of our governors, thousands of National Guardsmen and state police officers are protecting chemical facilities and nuclear power sites, key electrical grids and other potential targets. . . .

And, finally, we're strengthening the preparedness of our public health system. The Departments of Agriculture and Health and Human Services have increased field inspections of livestock and crops. Public health officials have increased medical surveillance in major cities. . . .

After our nation was attacked on September the 11th, 2001, America made a decision: We will not wait for our enemies to strike before we act against them. We're not going to permit terrorists and terror states to plot and plan and grow in strength while we do nothing.

The actions we're taking in Operation Liberty Shield are making this nation more secure. And the actions we're taking abroad against a terror network and against the regime in Iraq are removing a grave danger to all free nations. In every case, by acting today, we are saving countless lives in the future.

1. **How do Bush's word choices support his purpose to persuade readers of the necessity of Operation Iraqi Freedom?**

   **A** He uses words such as "regime" and "network" to describe the initiative.

   **B** He uses words such as "brilliantly" and "skill" to describe the troops on the ground.

   **C** He uses words such as "nightmare" and "murdered" to describe the atrocities happening.

   **D** He uses words such as "distracted" and "interrogating" to describe the work of the troops.

2. Read this sentence from the passage.

> Iraqi civilians attempting to flee to liberated areas have been shot and shelled from behind by Saddam's thugs.

Why does Bush use the word "thug" to describe the people working with Saddam Hussein?

**F** to communicate the idea that Hussein's soldiers are criminals

**G** to show that Hussein depends on soldiers who served in prison

**H** to highlight that Hussein has been resistant to attempts at diplomacy

**J** to emphasize that Hussein has been working with fighters from many nations

3. Read this excerpt from the text.

> The dictator's regime has ruled by fear and continues to use fear as a tool of domination to the end. Many Iraqis have been ordered to fight or die by Saddam's death squads. Others are pressed into service by threats against their children. Iraqi civilians attempting to flee to liberated areas have been shot and shelled from behind by Saddam's thugs. Schools and hospitals have been used to store military equipment. . . . Iraqis who show friendship toward coalition troops are murdered in cold blood by the regime's enforcers.

Which of the following terms or phrases does not convey Bush's negative feelings toward Saddam Hussein in this paragraph?

**A** dictator's regime

**B** death squads

**C** military equipment

**D** in cold blood

4. Which of the following words contributes to the speech's focus on safety?

**F** ally

**G** future

**H** information

**J** protections

5. Read this excerpt from the text.

> After our nation was attacked on September the 11th, 2001, America made a decision: We will not wait for our enemies to strike before we act against them. We're not going to permit terrorists and terror states to plot and plan and grow in strength while we do nothing.

Why did President Bush use the word "attacked" to describe what happened on September 11?

**A** to provide a neutral explanation of what happened on September 11

**B** to show that the United States was not responsible for the events of September 11

**C** to persuade listeners that the events of September 11 could not have been prevented

**D** to remind listeners of the violent nature of the events that occurred on September 11

## Analyzing and Evaluating Word Choice in Various Texts

Word choice is particularly important when a text is written for the purpose of persuasion. The author's word choices, including connotative language and figurative language, inform the reader about how the writer wants him or her to feel about the topic.

**Directions:** Read the text. Then do Numbers 6–11.

# From "Is It a Crime for a Citizen of the United States to Vote?"

*by Susan B. Anthony*

Friends and Fellow Citizens: I stand before you tonight under indictment for the alleged crime of having voted at the last presidential election, without having a lawful right to vote. It shall be my work this evening to prove to you that in thus voting, I not only committed no crime, but, instead, simply exercised my citizen's rights, guaranteed to me and all United States citizens by the National Constitution, beyond the power of any State to deny.

Our democratic-republican government is based on the idea of the natural right of every individual member thereof to a voice and a vote in making and executing the laws. We assert the province of government to be to secure the people in the enjoyment of their unalienable rights. We throw to the winds the old dogma that governments can give rights. Before governments were organized, no one denies that each individual possessed the right to protect his own life, liberty, and property. And when 100 or 1,000,000 people enter into a free government, they do not barter away their natural rights; they simply pledge themselves to protect each other in the enjoyment of them, through prescribed judicial and legislative tribunals. They agree to abandon the methods of brute force in the adjustment of their differences, and adopt those of civilization. . . .

The preamble of the Federal Constitution says:

"We, the people of the United States, in order to form a more perfect union, establish justice, insure domestic tranquility, provide for the common defense, promote the general welfare, and secure the blessings of liberty to ourselves and our posterity, do ordain and establish this Constitution for the United States of America."

It was we, the people; not we, the white male citizens; nor yet we, the male citizens; but we, the whole people, who formed the Union. And we formed it, not to give the blessings of liberty, but to secure them; not to the half of ourselves and the half of our posterity, but to the whole people—women as well as men. And it is a downright mockery to talk to women of their enjoyment of the blessings of liberty while they are denied the use of the only means of securing them provided by this democratic-republican government—the ballot.

6. **Susan B. Anthony chose the words in this speech to**

   F  warn people that women have the right to vote

   G  teach people that women have the right to vote

   H  notify people that women have the right to vote

   J  persuade people that women have the right to vote

7. **Anthony chose her words to influence which audience?**

   A  women

   B  politicians

   C  average citizens

   D  male landowners

8. **Read this sentence from the speech.**

> It shall be my work this evening to prove to you that in thus voting, I not only committed no crime, but, instead, simply exercised my citizen's rights, guaranteed to me and all United States citizens by the National Constitution, beyond the power of any State to deny.

**What does the word <u>exercised</u> mean as it is used in this sentence?**

F  eliminated

G  ignored

H  maintained

J  used

9. **Which of the following phrases is an example of figurative language?**

A  unalienable rights

B  throw to the winds

C  governments can give rights

D  protect each other

10. **Read this sentence from the speech.**

> And it is a downright mockery to talk to women of their enjoyment of the blessings of liberty while they are denied the use of the only means of securing them provided by this democratic-republican government—the ballot.

**Which idea is conveyed by the word "mockery"?**

F  It is silly to talk of rights when women are not able to vote.

G  It is difficult to talk of rights when women are not able to vote.

H  It is meaningless to talk of rights when women are not able to vote.

J  It is encouraging to talk of rights when women are not able to vote.

11. **How does Anthony want her audience to feel as a result of her word choices?**

A  angry

B  depressed

C  excited

D  hopeful

---

 **Test-Taking Tip**

Context clues can help you figure out the meaning of a word used in a test question. If you come across a test question that has an unfamiliar word, search the rest of the question for clues to its meaning. You can also refer to the test's introduction and directions for context clues.

---

## Writing Practice

A speech often aims to persuade listeners to agree with the speaker's beliefs or goals. A speechwriter uses carefully chosen words to evoke emotions and communicate a message.

**Directions:** In his speech about Operation Liberty Shield on pages 79 and 80, George W. Bush aimed to persuade listeners that the operation was necessary. Does his speech persuade you? Why or why not? Write an explanatory text analyzing Bush's word choices and effectively select examples from the text to explain how the speech affected you. Organize your ideas so that each new element builds on that which precedes it to create a unified whole.

This lesson will help you practice analyzing the development of ideas in fiction and nonfiction texts. Use it with Core Lesson 4.1 *Analyze the Development of Ideas* to reinforce and apply that knowledge.

| Key Concept | Core Skills |
|---|---|
| Every piece of writing has a structure. Writers develop their ideas in texts through organization. | • Recognize Organization<br>• Analyze Text Structure |

## Identifying Text Structure

Authors can organize their texts using one or more of five main structures. Using the structure of sequence, writers relate events in the order in which they happened or ideas in the order of importance. Often these texts include words such as *first, second, next,* and *last.* Another way writers organize their writing is by comparing or contrasting two or more ideas using words such as *although, both,* and *in contrast.* A third way to organize a text is through cause and effect. Words and phrases such as *so, therefore, since,* and *as a result* identify cause-and-effect structure. Description, the fourth type of structure, involves using vivid details to guide how a narrative unfolds. Using the description structure, writers often use terms that express spatial relationships: *above, to the right, next to.* Finally, writers who use the structure of problem and solution present a problem and one or more solutions. Texts written using this structure commonly include words and phrases such as *in order to* and *so that.*

**Directions:** Read the text. Then do Numbers 1–4.

## From *Sinking of the Titanic and Great Sea Disasters*
### edited by Logan Marshall

Ever was [an] ill-starred voyage more [promising] than when the *Titanic* . . . steamed majestically out of the port of Southampton. [The ship left] at noon on Wednesday, April 10th, bound for New York.

Elaborate preparations had been made for the maiden voyage. Crowds of eager watchers gathered to witness the departure. . . . [Everyone was] interested because of the notable people who were to travel aboard her. Friends and relatives of many of the passengers were at the dock to bid Godspeed to their departing loved ones. The passengers themselves were unusually gay and happy.

Majestic and beautiful the ship rested on the water, marvel of shipbuilding, worthy of any sea. As this new queen of the ocean moved slowly from her dock, no one questioned her construction. . . . [She had] an elaborate system of water-tight compartments, calculated to make her unsinkable. She had been pronounced the safest as well as the most [luxurious] Atlantic liner afloat.

There was silence just before the boat pulled out. . . . [Then] the heavy whistles sounded. The splendid Titanic, her flags flying and her band playing, churned the water and plowed heavily away.

Then . . . the people on board wav[ed] handkerchiefs and shout[ed] good-byes. . . . [Their voices] could be heard only as a buzzing murmur on shore. [Next, the *Titanic*] rode away on the ocean, proudly [and] majestically. . . .

*(Continued on next page)*

And so it was only her due that the *Titanic* steamed out of the harbor bound on her maiden voyage. . . . A thousand "God-speeds" were [called] after her, while [she dwarfed] every other vessel that she passed. . . .

In command of the *Titanic* was Captain E.J. Smith. . . . The next six officers, in the order of their rank, were Murdock, Lightollder [sic], Pitman, Boxhall, Lowe and Moody. Dan Phillips was chief wireless operator, with Harold Bride as assistant.

From the forward bridge, fully ninety feet above the sea, peered out the [kind] face of the ship's master. [He was] cool of aspect, deliberate of action, [and] impressive in [his confidence]. . . .

From far below the bridge sounded the strains of the ship's orchestra, playing a favorite air from "The Chocolate Soldier." All went as merry as a wedding bell. Indeed, among that gay ship's company were two score or more at least for whom the wedding bells had sounded. . . . Some were on their honeymoon tours. Others were returning to their motherland. . . .

[Who] would have [predicted] that within the span of six days that stately ship . . . would lie at the bottom of the Atlantic . . . ?

1. **What is the structure of this passage?**
   A sequence
   B cause and effect
   C compare and contrast
   D problem and solution

2. **Read this sentence from the text.**

   **A thousand "God-speeds" were [called] after her, while [she dwarfed] every other vessel that she passed. . . .**

   **What purpose does this sentence serve in the passage?**
   F to contrast the *Titanic* with other ships
   G to compare the *Titanic* with other ships
   H to describe the cause of the *Titanic*'s sinking
   J to describe the effect of the *Titanic*'s sinking

3. **Read this excerpt from the text.**

   **Then . . . the people on board wav[ed] handkerchiefs and shout[ed] good-byes. . . . [Their voices] could be heard only as a buzzing murmur on shore. [Next, the *Titanic*] rode away on the ocean, proudly [and] majestically. . . .**

   **Which word in the excerpt highlights the text structure of the passage?**
   A and
   B could
   C next
   D on

4. **Which excerpt from the passage provides a cause for the large crowds to have gathered at the departure of the *Titanic*?**
   F Elaborate preparations had been made. . . . Crowds of eager watchers gathered to witness the departure.
   G Friends and relatives . . . were at the dock to bid Godspeed to their departing loved ones.
   H She had been pronounced the safest as well as the most [luxurious] Atlantic liner afloat.
   J Then . . . the people on board wav[ed] handkerchiefs and shout[ed] good-byes.

## Variations in Organization

Chronological order (or time order) describes a sequence of events by relating what happened first, second, third, and so on. However, there are variations of this text structure. When writers interrupt the sequence to introduce events that took place before the story began, this is called flashback. Slow pacing adds details and descriptions so the plot moves along gradually. Fast pacing moves through events quickly in order to arrive at an important moment.

**Directions:** Read the text. Then do Numbers 5–8.

## From "The Adventure of the Dancing Men"
### *by Sir Arthur Conan Doyle*

Holmes had been seated for some hours in silence with his long, thin back curved over a chemical vessel in which he was brewing a particularly malodorous product. His head was sunk upon his breast, and he looked from my point of view like a strange, lank bird, with dull gray plumage and a black top-knot.

"So, Watson," said he, suddenly, "you do not propose to invest in South African securities?"

I gave a start of astonishment. Accustomed as I was to Holmes's curious facilities, this sudden intrusion into my most intimate thoughts was utterly inexplicable.

"How on earth do you know that?" I asked.

He wheeled around upon his stool, with a steaming test-tube in his hand, and a gleam of amusement in his deep-set eyes.

"Now, Watson, confess yourself utterly taken aback," said he.

"I am."

"I ought to make you sign a paper to that effect."

"Why?"

"Because in five minutes you will say that it is all so absurdly simple."

"I am sure I will say nothing of the kind."

"You see, my dear Watson"—he propped his test-tube in the rack, and began to lecture with the air of a professor addressing his class—"it is not really difficult to construct a series of inferences, each dependent upon its predecessor and each simple in itself. If, after doing so, one simply knocks out all the central inferences and presents one's audience with the starting-point and the conclusion, one may produce a startling, though possibly a meretricious, effect. Now, it was not really difficult, by an inspection of the groove between your left forefinger and thumb, to feel sure that you did *not* propose to invest your small capital in the gold fields."

"I see no connection."

"Very likely not; but I can quickly show you a close connection. Here are the missing links of the very simple chain: 1. You had chalk between your left finger and thumb when you returned from the club last night. 2. You put chalk there when you play billiards, to steady the cue. 3. You never play billiards except with Thurston. 4. You told me, four weeks ago, that Thurston had an option on some South African property which would expire in a month, and which he desired you to share with him. 5. Your check book is locked in my drawer, and you have not asked for the key. 6. You do not propose to invest your money in this manner."

*(Continued on next page)*

"How absurdly simple!" I cried.

"Quite so!" said he, a little nettled. "Every problem becomes very childish once it is explained to you. Here is an unexplained one. See what you can make of that, friend Watson." He tossed a sheet of paper upon the table, and turned once more to his chemical analysis.

I looked with amazement at the absurd hieroglyphics upon the paper.

"Why, Holmes, it is a child's drawing," I cried.

"Oh, that's your idea!"

"What else should it be?"

"That is what Mr. Hilton Cubitt, of Riding Thorpe Manor, Norfolk, is very anxious to know. This little conundrum came by the first post, and he was to follow by the next train. There's a ring at the bell, Watson. I should not be very much surprised if this were he."

A heavy step was heard upon the stairs, and an instant later there entered a tall, ruddy, clean-shaven gentleman, whose clear eyes and florid cheeks told of a life led far from the fogs of Baker Street. He seemed to bring a whiff of his strong, fresh, bracing, east-coast air with him as he entered. Having shaken hands with each of us, he was about to sit down, when his eye rested upon the paper with the curious markings, which I had just examined and left upon the table.

"Well, Mr. Holmes, what do you make of these?" he cried. "They told me that you were fond of queer mysteries, and I don't think you can find a queerer one than that. I sent the paper on ahead, so that you might have time to study it before I came."

"It is certainly rather a curious production," said Holmes. "At first sight it would appear to be some childish prank. It consists of a number of absurd little figures dancing across the paper upon which they are drawn. Why should you attribute any importance to so grotesque an object?"

"I never should, Mr. Holmes. But my wife does. It is frightening her to death. She says nothing, but I can see terror in her eyes. That's why I want to sift the matter to the bottom."

Holmes held up the paper so that the sunlight shone full upon it. It was a page torn from a notebook. The markings were done in pencil. . . .

Holmes examined it for some time, and then, folding it carefully up, he placed it in his pocketbook.

"This promises to be a most interesting and unusual case," said he. "You gave me a few particulars in your letter, Mr. Hilton Cubitt, but I should be very much obliged if you would kindly go over it all again for the benefit of my friend, Dr. Watson."

5.  **Read this excerpt from the text.**

> **A heavy step was heard upon the stairs, and an instant later there entered a tall, ruddy, clean-shaven gentleman, whose clear eyes and florid cheeks told of a life led far from the fogs of Baker Street. He seemed to bring a whiff of his strong, fresh, bracing, east-coast air with him as he entered. Having shaken hands with each of us, he was about to sit down, when his eye rested upon the paper with the curious markings, which I had just examined and left upon the table.**

**Which text structure is used in the paragraph?**

A  cause and effect

B  chronological order

C  problem and solution

D  compare and contrast

6. **Read this sentence from the text.**

> If, after doing so, one simply knocks out all the central inferences, each dependent upon its predecessor and each simple in itself.

**What does the word** <u>inferences</u> **mean as it is used in this sentence?**

F   conclusions

G   evidence

H   reasoning

J   statements

7. **Read this excerpt from the text.**

> . . . Here are the missing links of the very simple chain: 1. You had chalk between your left finger and thumb when you returned from the club last night. 2. You put chalk there when you play billiards, to steady the cue. 3. You never play billiards except with Thurston. 4. You told me, four weeks ago, that Thurston had an option on some South African property which would expire in a month, and which he desired you to share with him. 5. Your check book is locked in my drawer, and you have not asked for the key. 6. You do not propose to invest your money in this manner.

**What is the structure of the ideas in the excerpt?**

A   Holmes uses flashbacks to relate the events of the simple chain.

B   Holmes uses fast pacing to relate the events of the simple chain.

C   Holmes uses slow pacing to relate the events of the simple chain.

D   Holmes uses compare and contrast to relate the events of the simple chain.

8. **Which summary reflects the order in which events occur in the passage?**

F   Holmes brews something in a chemical vessel. Holmes tells Watson the six missing links of the simple chain. Holmes holds up a piece of paper in the sunlight. Mr. Hilton Cubitt rings the doorbell.

G   Holmes brews something in a chemical vessel. Mr. Hilton Cubitt rings the doorbell. Holmes tells Watson the six missing links of the simple chain. Holmes holds up a piece of paper in the sunlight.

H   Holmes brews something in a chemical vessel. Holmes holds up a piece of paper in the sunlight. Holmes tells Watson the six missing links of the simple chain. Mr. Hilton Cubitt rings the doorbell.

J   Holmes brews something in a chemical vessel. Holmes tells Watson the six missing links of the simple chain. Mr. Hilton Cubitt rings the doorbell. Holmes holds up a piece of paper in the sunlight.

 **Test-Taking Tip**

The more you practice identifying the text structure of a passage, the more confident you will be as a reader. By noticing words that are specific to particular text structures, like *first* and *as a result*, you will understand what kind of passage you are reading. Looking for words like this when reading a passage on a test will help you understand the text and the questions that follow.

## Language Practice

A sentence can be simple, compound, complex, or compound-complex. A simple sentence contains one independent clause (a clause that can stand alone). Rarely will a reader encounter a sequence of simple sentences in a text, however. Varying sentence structure makes the text more engaging and expresses relationships among ideas more clearly. A compound sentence joins two independent clauses with a comma followed by a coordinating conjunction. Coordinating conjunctions include *and, but, or,* and *so.* A complex sentence contains one independent clause and one or more dependent clauses (clauses that can't stand alone). The dependent clause is joined to the main clause by a conjunction such as *after, although, because, if,* or *until.* The dependent clause may come at the beginning of the sentence (followed by a comma) or at the end (with no comma between the clauses). A compound-complex sentence contains two or more independent clauses and at least one dependent clause.

**Directions:** Read the draft of an excerpt from an article. Then do Numbers 9 through 12.

[1]Parrots are affectionate and entertaining pets. [2]They also cost of lot of money and time. [3]Let's say you decide to get a parrot. [4]There are several things you'll need right away. [5]You'll need a cage. [6]You should fill the cage with a variety of toys. [7]Your bird will also need a variety of foods, such as seeds, nuts, and lots of juicy fresh fruit. [8]You will also need to spend several hours a day taking care of your bird. [9]You have to feed your bird and clean its cage. [10]Parrots need affection. [11]You have to spend time cuddling your bird.

9. **Which option best combines sentences 1 and 2?**

   **A**  Parrots are affectionate and entertaining pets and are expensive, too.

   **B**  Parrots are affectionate and entertaining pets, and cost money and time.

   **C**  Parrots are affectionate and entertaining pets, but they cost a lot of money and time.

   **D**  Parrots are affectionate and entertaining pets since they cost a lot of money and time.

10. **Which option best combines sentences 3 and 4?**

   **F**  If you decide to get a parrot, there are several things you'll need right away.

   **G**  Let's say you decide to get a parrot so you'll need several things right away.

   **H**  Let's say you decide to get a parrot and several things you'll need right away.

   **J**  If you decide to get a parrot, but there are several things you'll need right away.

11. **Which option best combines sentences 5 and 6?**

   **A**  You'll need a cage and a variety of toys.

   **B**  You'll need a cage but fill it with a variety of toys.

   **C**  You'll need a cage, and fill it with a variety of toys.

   **D**  You'll need a cage, which you should fill with a variety of toys.

12. **Which the option best combines sentences 9, 10, and 11?**

   **F**  You have to feed your bird, clean its cage, and cuddle it when parrots need affection.

   **G**  You have to feed your bird, clean its cage, and cuddle your bird, since parrots need affection.

   **H**  Not only do you have to feed your bird and clean its cage, and parrots need affection, so you have to spend time cuddling your bird.

   **J**  Not only do you have to feed your bird and clean its cage, but, since parrots need affection, you have to spend time cuddling your bird.

## Writing Practice

Using transition words that are specific to a text structure helps writers develop their ideas. For example, texts organized by sequence may include words such as *yesterday, after that, next,* and *later.* Authors of compare-and-contrast texts use words and phrases such as *both, too,* and *have in common* to show how two subjects are alike. To show how two subjects are different, authors use words and phrases such as *but, on the other hand,* and *however.*

**Directions:** Write an explanatory text to compare and contrast how Sherlock Holmes and another fictional detective, Hercule Poirot, solve mysteries. Before you begin planning and writing, reread "The Adventure of the Dancing Men" and read the excerpt from *The Mysterious Affair at Styles* below and on the following pages. Analyze how the authors develop their ideas using their detective characters. Develop the text thoroughly by selecting the most significant and relevant details and quotations. Make sure you use words that are specific to the compare-and-contrast text structure.

## From "The Adventure of the Dancing Men"
### *by Sir Arthur Conan Doyle*

Holmes had been seated for some hours in silence with his long, thin back curved over a chemical vessel in which he was brewing a particularly malodorous product. His head was sunk upon his breast, and he looked from my point of view like a strange, lank bird, with dull gray plumage and a black top-knot.

"So, Watson," said he, suddenly, "you do not propose to invest in South African securities?"

I gave a start of astonishment. Accustomed as I was to Holmes's curious facilities, this sudden intrusion into my most intimate thoughts was utterly inexplicable.

"How on earth do you know that?" I asked.

He wheeled around upon his stool, with a steaming test-tube in his hand, and a gleam of amusement in his deep-set eyes.

"Now, Watson, confess yourself utterly taken aback," said he.

"I am."

"I ought to make you sign a paper to that effect."

"Why?"

"Because in five minutes you will say that it is all so absurdly simple."

"I am sure I will say nothing of the kind."

"You see, my dear Watson"—he propped his test-tube in the rack, and began to lecture with the air of a professor addressing his class—"it is not really difficult to construct a series of inferences, each dependent upon its predecessor and each simple in itself. If, after doing so, one simply knocks out all the central inferences and presents one's audience with the starting-point and the conclusion, one may produce a startling, though possibly a meretricious, effect. Now, it was not really difficult, by an inspection of the groove between your left forefinger and thumb, to feel sure that you did *not* propose to invest your small capital in the gold fields."

"I see no connection."

*(Continued on next page)*

"Very likely not; but I can quickly show you a close connection. Here are the missing links of the very simple chain: 1. You had chalk between your left finger and thumb when you returned from the club last night. 2. You put chalk there when you play billiards, to steady the cue. 3. You never play billiards except with Thurston. 4. You told me, four weeks ago, that Thurston had an option on some South African property which would expire in a month, and which he desired you to share with him. 5. Your check book is locked in my drawer, and you have not asked for the key. 6. You do not propose to invest your money in this manner."

"How absurdly simple!" I cried.

"Quite so!" said he, a little nettled. "Every problem becomes very childish once it is explained to you. Here is an unexplained one. See what you can make of that, friend Watson." He tossed a sheet of paper upon the table, and turned once more to his chemical analysis.

I looked with amazement at the absurd hieroglyphics upon the paper.

"Why, Holmes, it is a child's drawing," I cried.

"Oh, that's your idea!"

"What else should it be?"

"That is what Mr. Hilton Cubitt, of Riding Thorpe Manor, Norfolk, is very anxious to know. This little conundrum came by the first post, and he was to follow by the next train. There's a ring at the bell, Watson. I should not be very much surprised if this were he."

A heavy step was heard upon the stairs, and an instant later there entered a tall, ruddy, clean-shaven gentleman, whose clear eyes and florid cheeks told of a life led far from the fogs of Baker Street. He seemed to bring a whiff of his strong, fresh, bracing, east-coast air with him as he entered. Having shaken hands with each of us, he was about to sit down, when his eye rested upon the paper with the curious markings, which I had just examined and left upon the table.

"Well, Mr. Holmes, what do you make of these?" he cried. "They told me that you were fond of queer mysteries, and I don't think you can find a queerer one than that. I sent the paper on ahead, so that you might have time to study it before I came."

"It is certainly rather a curious production," said Holmes. "At first sight it would appear to be some childish prank. It consists of a number of absurd little figures dancing across the paper upon which they are drawn. Why should you attribute any importance to so grotesque an object?"

"I never should, Mr. Holmes. But my wife does. It is frightening her to death. She says nothing, but I can see terror in her eyes. That's why I want to sift the matter to the bottom."

Holmes held up the paper so that the sunlight shone full upon it. It was a page torn from a notebook. The markings were done in pencil. . . .

Holmes examined it for some time, and then, folding it carefully up, he placed it in his pocketbook.

"This promises to be a most interesting and unusual case," said he. "You gave me a few particulars in your letter, Mr. Hilton Cubitt, but I should be very much obliged if you would kindly go over it all again for the benefit of my friend, Dr. Watson."

# From *The Mysterious Affair at Styles*

*by Agatha Christie*

In a few minutes I was knocking at the door of Leastways Cottage.

. . . A window above me was cautiously opened, and Poirot himself looked out.

He gave an exclamation of surprise at seeing me. In a few brief words, I explained the tragedy that had occurred, and that I wanted his help. . . .

In a few moments he had unbarred the door, . . . and I related the whole story, keeping back nothing, and omitting no circumstance, however insignificant. . . .

I told him of my awakening, of Mrs. Inglethorp's dying words, of her husband's absence, of the quarrel the day before, of the scrap of conversation between Mary and her mother-in-law that I had overheard, of the former quarrel between Mrs. Inglethorp and Evelyn Howard, and of the latter's innuendoes.

I was hardly as clear as I could wish. I repeated myself several times, and occasionally had to go back to some detail that I had forgotten. Poirot smiled kindly on me.

"The mind is confused? Is it not so? Take time, mon ami [my friend]. You are agitated; you are excited—it is but natural. Presently, when we are calmer, we will arrange the facts, neatly, each in his proper place. We will examine—and reject. Those of importance we will put on one side; those of no importance, pouf!"—he screwed up his cherub-like face, and puffed comically enough—"blow them away!"

"That's all very well," I objected, "but how are you going to decide what is important, and what isn't? That always seems the difficulty to me."

Poirot shook his head energetically. He was now arranging his moustache with exquisite care.

"Not so. Voyons [Let's see]! One fact leads to another—so we continue. Does the next fit in with that? A merveille [wonder]! Good! We can proceed. This next little fact—no! Ah, that is curious! There is something missing—a link in the chain that is not there. We examine. We search. And that little curious fact, that possibly paltry little detail that will not tally, we put it here!" He made an extravagant gesture with his hand. "It is significant! It is tremendous!"

"Y—es—"

"Ah!" Poirot shook his forefinger so fiercely at me that I quailed before it. "Beware! Peril to the detective who says: 'It is so small—it does not matter. It will not agree. I will forget it.' That way lies confusion! Everything matters."

"I know. You always told me that. That's why I have gone into all the details of this thing whether they seemed to me relevant or not."

"And I am pleased with you. You have a good memory, and you have given me the facts faithfully. Of the order in which you present them, I say nothing—truly, it is deplorable! But I make allowances—you are upset. To that I attribute the circumstance that you have omitted one fact of paramount importance."

"What is that?" I asked.

"You have not told me if Mrs. Inglethorp ate well last night."

I stared at him. Surely the war had affected the little man's brain. . . .

"I don't remember," I said. "And, anyway, I don't see—"

"You do not see? But it is of the first importance."

*(Continued on next page)*

"I can't see why," I said, rather nettled. "As far as I can remember, she didn't eat much. She was obviously upset, and it had taken her appetite away. That was only natural."

"Yes," said Poirot thoughtfully, "it was only natural." . . .

"Poirot," I said, "I wish you would tell me why you wanted to know if Mrs. Inglethorp ate well last night?" . . .

"I do not mind telling you—though, as you know, it is not my habit to explain until the end is reached. The present contention is that Mrs. Inglethorp died of strychnine poisoning, presumably administered in her coffee. . . . Something may arise at the autopsy to explain it. In the meantime, remember it."

_____

_____

_____

_____

_____

_____

_____

_____

_____

_____

_____

_____

_____

_____

_____

_____

This lesson will help you practice identifying text structure and understand how text structure impacts key ideas. Use it with Core Lesson 4.2 *Analyze How Structure Impacts Key Ideas* to reinforce and apply your knowledge.

| Key Concept | Core Skills |
| --- | --- |
| Authors structure what they write to communicate and reinforce key ideas. | • Analyze the Relationship between Paragraphs<br>• Understand Organization |

## Identifying Text Structures

Writers organize their work to help readers understand their ideas. They often use one of the five most common structures—sequence, compare and contrast, cause and effect, description, and problem and solution.

A text with a sequence text structure places events in time order. Another type of sequence is order of importance in which the most important point is presented first or at the end of the text. In texts that use compare-and-contrast structure, a writer compares, contrasts, or compares and contrasts ideas. Cause-and-effect texts describe how events cause other events. An event can have multiple causes or multiple effects. Texts that have a description text structure use the five senses to paint a vivid picture. Finally, problem-and-solution texts offer one or more solutions to a problem.

**Directions:** Read the text. Then do Numbers 1–4.

# From "Graduated Driver Licensing"
### *by the National Safety Council*

1   The National Safety Council is a leader in promoting Graduated Driver Licensing (GDL).

2   GDL is a novice driver licensing system that is proven effective at reducing teen drivers' high crash risk by 20–40%. States with stronger, comprehensive GDL systems see a higher reduction in teen crashes. GDL reduces teen driver exposure to high crash risk situations, such as nighttime driving and teen passengers.

3   GDL systems have three stages of licensure:
   1. A learner's permit that allows driving only while supervised by a fully licensed driver.
   2. An intermediate (sometimes called provisional) license that allows unsupervised driving under certain restrictions including nighttime and passenger limits.
   3. A full license.

4   All new drivers can make wrong decisions behind the wheel. However teens are the most at jeopardy. They bring to the road a unique mix of inexperience, distraction, peer pressure and a tendency to underestimate risk. . . .

5   Most Americans typically learn to drive during the teen years, when the brain is not fully mature yet. Recent research is beginning to give us insight into why many teens have difficulty regulating risk-taking behavior:
   • The area of the brain that weighs consequences, suppresses impulses and organizes thoughts does not fully mature until about age 25.
   • Hormones are more active in teens, which influence the brain's neurochemicals that regulate excitability and mood. The result can be thrill-seeking behavior and experiences that create intense feelings.

*(Continued on next page)*

6    Learning to regulate driving behavior comes with time and practice. Defensive Driving Course-Alive at 25® offers a balanced approach to help teens not only regulate their own driving behavior, but also help them deal with the actual issues that can influence their driving behavior.

7    Driver education programs play a role in preparing teens to drive, but should not be viewed as the end of the learning-to-drive process. In order to develop safe driving skills, inexperienced drivers need opportunities to improve through gradual exposure to increasingly challenging driving tasks. Teens become safer drivers with more driving experience.

8    In some states, the completion of driver education qualifies a teen for full driving privileges. The National Safety Council believes this is not a wise approach. Research shows that significant hours of behind-the-wheel experience are necessary to reduce crash risk. Parent involvement and Graduated Driver Licensing play important roles in developing skills.

9    DriveitHOME is a new program offering specially created resources to help parents keep their teens safer on the roads, especially after a teen gets a driver's license. Designed by parents for parents, the unique program includes an interactive website featuring engaging videos, practice tips and other critical resources. Parents can sign up to receive weekly practice tips and suggestions via e-mail, and are encouraged to share their own teaching techniques and experiences.

1.   **Read this excerpt from the text.**

> **GDL systems have three stages of licensure:**
> 1. **A learner's permit that allows driving only while supervised by a fully licensed driver.**
> 2. **An intermediate (sometimes called provisional) license that allows unsupervised driving under certain restrictions including nighttime and passenger limits.**
> 3. **A full license.**

   **Which text structure best describes the way the ideas in this excerpt are organized?**

   **A**  sequence

   **B**  cause and effect

   **C**  order of importance

   **D**  compare and contrast

2.   **Which sentence from the passage offers one solution to the problem of teen drivers' high crash risk?**

   **F**  All new drivers can make wrong decisions behind the wheel.

   **G**  However teens are the most at jeopardy.

   **H**  They bring to the road a unique mix of inexperience, distraction, peer pressure and a tendency to underestimate risk.

   **J**  Teens become safer drivers with more driving experience.

3.   **Which paragraph from the passage presents causes for why teens have difficulty managing risky behavior behind the wheel?**

   **A**  paragraph 2 (beginning with "GDL is a novice driver licensing system . . .")

   **B**  paragraph 3 (beginning with "GDL systems have three stages of licensure . . .")

   **C**  paragraph 5 (beginning with "Most Americans typically learn to drive . . .")

   **D**  paragraph 7 (beginning with "Driver education programs play a role . . .")

4. **Which sentence from the passage describes an effect of the GDL?**

   **F** States with stronger, comprehensive GDL systems see a higher reduction in teen crashes.

   **G** Learning to regulate driving behavior comes with time and practice.

   **H** In some states, the completion of driver education qualifies a teen for full driving privileges.

   **J** Designed by parents for parents, the unique program includes an interactive website featuring engaging videos, practice tips and other critical resources.

## Text Structure and Key Ideas

Understanding where writers place important information can help readers identify the significant ideas in a text. Often a writer emphasizes an idea by placing it at the beginning or the end of a text.

**Directions:** Read the text. Then do Numbers 5–8.

# Adapted from the Writings and Observations of Charles Fort

1   A tremendous number of little toads, one or two months old, fell from a great thick cloud that appeared suddenly in a clear sky, in August 1804, near Toulouse, France, according to a letter from Prof. Pontus to M. Arago. (*Comptes Rendus*, 3-54.)

2   An issue of *Scientific American* magazine, dated July 12, 1873, reported that "A shower of frogs which darkened the air and covered the ground for a long distance is the reported result of a recent rainstorm at Kansas City, MO."

3   Some experts claim that small frogs and toads have never fallen from the sky, but in every purported case were "on the ground in the first place," or that there have been such falls "up from one place in a whirlwind, and down in another."

4   See, for instance, *Leisure Hours*, 3-779 for accounts of small frogs, or toads, said to have been seen to fall from the sky. The writer says that all observers were mistaken and that the frogs or toads must have fallen from trees or other places overhead.

5   There are, it must be said, cases where the possibility of fallen frogs having "been there in the first place" is quite remote:

6   Little frogs were found in London, after a heavy storm (July 30, 1838, *Notes and Queries*, 8-7-437).

7   Little toads were found in a desert, after a rainfall (Notes and Queries, 8-8-493).

8   At the same time, I do not completely dismiss the conventional explanation of whirlwinds as the [reason for] falling frogs. I think that there have likely been such occurrences. In the *London Times*, July 4, 1883, there is an account of a shower of twigs and leaves and tiny toads in a storm upon the slopes of the Apennines. This may have indeed been the work of a whirlwind.

9   That is one specific case, however. In others, while it is easy to say that small frogs that have fallen from the sky had been scooped up by a whirlwind, this gives no regard for mud, debris from the bottom of a pond, floating vegetation, or loose things from the shores. To accept a whirlwind as the cause, one would need to accept that a whirlwind somehow, very precisely, picked up frogs alone.

*(Continued on next page)*

10   There is also the fact that, of all instances I have studied that attribute the fall of small frogs or toads to whirlwinds, only one actually identifies or places the whirlwind. Also, it seems to me that a pond going up would be quite as interesting as frogs coming down, and that anybody who had lost a pond would be heard from. Yet in *Symons' Meteorological Magazine*, a fall of small frogs, near Birmingham, England, June 30, 1892, is attributed to a specific whirlwind, without a word as to any special pond that had contributed. And something else that strikes my attention here is that these frogs are described as almost white.

11   I am afraid there is no escape for us: we shall have to accept that upon this earth exist some still-unknown locations: places with white frogs in them.

5.  **Why does the author begin the passage with the observations of frog and toad sightings?**
   A   to present a solution for the problem of frogs and toads falling in France
   B   to show the problem that frog and toad sightings posed in London and France
   C   to reveal instances of frog and toad sightings before exploring what may have happened to cause the events
   D   to contrast the effects of frog and toad sightings in London with the effects of frog and toad sightings in the United States

6.  **Which paragraph from the passage begins with the author's skepticism about a possible cause of frog and toad sightings?**
   F   paragraph 2 (beginning with "An issue of *Scientific American* . . .")
   G   paragraph 3 (beginning with "Some experts claim . . .")
   H   paragraph 4 (beginning with "See, for instance, . . .")
   J   paragraph 10 (beginning with "There is also the fact that, . . .")

7.  **Read this sentence from the passage.**

   **There are, it must be said, cases where the possibility of fallen frogs having "been there in the first place" is quite remote.**

   **What does the word remote mean as it is used in this sentence?**
   A   device
   B   distant
   C   unfriendly
   D   unlikely

8.  **Which sentence from the passage reveals a possible cause of frogs and toads falling from the sky?**
   F   Little frogs were found in London, after a heavy storm.
   G   Little toads were found in a desert, after a rainfall.
   H   [A] shower of twigs and leaves and tiny toads [fell] . . . upon the slopes of the Apennines.
   J   This may have indeed been the work of a whirlwind.

**Test-Taking Tip**

When you approach a test prompt that requires you to write an essay, identify the text structure that will best fit your response. For example, if you are asked to write about the causes and effects of a natural disaster, you might want to write the causes first and then write about the effects. Knowing different types of text structures will help you decide how to organize your essay and how to determine the best place to write your ideas within each paragraph.

## Writing Practice

Authors use a variety of text structures to convey their ideas. In a well-structured passage, however it is organized, each section links to those before and after it to convey key ideas effectively.

**Directions:** Write an informative text to compare and contrast the structure of the two passages in this lesson: "Graduated Driver Licensing" on pages 95 and 96 and the writings of Charles Fort on pages 97 and 98. Analyze the relationship between sections of text in each passage, and evaluate how well the structure conveys key ideas. Use the most significant and relevant examples from the text as evidence in your response.

This lesson will help you practice analyzing the effects of transitional and signal words in nonfiction texts. Use it with Core Lesson 4.3 *Analyze the Effects of Transitional and Signal Words* to reinforce and apply your knowledge.

| Key Concept | Core Skills |
|---|---|
| Writers use certain words and phrases to link ideas within sentences and between sentences. | • Determine the Relationships among Ideas<br>• Analyze Transitions between Paragraphs |

## Locating Transitions

Transitions are shifts in the text that show the writer has moved from one idea to the next. Transitions can happen between paragraphs or within paragraphs. The best way to locate transitions is to look for signal words or phrases. Signal words and phrases express the following relationships: addition, time order, relative location, relative importance, cause and effect, comparison, contrast, example, and conclusion.

**Directions:** Read the text. Then do Numbers 1–5.

# How to Choose the Right Dog for You

1    Raising a puppy can be a great experience, but choosing a puppy is a big decision. You want to get the kind of dog that's right for you and your family. In addition, you want to pick a healthy puppy that will grow up to be a loyal pet for many years. How do you find the right puppy? Experts agree that you should follow several steps to ensure you choose the right pet.

2    First, before buying a dog, make sure you are getting the right kind of pet for your family. Think carefully about the breeds you are interested in, and decide which one will be best for your home. For instance, if you have young children who like to romp and play, you will probably want to get a breed that is large enough to play with your children. A Chihuahua, for instance, would not be a good choice, because it could be hurt easily while playing. On the other hand, the dog you choose should not be a large or aggressive breed if your children are very small. Seek advice from a dog breeder or veterinarian before making a choice.

3    After choosing the kind of dog you want, begin looking around. In general, large stores that sell puppies are not the best place to find a puppy because a dog from there might have health problems. Instead of heading for a large store, consider a reputable private breeder. If a private breeder is too expensive, you also might consider getting a dog from your city's animal shelter. When you get a dog from the animal shelter, you often only have to pay for the dog's license and required shots.

4    When you pick out a puppy from a litter, observe the puppies carefully from a distance and choose a puppy whose character you like.

5    After you have narrowed your choice to one puppy, examine it carefully. Inspect the dog to make sure its skin and fur look healthy. Make sure the puppy doesn't have ticks or fleas, and check its gums. Pink gums indicate good health, whereas white gums could indicate anemia caused by heartworm.

6    After you get your puppy home, continue to observe it to make sure it is the dog for you. If you need further advice, check with the breeder or your vet. If you follow the steps above, you will have a fine pet that will give you and your family years of loyalty and companionship.

1. **Read this excerpt from the text.**

   Raising a puppy can be a great experience, but choosing a puppy is a big decision. You want to get the kind of dog that's right for you and your family. In addition, you want to pick a healthy puppy that will grow up to be a loyal pet for many years. How do you find the right puppy? Experts agree that you should follow several steps to ensure you choose the right pet.

   **Which phrase in the paragraph is a signal phrase?**

   **A** that's right

   **B** in addition

   **C** for many

   **D** to ensure

2. **According to the passage, the first step in selecting the proper dog is to**

   **F** begin looking around to find the right dog

   **G** think about the best breeds for your family

   **H** narrow your choice to one puppy and examine it

   **J** continue to observe the dog to make sure it is the right fit

3. **What does the signal phrase <u>on the other hand</u> reveal about the shift in ideas in paragraph 2?**

   **A** It provides an example of large or aggressive breeds.

   **B** It shows the effect of buying a small Chihuahua breed.

   **C** It compares the small Chihuahua breed to a large or aggressive breed.

   **D** It contrasts the small Chihuahua breed with a large or aggressive breed.

4. **The signal phrase <u>for instance</u> is used twice in paragraph 2. Which transition does this signal phrase <u>show?</u>**

   **F** It shows what happens in time order after bringing a Chihuahua home.

   **G** It shows an effect of buying a Chihuahua on families with young children.

   **H** It reveals a relative location about the best places to find and buy different dogs.

   **J** It provides examples of dogs that might or might not be appropriate for families with young children.

5. **Read this excerpt from the text.**

   When you pick out a puppy from a litter, observe the puppies carefully from a distance and choose a puppy whose character you like.

   After you have narrowed your choice to one puppy, examine it carefully. Inspect the dog to make sure its skin and fur look healthy. Make sure the puppy doesn't have ticks or fleas, and check its gums. Pink gums indicate good health, whereas white gums could indicate anemia caused by heartworm.

   **What does the signal word <u>after</u> reveal about the relationship between ideas in the two paragraphs?**

   **A** The word <u>after</u> signals a contrast.

   **B** The word <u>after</u> signals a shift in time.

   **C** The word <u>after</u> signals that examples will follow.

   **D** The word <u>after</u> signals that a conclusion will be revealed.

## Analyzing Transitions

Transitions, whether they come between sentences or between paragraphs, tell the reader to slow down and focus on how the ideas have shifted. If signal words have not been used, you can infer transitions by paying attention to the relationship between ideas.

**Directions:** Read the text. Then do Numbers 6–10.

## Why NASA Deserves Our Continued (If Not Increased) Support

1    The Space Age began in 1957, with the Soviet Union's successful launch of the unmanned *Sputnik 1*. The first manned space mission came a mere four years later, in 1961, when Soviet cosmonaut Yuri Gagarin became the first human being to orbit Earth. During the five decades since, human beings have explored outer space in the same way that Europeans explored the hitherto unfamiliar expanses of the Americas during the Age of Exploration—by physically going there. Impressive accomplishments—sending humans to the moon, manually placing the *Hubble* telescope in Earth's orbit—can be credited to the United States National Aeronautics and Space Administration (NASA). Yet, despite NASA's extraordinary history, there has been continual discussion as to whether its continued existence is justified. Today we can state that the answer is "By all means, yes."

2    Let's begin our analysis of this assertion by addressing the primary objection to it—the United States cannot afford the expense. Space exploration costs a great deal of money. However, it is a mistake to think of NASA's budget as a waste of money that would be better spent on Earth. It is spent on Earth. When President Eisenhower created the agency in 1958, he said that one purpose for it was the development of new technologies adaptable for everyday use. NASA has excelled in this regard. To date, the organization has secured more than 6,000 patents, many of which have driven innovation in other fields. Thousands of inventions, such as cordless tools, water filters, smoke detectors, medical devices, cell phones, and home entertainment systems, can trace their technological lineage to one or more of NASA's patents.

3    Moreover, this pioneering of knowledge points to related advantages to space exploration—it answers questions about the material world and how it works, and it also leads to new questions that, when answered, uncover still further knowledge. Surely this potential for learning is as expansive as space itself. Who knows what remains to be discovered about the universe and our place in it? Perhaps we'll stumble upon new supplies of needed natural resources, new clues about the origins of life, or even new forms of life itself—some of which, it isn't far-fetched to consider, might have much in common with us and perhaps a thing or two to teach us.

4    As we think about all of this, we should also look at our world's likely future. There is no guarantee that humankind must forever survive and develop. Some claim that there is an increasing amount of evidence that the opposite outcome is likely. The world's population is growing at an ever-faster rate, but we have limited natural resources. There are at present more than 7 billion human beings on Earth, many already living in poverty. The United States Census Bureau estimates that there will be more than 9 billion humans by 2050. It seems unwise, therefore, not to put some effort toward finding new places for humans to live. This idea might seem like science fiction at present, but one decade's sci-fi is the next decade's science fact.

5    Finally, let's ponder a proposition that few people would dispute. Whatever the cause is, a spirit of curiosity and adventure is part of what it means to be a human being. To state that this inquisitiveness must be limited to the world in which we find ourselves ignores the fact that we would know little about our world if not for that spirit of adventure. To squelch our natural urge to explore space is to deny our very humanity.

6. **Which shift in ideas occurs between the first and second paragraphs?**

   F The first paragraph provides NASA's history, and the second paragraph provides examples of NASA's new technologies.

   G The first paragraph presents the problems of space exploration, and the second paragraph provides a solution to that problem.

   H The first paragraph provides information about the beginning of space exploration, and the second paragraph reveals a shift in time order.

   J The first paragraph presents some of NASA's accomplishments, and the second paragraph concludes that NASA should not be funded anymore.

7. **Read this sentence from the text.**

   Let's begin our analysis of this assertion by addressing the primary objection to it: the United States cannot afford the expense.

   **What does the word assertion mean as it is used in this sentence?**

   A command

   B declaration

   C question

   D request

8. **Read this sentence from the text.**

   Thousands of inventions, such as cordless tools, water filters, smoke detectors, medical devices, cell phones, and home entertainment systems, can trace their technological lineage to one or more of NASA's patents.

   **Which signal phrase could be placed at the beginning of this sentence?**

   F In brief

   G By contrast

   H For instance

   J In conclusion

9. **Read this excerpt from the text.**

   Finally, let's ponder a proposition that few people would dispute. Whatever the cause, a spirit of curiosity and adventure is part of what it means to be a human being. To state that this inquisitiveness must be limited to the world in which we find ourselves ignores the fact that we would know little about our world if not for that spirit of adventure. To squelch our natural urge to explore space is to deny our very humanity.

   **Which of the following statements is true?**

   A The word finally signals the relative location of ideas from the passage.

   B The word finally signals a conclusion of ideas presented in the passage.

   C The word whatever signals a contrast with the other ideas in the passage.

   D The word whatever signals a cause of events that is presented in the rest of the passage.

10. **Which type of transition does the word "moreover" signal?**

    F addition

    G cause

    H conclusion

    J effect

## Test-Taking Tip

When responding to a writing prompt on a test, reread your sentences to make sure that your signal words and phrases make sense in context. Signal words or phrases that have similar meanings cannot necessarily be used interchangeably. Suppose you wanted to write a sentence that contrasted apples and oranges, for example: "Unlike oranges, apples have an edible, thin peel." You might remember that "in spite of" is another signal phrase that shows contrast. Even so, you would not be able to substitute "in spite of" for "unlike" in this sentence. Rereading each sentence that contains a signal word or phrase should help you decide whether you used the right signal word or phrase.

## Writing Practice

Transitions and signal words build relationships among ideas and can make a text more powerful and coherent. In an argument, they connect and build on key points.

**Directions:** Reread the following passage in support of NASA. Then read the second passage, which argues against funding for NASA. Which side are you on? Write an argument to support the claim for or against continued funding for NASA. Support your claim with examples from the texts. Use appropriate and varied transitions to link the major sections of your text, create cohesion, and clarify the relationships among ideas and concepts.

## Why NASA Deserves Our Continued (If Not Increased) Support

The Space Age began in 1957, with the Soviet Union's successful launch of the unmanned *Sputnik 1*. The first manned space mission came a mere four years later, in 1961, when Soviet cosmonaut Yuri Gagarin became the first human being to orbit Earth. During the five decades since, human beings have explored outer space in the same way that Europeans explored the hitherto unfamiliar expanses of the Americas during the Age of Exploration—by physically going there. Impressive accomplishments—sending humans to the moon, manually placing the *Hubble* telescope in Earth's orbit—can be credited to the United States National Aeronautics and Space Administration (NASA). Yet, despite NASA's extraordinary history, there has been continual discussion as to whether its continued existence is justified. Today we can state that the answer is "By all means, yes."

Let's begin our analysis of this assertion by addressing the primary objection to it—the United States cannot afford the expense. Space exploration costs a great deal of money. However, it is a mistake to think of NASA's budget as a waste of money that would be better spent on Earth. It *is* spent on Earth. When President Eisenhower created the agency in 1958, he said that one purpose for it was the development of new technologies adaptable for everyday use. NASA has excelled in this regard. To date, the organization has secured more than 6,000 patents, many of which have driven innovation in other fields. Thousands of inventions, such as cordless tools, water filters, smoke detectors, medical devices, cell phones, and home entertainment systems, can trace their technological lineage to one or more of NASA's patents.

Moreover, this pioneering of knowledge points to related advantages to space exploration—it answers questions about the material world and how it works, and it also leads to new questions that, when answered, uncover still further knowledge. Surely this potential for learning is as expansive as space itself. Who knows what remains to be discovered about the universe and our place in it? Perhaps we'll stumble upon new supplies of needed natural resources, new clues about the origins of life, or even new forms of life itself—some of which, it isn't far-fetched to consider, might have much in common with us and perhaps a thing or two to teach us.

*(Continued on next page)*

As we think about all of this, we should also look at our world's likely future. There is no guarantee that humankind must forever survive and develop. Some claim that there is an increasing amount of evidence that the opposite outcome is likely. The world's population is growing at an ever-faster rate, but we have limited natural resources. There are at present more than 7 billion human beings on Earth, many already living in poverty. The United States Census Bureau estimates that there will be more than 9 billion humans by 2050. It seems unwise, therefore, not to put some effort toward finding new places for humans to live. This idea might seem like science fiction at present, but one decade's sci-fi is the next decade's science fact.

Finally, let's ponder a proposition that few people would dispute. Whatever the cause is, a spirit of curiosity and adventure is part of what it means to be a human being. To state that this inquisitiveness must be limited to the world in which we find ourselves ignores the fact that we would know little about our world if not for that spirit of adventure. To squelch our natural urge to explore space is to deny our very humanity.

# From "Options for Reducing the Deficit: 2014 to 2023"

### *by the Congressional Budget Office*

NASA's Human Exploration and Operations programs focus on developing systems and capabilities required to explore deep space while continuing operations in low-Earth orbit. The exploration programs fund research and development of the next generation of systems for deep space exploration. [The programs also] provide technical and financial support to the commercial space industry. . . . NASA's space operations programs involve . . . using the International Space Station [and] providing space communications capabilities.

This [deficit reduction] option would terminate NASA's human space exploration and space operations programs, except for those necessary [for] space communications. . . . The agency's science and aeronautics programs and robotic space missions would continue. Eliminating those human space programs would save $73 billion between 2015 and 2023. . . .

The main argument for this option is that increased capabilities in electronics and information technology have generally reduced the need for humans to fly space missions. The scientific instruments used to gather knowledge in space rely much less (or not at all) on nearby humans to operate them. NASA and other federal agencies have increasingly adopted that approach in their activities on Earth. . . . [These activities use] robots to perform missions without putting humans in harm's way. For example, NASA has been using remotely piloted vehicles to track hurricanes over the Atlantic Ocean at much longer distances than those for which tracking aircraft are conventionally piloted.

Eliminating humans from spaceflights would avoid risk to human life. [It] would [also] decrease the cost of space exploration by reducing the weight and complexity of the vehicles needed for the missions. (Unlike instruments, humans need water, air, food, space to move around in, and rest.) In addition, by replacing people with instruments, the missions could be made one way. [R]eturn would be necessary only when the mission required it, such as to collect samples for further analysis. [T]hus, . . . the cost, weight, and complexity of return and reentry into the Earth's atmosphere [would be eliminated].

A major argument against this option is that eliminating human spaceflight from the orbits near Earth would end the technical progress necessary to prepare for human missions to Mars. . . . Moreover, if, in the future, robotic missions proved too limiting, then human space efforts would have to be restarted. Another argument against this option is that there may be some scientific advantage to having humans at the International Space Station to conduct experiments in microgravity. . . . (However, the International Space Station is currently scheduled to be retired in 2020. . . .)

This lesson will help you practice analyzing an author's purpose and point of view in two informational texts. Use it with Core Lesson 5.1 *Determine Author's Purpose and Point of View* to reinforce and apply your knowledge.

### Key Concept

Authors have a reason for writing, and they often have an opinion about the topic of their writing.

### Core Skills

- Determine Author's Purpose
- Establish Point of View

## Identifying an Author's Purpose

Authors write texts for a specific purpose. A text may be written to inform the reader about a topic, to persuade the reader to think a certain way, or to entertain him or her.

**Directions:** Read the text. Then do Numbers 1–4.

# The Nature of Waves

A **wave** is a periodic or harmonic disturbance in space or through a medium (water, for instance) by which energy is transmitted. Water, sound, and light travel in waves. The illumination a lamp provides comes from light waves, and the music emanating from a stereo comes from sound waves. The powers to preserve food and warm it come from electromagnetic waves, and the power that transmits signals to a television comes from radio waves. The energy that gives a waterbed its soothing motion comes from water waves.

**Types of Properties of Waves**

Waves transmit energy in different ways, and all phases of matter transmit waves. An example of a solid transmitting wave energy is an earthquake that takes place when rocks are under pressure and snap or slide into new positions. Waves that are felt and seen in water are examples of a liquid transmitting wave energy. Gases also transmit wave energy, as in an explosion, when heat, sound, and light waves are generated. Two basic types of waves exist: longitudinal waves and transverse waves.

**Longitudinal Wave**

Particles of the medium move back and forth in the same direction as the wave itself moves. An example of a longitudinal wave is a sound wave that occurs when a tuning fork is tapped. When a tuning fork is tapped, the prongs move from right to left in a rapid periodic motion. A sound wave is produced, and it moves parallel (right and left) to the moving prong.

**Transverse Wave**

Particles of the medium move at right angles to the direction of the wave's movement. An example of a transverse wave is one that occurs when a pebble is tossed into a still pond. When a stone is dropped into a pond, the waves produced appear to move outward. These waves move at right angles to the dropped stone.

**Wave Attributes**

Waves have two components, a crest and a trough. A **crest** is the point of highest displacement in a wave, and a **trough** is the point of lowest displacement. Crests and troughs are easily visible in water waves.

*(Continued on next page)*

Two specific characteristics of a wave are length and frequency:

- **Wavelength** is defined as the distance between two successive wave crests or two successive wave troughs.

- **Wave frequency** is the number of wave crests that pass a given point per second.

Therefore, the shorter the wavelength is, the higher the wave frequency will be. In fact, a wave's speed equals the wavelength times the wave frequency.

When a source of a wave is in motion, a compression of the wavelength is detected. This can be demonstrated with sound waves. As a train passes while you are standing on the platform, you will notice a distinct drop in the pitch or sound quality. This drop in sound pitch is heard by the observers standing on the side during an automotive race such as the Indianapolis 500. Water waves demonstrate the same compression in the direction of motion. The water waves in the front of a boat are squeezed together, while those at the rear of the boat are far apart. This is referred to as the **Doppler Effect**. Scientists use the Doppler Effect to forecast tornadoes and to detect the motion of stars in our galaxy.

**Sound Wave**

Sound waves are longitudinal waves. A musical pitch, or tone, is heard when there is a definite frequency to a wave—the lower the frequency, the lower the tone. For example, the frequency of a bass speaker in a stereo system is lower than a tweeter, or high-frequency speaker, because the low-pitched sound of the bass results from a lower number of vibrations per second.

1. **Which phrase best describes the author's purpose for this passage?**

   **A**  to inform

   **B**  to persuade

   **C**  to entertain

   **D**  to express emotion

2. **Read this sentence from the text.**

   **This drop in sound pitch is heard by the observers standing on the side during an automotive race such as the Indianapolis 500.**

   **How does this sentence support the author's purpose?**

   **F**  It gives the reader the desire to attend a race.

   **G**  It helps the reader visualize the excitement of a car race.

   **H**  It gives an example to illustrate compression in sound waves.

   **J**  It helps the reader understand the need to be careful around machinery.

3. **Read this sentence from the text.**

   **An example of a transverse wave is one that occurs when a pebble is tossed into a still pond.**

   **How does this sentence from the "Transverse Wave" section support the author's purpose?**

   **A**  It teaches about transverse waves by providing an example.

   **B**  It provides vivid sensory details to spark the reader's imagination.

   **C**  It provides a reason for the reader to agree with the author's viewpoint.

   **D**  It uses figurative language to help the reader enjoy reading the passage.

**4.** **Read this sentence from the text.**

> Wave frequency is the number of wave crests that pass a given point per second.

**Which definition fits the word <u>frequency</u> as it is used in this passage?**

**F** how often something happens

**G** what tunes you in to a radio station

**H** the proportion of one type of item in a group

**J** the number of times an electric current changes direction

## Recognizing an Author's Point of View

Point of view is the author's attitude toward a topic. A point of view may be positive, negative, or neutral. It may be expressed directly or implied.

**Directions:** Read the text. Then do Numbers 5–9.

# From "Selected Speeches of George W. Bush 2001–2008"

*by George W. Bush*

Both parties have been talking about education reform for quite a while. It's time to come together to get it done so that we can truthfully say in America, "No child will be left behind—not one single child."

We share a moment of exceptional promise—a new administration, a newly sworn-in Congress, and we have a chance to think anew and act anew.

All of us are impatient with the old lines of division. All of us want a different attitude here in the nation's capital. All in this room, as well as across the country, know things must change.

We must confront the scandal of illiteracy in America, seen most clearly in high-poverty schools, where nearly 70 percent of fourth graders are unable to read at a basic level. We must address the low standing of [American] test scores amongst industrialized nations in math and science, the very subjects most likely to affect our future competitiveness. We must focus the spending of federal tax dollars on things that work. Too often we have spent without regard for results, without judging success or failure from year to year.

We must face up to the plague of school violence, with an average of 3 million crimes committed against students and teachers inside public schools every year. That's unacceptable in our country. Change will not come by adding a few new federal programs to the old. If we work only at the edges, our influence will be confined to the margins. We need real reform.

Change will not come by disdaining or dismantling the federal role of education. I believe strongly in local control of schools. I trust local folks to chart the path to excellence. But educational excellence for all is a national issue, and at this moment is a presidential priority. I've seen how real education reform can lift up scores in schools and effectively change lives.

And real education reform reflects four basic commitments. First, children must be tested every year in reading and math. Every single year. Not just in the third grade or the eighth grade, but in the third, fourth, fifth, sixth and seventh and eighth grade. . . . Without yearly testing, we don't know who is falling behind and who needs help. Without yearly testing, too often we don't find failure until it is too late to fix. . . .

*(Continued on next page)*

Secondly, the agents of reform must be schools and school districts, not bureaucracies. Teachers and principals, local and state leaders must have the responsibility to succeed and the flexibility to innovate. One size does not fit all when it comes to educating the children in America. School districts, school officials, educational entrepreneurs should not be hindered by excessive rules and red tape and regulation.

. . . If local schools do not have the freedom to change, they cannot be held accountable for failing to change. Authority and accountability must be aligned at the local level, or schools will have a convenient excuse for failure. "I would have done it this way, but some central office or Washington, D.C., caused me to do it another way."

. . . Third, many of our schools, particularly low-income schools, will need help in the transition to higher standards. When a state sets standards, we must help schools achieve those standards.

We must measure, we must know; and if a school or school district falls short, we must understand that help should be applied. . . . Once failing schools are identified, we will help them improve. . . . We want success, and when schools are willing to accept the reality that the accountability system points out and are willing to change, we will help them.

Fourth, American children must not be left in persistently dangerous or failing schools. When schools do not teach and will not change, parents and students must have other meaningful options. And when children or teenagers go to school afraid of being threatened or attacked or worse, our society must make it clear it's the ultimate betrayal of adult responsibility.

Parents and children who have only bad options must eventually get good options, if we are to succeed all across the country. . . .

These four principles are the guides to our education reform package. Yet today I'm offering more than principles. I'm sending a series of specific proposals to the United States Congress; my own blueprint for reform. I want to begin our discussion in detail with the members of the House and the Senate, because I know we need to act by this summer so that the people at the local level can take our initiatives and plan for the school year beginning next fall.

. . . If somebody's got a better idea, I hope they bring it forward, because the secretary and I will listen.

We've got one thing in mind: an education system that's responsive to the children, an education system that educates every child, an education system that I'm confident can exist; one that's based upon sound fundamental curriculum, one that starts teaching children to read early in life, one that focuses on systems that do work, one that heralds our teachers and makes sure they've got the necessary tools to teach, but one that says every child can learn. And in this great land called America, no child will be left behind.

5. **Which statement best expresses the author's point of view?**

   **A** High standards leave some children behind.

   **B** Parents and children have too many choices in education.

   **C** The education system is not working and needs to be changed.

   **D** Education in the United States allows everyone to be successful.

6. **Which word best describes the author's point of view about the education system in the United States at the time of the speech?**

   **F** negative

   **G** neutral

   **H** optimistic

   **J** positive

7. **Which phrase best describes the author's purpose for this passage?**

   **A** to inform

   **B** to explain

   **C** to entertain

   **D** to persuade

8. **According to the author's point of view, what is most needed in the United States educational system?**

   **F** diversity

   **G** leaders

   **H** money

   **J** reform

9. **Which is not a suggestion the author lists to support his point of view?**

   **A** Create a uniform model for all children.

   **B** Help children transition to higher standards.

   **C** Test children every year in math and reading.

   **D** Allow children to leave dangerous or failing schools.

## Language Practice

In punctuation, an ellipsis is a series of three dots (. . .). If an ellipsis is used in the middle of a text, it indicates that a word or words—or even sentences—have been left out. Sometimes a writer may insert words in brackets to show the connections between the ideas separated by the ellipsis.

**Directions:** Read this paragraph from an article. Then do Numbers 10 and 11.

The Portuguese explorer Ferdinand Magellan should be known as the greatest navigator of all time. The fleet under his command discovered the Strait of Magellan, a passageway at the tip of South America that connects the Atlantic and Pacific oceans. Although he died before his voyage was completed, his navigational planning helped his crew finish their trip around the world. Magellan's discovery of the Strait of Magellan helped other explorers learn more about the Pacific Ocean. The most important result was that his long voyage proved that the world is actually round.

10. **Which sentence correctly uses ellipsis to indicate that text has been left out from the underlined sentence in the original source?**

    **F** The . . . explorer Ferdinand Magellan should be known as the greatest navigator of all time.

    **G** The Portuguese explorer Ferdinand Magellan . . . should be known as the greatest navigator of all time.

    **H** The Portuguese explorer Ferdinand Magellan should be known as . . . the greatest navigator of all time.

    **J** The Portuguese explorer Ferdinand Magellan should be known as the greatest navigator of all time. . . .

**11. Which sentence properly uses an ellipsis in a quotation from the text?**

A The author believes Magellan is important because he "helped other explorers learn more about the Pacific Ocean . . . proved that the world is actually round."

B The author believes Magellan is important because he "helped other explorers learn more about the Pacific Ocean . . . [and] his long voyage proved that the world is actually round."

C The author says Magellan is important because his "discovery helped other explorers learn more about the Pacific Ocean [and] his long voyage proved that the world is actually round."

D The author says Magellan is important because he "discovered . . . the Strait of Magellan helped other explorers learn more about the Pacific Ocean [and] proved the world is round."

**Directions:** Read this paragraph from an article. Then do Numbers 12 and 13.

Humorists tell a story gravely, concealing the fact that they even dimly suspect that there is anything funny about it. They let the humor work its magic unassisted. Comic storytellers, however, announce beforehand that a story is one of the funniest they have ever heard. They blurt it out with impatient delight and are the first to laugh when they get through. Sometimes, if they get a laugh, they are so happy that they will repeat the point of the story and glance around from face to face, hoping to collect a second laugh. It is a pathetic thing to see.

**12. Which option correctly shows that text has been left out from the underlined sentences in the original source?**

F Humorists . . . let the humor work its magic unassisted.

G Humorists tell a story gravely, [letting] the humor work its magic unassisted.

H Humorists tell a story gravely. They let the humor work its magic unassisted.

J Humorists tell a story gravely, . . . concealing the fact that they even dimly suspect that there is anything funny about it.

**13. Which quotation correctly shows that text has been left out from the original source?**

A The author explains, "Comic storytellers, however, are the first to laugh when they get through."

B The author explains, "Comic storytellers . . . announce beforehand that a story is one of the funniest they have ever heard [and] are the first to laugh when they get through."

C The author explains, "Comic storytellers announce beforehand that a story is one of the funniest they have ever heard . . . and are the first to laugh when they get through."

D The author explains, "Comic storytellers . . . announce beforehand that a story is one of the funniest they have ever heard . . . and are the first to laugh when they get through."

## Test-Taking Tip

When reading test questions, note key words that help you understand what the question is asking. For example, you might write the words *point of view* or *author's purpose.*

# Writing Practice

People have different ideas about how to improve the education system in the United States. George W. Bush stated his administration's viewpoint in his "No Child Left Behind" speech.

**Directions:** Write an argument in which you assert your own point of view about the ideas in Bush's speech, found on pages 109 and 110. State your point of view clearly, citing specific significant and relevant examples from the speech as you analyze Bush's viewpoint and share your own. Support your claims using valid reasoning and relevant and sufficient evidence.

_____

_____

_____

_____

_____

_____

_____

_____

_____

_____

_____

_____

_____

_____

_____

_____

_____

This lesson will help you practice using two texts to analyze how an author's purpose determines the text structure. Use it with Core Lesson 5.2 *Analyze How Author's Purpose Determines Structure* to reinforce and apply your knowledge.

## Key Concept

Authors choose specific text structures to clarify what they want to say. The text structures engage the reader and help authors achieve a purpose.

## Core Skills

- Analyze Text Structure
- Determine Author's Purpose

## Text Structure in Informational Texts

All authors have a purpose for writing. The most common purposes are to inform, to persuade, and to entertain. An author of an informational text chooses an organization, or structure, that supports the purpose for writing. Common text structures include sequence, compare and contrast, cause and effect, description, and problem and solution.

**Directions:** Read the text. Then do Numbers 1–4.

# Earth Science: The Study of Earth

**Earth science** is the study of Earth's origins and the forces at work that are constantly changing the surface of the planet. Earth science differs from the life sciences in that Earth science focuses on nonliving things rather than living things. It is a very broad field that covers the subjects of astronomy, geology, meteorology, paleontology, and oceanography.

### Astronomy: The Study of Space

One of the oldest fields of study in science deals with how Earth was created and how this planet fits into the design of the universe. **Astronomy** is the study of the size, movements, and composition of the planets, stars, and other deep-space objects. By observing objects in space, astronomers hope to understand how our planet was created and how it evolved. A number of important theories have been advanced to explain the beginning of Earth and its universe.

### The Beginning of the Universe

According to the leading theory, known as the **big bang theory**, a "cosmic egg" made up of dust and gas containing all the matter in the universe exploded. This explosion occurred 15 to 20 billion years ago, creating the basic atoms of our lightest gases from which the stars formed. The big bang theory accounts for the measured expansion of the universe and the background radiation found in all directions in outer space. According to the **open universe theory**, the universe will either continue the expansion indefinitely or begin a collapse. A different theory, called the **closed universe theory**, predicts that the total mass of the universe is large enough to gather up all matter into a concentrated central point and then gravitationally collapse at some point in the distant future. This collapse is referred to as the "big crunch."

The most distant (but unknown) objects detected by science are known as **quasars** (quasi-stellar radio sources). The light and energy that has arrived from these objects is about 16 billion years old. It is likely that the energy that we receive now came from these objects during their formation. Every time scientists investigate deep-space objects, they must remember that information we receive now took time to get to Earth. Even the light from the sun takes eight minutes to reach Earth. The nearest star to the sun is Alpha Centauri, which is more than four light years away.

1. **What is the author's main purpose for writing this piece?**

   **A** to inform

   **B** to entertain

   **C** to persuade

   **D** to express emotions

2. **Which best describes the overall structure of this passage?**

   **F** sequence

   **G** description

   **H** cause and effect

   **J** compare and contrast

3. **How does the overall structure help the author achieve the purpose for writing?**

   **A** It helps the reader compare Earth science and life sciences.

   **B** It helps the reader understand which topics are included in Earth science.

   **C** It helps the reader understand the order in which astronomy theories were developed.

   **D** It helps the reader understand how lack of funding causes limits on astronomy research.

4. **Read this excerpt from the passage.**

   > **According to the leading theory, known as the big bang theory, a "cosmic egg" made up of dust and gas containing all the matter in the universe exploded. This explosion occurred 15 to 20 billion years ago, creating the basic atoms of our lightest gases from which the stars formed. The big bang theory accounts for the measured expansion of the universe and the background radiation found in all directions in outer space. According to the open universe theory, the universe will either continue the expansion indefinitely or begin a collapse. A different theory, called the closed universe theory, predicts that the total mass of the universe is large enough to gather up all matter into a concentrated central point and then gravitationally collapse at some point in the distant future. This collapse is referred to as the "big crunch."**

   **Which best describes the structure of this paragraph?**

   **F** sequence

   **G** description

   **H** cause and effect

   **J** compare and contrast

 **Test-Taking Tip**

When you are answering a multiple-choice question, read the question and formulate an answer in your head. Then read the answer choices. Choose the answer that is most similar to your answer. Following these steps will help you eliminate answer choices that are definitely incorrect.

## Text Structure in Literary Texts

Like authors of informational texts, literary writers also choose text structures that convey their purposes. These text structures are similar to those used by informational writers. Sometimes literary writers enhance the text structure with special techniques such as alternating viewpoints, flashback, and parallel plots.

**Directions:** Read the text. Then do Numbers 5–10.

## From "The Masque of the Red Death"
### *by Edgar Allan Poe*

[T]hese other apartments were densely crowded, and in them beat feverishly the heart of life. And the revel went whirlingly on, until at length there commenced the sounding of midnight upon the clock. And then the music ceased, as I have told; and the evolutions of the waltzers were quieted; and there was an uneasy cessation of all things as before. But now there were twelve strokes to be sounded by the bell of the clock. . . . [B]efore the last echoes of the last chime had utterly sunk into silence, there were many individuals in the crowd who had found leisure to become aware of the presence of a masked figure which had arrested the attention of no single individual before. And the rumor of this new presence having spread itself whisperingly around, there arose at length from the whole company a buzz, or murmur, expressive of disapprobation and surprise—then, finally, of terror, of horror, and of disgust.

In an assembly of phantasms such as I have painted, it may well be supposed that no ordinary appearance could have excited such sensation. In truth the masquerade license of the night was nearly unlimited; but the figure in question had out-Heroded Herod, and gone beyond the bounds of even the prince's indefinite decorum. There are chords in the hearts of the most reckless which cannot be touched without emotion. Even with the utterly lost, to whom life and death are equally jests, there are matters of which no jest can be made. The whole company, indeed, seemed now deeply to feel that in the costume and bearing of the stranger neither wit nor propriety existed.

The figure was tall and gaunt, and shrouded from head to foot in the habiliments of the grave. The mask which concealed the visage was made so nearly to resemble the countenance of a stiffened corpse that the closest scrutiny must have had difficulty in detecting the cheat. And yet all this might have been endured, if not approved, by the mad revellers around. But the mummer had gone so far as to assume the type of the Red Death. His vesture was dabbled in blood—and his broad brow, with all the features of the face, was besprinkled with the scarlet horror.

When the eyes of Prince Prospero fell upon this spectral image (which with a slow and solemn movement, as if more fully to sustain its role, stalked to and fro among the waltzers) he was seen to be convulsed, in the first moment with a strong shudder either of terror or distaste; but, in the next, his brow reddened with rage.

5. **What is the author's purpose for writing this piece?**

   **A**  to inform

   **B**  to entertain

   **C**  to persuade

   **D**  to express emotions

6. **Which term best describes the overall text structure of this passage?**

   **F**  sequence

   **G**  flashback

   **H**  parallel plots

   **J**  problem and solution

7. **How does the text structure help achieve the author's purpose for writing?**

   **A** It helps the reader follow the events that occur during the masked ball.

   **B** It helps the reader see the events at the masked ball from various perspectives.

   **C** It helps the reader compare the feelings and actions of several characters at the masked ball.

   **D** It helps the reader understand how earlier events influenced the masked character's current actions.

8. **Which technique does the author use to help tell the story?**

   **F** flashbacks

   **G** parallel plots

   **H** time-order words

   **J** alternating viewpoints

9. **Read this sentence from the story.**

   > When the eyes of Prince Prospero fell upon this spectral image (which with a slow and solemn movement, as if more fully to sustain its role, stalked to and fro among the waltzers) he was seen to be convulsed, in the first moment with a strong shudder either of terror or distaste; but, in the next, his brow reddened with rage.

   **What does the word <u>sustain</u> mean as it is used in this sentence?**

   **A** nourish

   **B** keep up

   **C** undergo

   **D** withstand

10. **Read the story events, and then choose the correct sequence.**

    **i.** People were disturbed by the way the masked character was dressed.

    **ii.** The prince became angry.

    **iii.** People began to notice a masked character.

    **iv.** The music stopped at midnight, and the party got quiet.

    **Which list shows the correct sequence of events?**

    **F** i, ii, iii, iv

    **G** ii, iv, iii, i

    **H** iii, iv, ii, i

    **J** iv, iii, i, ii

---

 **Test-Taking Tip**

When possible, use your life experiences as the basis for your essay on a test. If you are writing about something you know well, you will feel more confident and engaged. In addition, you will have a ready supply of real-life examples to use as evidence to support your ideas.

---

### Writing Practice

Authors of literary texts use a variety of structures and techniques to accomplish the same general purpose. Their choices may depend on the mood or effect they want to create in a particular story, or simply their own personal style.

**Directions:** Choose an alternate structure for "The Masque of the Red Death" on page 116, and explain how and why you would tell the story using that structure. What special techniques would you use, and why? In what ways would your version of the story differ from Poe's? Would your purpose be the same as his? Select concrete details, quotations, and examples appropriate to your target audience from the text in your explanatory text.

This lesson will help you practice inferring the author's purpose in two informational texts. Use it with Core Lesson 5.3 *Infer Author's Purpose* to reinforce and apply your knowledge.

## Key Concept

When an author does not explicitly state the purpose for writing a text, readers can use their prior knowledge and details from the text to infer the author's purpose.

## Core Skills

- Use a Graphic Organizer
- Determine the Implicit Purpose in a Text

## Inferring the Author's Purpose

Authors write with a specific purpose in mind. They might want to inform you about a topic, to persuade you to think a certain way, or to entertain you. They might even have more than one purpose. However, authors do not always state the purpose explicitly. Sometimes you have to infer it by using context, details, and your own knowledge of the topic.

**Directions:** Read the text. Then do Numbers 1–5.

---

# MEMO

**Date:** October 15

**To:** All Medical Staff

**From:** Wendy Lockwood, Human Resources Manager

**Subject:** Hand-washing guidelines

This memo is a follow-up to the recent training about workplace hygiene and safety. We would like to outline the key points addressed in the training about clean hands in the workplace. These guidelines are crucial for all medical staff to follow. However, they also serve as common-sense hygiene tips for everyone in a workplace setting.

To ensure that all germs and bacteria are released, be sure to follow these steps:

1. Place hands together under warm water. Using antibacterial soap, rub your hands together for at least 20 seconds.
2. Thoroughly wash both sides of the hands, the wrists, and under the fingernails.
3. Rinse well.
4. Completely dry your hands using a clean towel, which helps remove the germs. If using a disposable towel, be sure to throw it in the trash.

If water is not available, use an alcohol-based hand sanitizer. Place a small dollop of the product on the palm of one hand, and then rub it all over your hands and fingers until it dries.

Frequent hand-washing can help you and others avoid illness. You should wash your hands

- after using the bathroom.
- before and after eating or preparing food (especially raw meat).
- after sneezing, coughing, or blowing your nose.
- before and after tending to a wound.

---

*(Continued on next page)*

- after handling trash and/or hazardous materials.
- after touching objects contaminated by floodwater or sewage.
- after handling animals or their waste.
- when your hands are visibly dirty.

This information and a recording of last week's training presentation are available on our company's intranet. We strongly encourage all medical staff to review the information. Please help us adhere to the highest standards possible, ensuring the health and safety of our cohorts and patients.

Source: Centers for Disease Control and Prevention: www.cdc.gov/handwashing/

1. **Wendy Lockwood's purposes for writing the memo are to persuade and to**

   A  inform readers

   B  express emotions

   C  entertain students

   D  describe situations

2. **The author's main reason for including the bullet points is to convey that**

   F  hands are susceptible to getting dirty

   G  people who are sick can spread disease

   H  animals should not be present in the workplace

   J  hands can become contaminated in many ways

3. **Read this excerpt from the text.**

   **You should wash your hands . . . after handling trash and/or hazardous materials**

   **What does the word hazardous mean as it is used in this sentence?**

   A  dangerous

   B  dirty

   C  slippery

   D  unpleasant

4. **Which phrase states the implied author's purpose of the text?**

   F  to reduce training costs for the hospital

   G  to prevent the spread of disease in the hospital

   H  to highlight the work of researchers in the hospital

   J  to address complaints from patients about the hospital

5. **Which word could most logically be added to this memo?**

   A  comfortable

   B  crucial

   C  pleasant

   D  unhelpful

## Using Context to Infer Implicit Purpose

When authors do not state why they are writing, you can use your knowledge and the details in the text to infer the purpose. It is also helpful to consider the author and the context.

**Directions:** Read the text. Then do Numbers 6–9.

# From "A War That Is Finished"

*by President Gerald R. Ford, April 23, 1975*

Instead of my addressing the image of America, I prefer to consider the reality of America. It is true that we have launched our bicentennial celebration without having achieved human perfection, but we have attained a very remarkable self-governed society that possesses the flexibility and the dynamism to grow and undertake an entirely new agenda, an agenda for America's third century.

So, I ask you to join me in helping to write that agenda. I am as determined as a president can be to seek national rediscovery of the belief in ourselves that characterized the most creative periods in our nation's history. The greatest challenge of creativity, as I see it, lies ahead.

We, of course, are saddened indeed by the events in Indochina. But these events, tragic as they are, portend neither the end of the world nor of America's leadership in the world.

Let me put it this way, if I might. Some tend to feel that if we do not succeed in everything everywhere, then we have succeeded in nothing anywhere. I reject categorically such polarized thinking. We can and we should help others to help themselves. But the fate of responsible men and women everywhere, in the final decision, rests in their own hands, not in ours.

America's future depends upon Americans—especially your generation, which is now equipping itself to assume the challenges of the future, to help write the agenda for America.

Earlier today, in this great community, I spoke about the need to maintain our defenses. Tonight, I would like to talk about another kind of strength, the true source of American power that transcends all of the deterrent powers for peace of our armed forces. I am speaking here of our belief in ourselves and our belief in our nation.

Abraham Lincoln asked, in his own words, and I quote, "What constitutes the bulwark of our own liberty and independence?" And he answered, "It is not our frowning battlements or bristling seacoasts, our army or our navy. Our defense is in the spirit which prized liberty as the heritage of all men, in all lands everywhere."

It is in this spirit that we must now move beyond the discords of the past decade. It is in this spirit that I ask you to join me in writing an agenda for the future.

6. **The speaker was the president of the United States. Which statement about the presidency is <u>most</u> relevant in determining the purpose of Ford's speech?**

   F  The president is elected every four years.

   G  The president leads his or her political party.

   H  The president guides the nation and the military.

   J  The president signs legislation written by Congress.

7. **Which contextual information is <u>most</u> relevant in determining the purpose of Ford's speech?**

   A  Some Americans were discouraged by the Vietnam War.

   B  The speech was made at Tulane University in Louisiana.

   C  President Ford served in the United States Navy during World War II.

   D  Many celebrations were held to celebrate the United States bicentennial.

8. **Which sentence from the speech best conveys Ford's overall purpose?**

 F Instead of my addressing the image of America, I prefer to consider the reality of America.

 G We, of course, are saddened indeed by the events in Indochina.

 H I am speaking here of our belief in ourselves and our belief in our nation.

 J It is in this spirit, that I ask you to join me in writing an agenda for the future.

9. **What was President Ford's main purpose for delivering this speech?**

 A to explain ideas

 B to inform students

 C to persuade people

 D to express emotion

 **Test-Taking Tip**

If you are unsure of the answer to a question, note the question number and move on. Continuing with the remaining questions might help you figure out the answer to a difficult question. At the end of the test, if you have time, you can return to the questions you noted but didn't answer.

## Writing Practice

In Gerald Ford's speech "A War That Is Finished," the former president said, "We can and we should help others to help themselves. But the fate of responsible men and women everywhere, in the final decision, rests in their own hands, not in ours." A week later, North Vietnam captured Saigon. By then, American civilians and military had evacuated.

**Directions:** Reread the excerpt from Ford's speech, below. Then read an excerpt from a memo from the State Department, which follows Ford's speech. On the basis of these two passages, do you agree with Ford's statement? Why or why not? Write an argument to support your position. Establish the significance of your claim, and use the most relevant evidence from both passages to support your argument. Use precise language and techniques, and include specific examples of rhetoric from each source that helped you form your opinion.

### From "A War That Is Finished"

*by President Gerald R. Ford, April 23, 1975*

Instead of my addressing the image of America, I prefer to consider the reality of America. It is true that we have launched our bicentennial celebration without having achieved human perfection, but we have attained a very remarkable self-governed society that possesses the flexibility and the dynamism to grow and undertake an entirely new agenda, an agenda for America's third century.

So, I ask you to join me in helping to write that agenda. I am as determined as a president can be to seek national rediscovery of the belief in ourselves that characterized the most creative periods in our nation's history. The greatest challenge of creativity, as I see it, lies ahead.

We, of course, are saddened indeed by the events in Indochina. But these events, tragic as they are, portend neither the end of the world nor of America's leadership in the world.

*(Continued on next page)*

Chapter 5 | **Lesson 3** | Infer Author's Purpose

Let me put it this way, if I might. Some tend to feel that if we do not succeed in everything everywhere, then we have succeeded in nothing anywhere. I reject categorically such polarized thinking. We can and we should help others to help themselves. But the fate of responsible men and women everywhere, in the final decision, rests in their own hands, not in ours.

America's future depends upon Americans—especially your generation, which is now equipping itself to assume the challenges of the future, to help write the agenda for America.

Earlier today, in this great community, I spoke about the need to maintain our defenses. Tonight, I would like to talk about another kind of strength, the true source of American power that transcends all of the deterrent powers for peace of our armed forces. I am speaking here of our belief in ourselves and our belief in our nation.

Abraham Lincoln asked, in his own words, and I quote, "What constitutes the bulwark of our own liberty and independence?" And he answered, "It is not our frowning battlements or bristling seacoasts, our army or our navy. Our defense is in the spirit which prized liberty as the heritage of all men, in all lands everywhere."

It is in this spirit that we must now move beyond the discords of the past decade. It is in this spirit that I ask you to join me in writing an agenda for the future.

# From "Lessons of Viet-Nam"
### by the United States Department of State, May 9, 1975

Foremost among the criteria we might . . . employ in making judgments about our commitments is the . . . strength and will of our prospective ally—its ability to help itself. Although the Vietnamese government we supported was far more humane than its adversary, it was . . . unable to mobilize effectively the support of its people in the face of an implacable, disciplined enemy. Without such support, ultimate defeat was probably inevitable. . . .

In effect, we allowed saving South Viet-Nam to become more important to us than it was for the South Vietnamese themselves. In the future, we should gauge our support to our allies' efforts, and their successes. If they cannot do the job, we will be unable to do it for them.

We should be fully aware of the fragility of governments which rest . . . on the support of the military. This was not the chief cause of South Viet-Nam's downfall. . . . [However,] the inflexibility and narrowness of judgment of an increasingly isolated leadership in the face of unyielding North Vietnamese pressure played a role in the nation's ultimate collapse. . . .

We should admit our own imperfect understanding of the political dynamics of foreign (particularly Asian) societies. In Viet-Nam we persistently looked at political conditions, and made our judgments, from . . . a Western perspective.

. . . We should not assume, as we did in 1963, that we know what is best for a country and proceed . . . to [precipitate] a situation with unknown and possibly disastrous consequences. Nor should we take the opposite tack—allying ourselves too rigidly with a leadership whose diminishing mandate we may not be able to perceive. . . .

If we were ever to become involved again in an effort of the magnitude of Viet-Nam, we could make things somewhat easier for ourselves by improving the ways we attempt to manage our involvement. It can be argued that, in addition to having very little control over what South Viet-Nam did, we were never in firm control of our own resources, whether military, economic or political. A diffusion of responsibility and control compounded our difficulties.

We should guard against biased intelligence and analysis to support policy goals, as happened in Viet-Nam particularly during the height of our involvement.

*(Continued on next page)*

Related to this, we should be wary of "advocacy reporting" from our missions and within the bureaucracy at home. A particularly virulent form of "localitis" affected many capable and dedicated individuals working in or on Viet-Nam. They were intensely committed, to a worthy goal, but personal commitment sometimes blurred judgment. . . .

We should recognize that no amount of cajolery can create public support for a foreign undertaking where none already exists. (Thus, our commitments must be related to perceived national interests.) An Administration, by active leadership, can only energize latent support.

Having become involved in a difficult foreign project, we should not attempt to mislead public opinion or the Congress as to its duration or the level of sacrifice it will require. We should not profess to see lights at the end of tunnels. We should not employ short-term rationales, out of short-term expediency, when in fact much remains to be done. . . .

Consistent with the requirements of military security, our basic policy decisions should be publicly stated and defended.

This lesson will help you practice analyzing how authors differentiate and support their positions. Use it with Core Lesson 5.4 *Analyze How Authors Differentiate Their Positions* to reinforce and apply your knowledge.

## Key Concept

Authors can strengthen their position by acknowledging viewpoints that differ from theirs and by using evidence or reasoning to refute them.

## Core Skills

- Identify an Author's Position
- Evaluate Arguments

## Identifying an Author's Position

To support their positions, or opinions, on a topic, authors often introduce other viewpoints. These viewpoints can be complementary or conflicting. Writers can then strengthen their position in one of two ways. They can show how the complementary viewpoints support their position, or they can disprove, or refute, conflicting viewpoints or show that those viewpoints are unreasonable.

**Directions:** Read the text. Then do Numbers 1–4.

# From *1911 California voters' information manual*
### *by Assemblyman H.G. Cattell*

1    Women should have equal political rights with men as provided for in Senate Constitutional Amendment No. 8 because—

2    Women are equal to men intellectually. In fact, if we take the number of graduates from our schools and colleges, we must admit that they are farther advanced mentally.

3    Women should not be subject to taxation without representation any more than men. "Consent of the governed" means women as well as men, for they are subject to government as well as men.

4    Women are recognized in the family as a large part of the governing force. The state is only a large family composed of both sexes. Why should she not be considered in the government of the larger family?

5    Women have been given suffrage in numerous countries and in several states in this Union, and partial suffrage in nearly all civilized countries. We have no knowledge of such action having proved to be a failure or of such laws being repealed. Of course, [this] would be done were the experiment not a success.

6    Women are better morally, as evidenced by the criminals in the penitentiaries. For example, in the penitentiaries in California we have about three thousand men and about thirty women. The cases tried before the police courts probably average about the same. We must, therefore, admit that women would be a great factor in promoting honesty, equity and morality if given the ballot.

7    It is argued that all women do not wish to vote. The same argument applies to men. It has become common practice on election days to send [transportation] for a large percent of the male voters, and many who go voluntarily do so from a sense of duty. Women, being more faithful to duty, will exercise their right of franchise and do it cheerfully. Besides, their presence on such occasions will . . . guarantee that everything will be carried on respectably.

*(Continued on next page)*

8    Women who are in touch with public affairs are none the less womanly. On the contrary, they are better and more companionable wives, more interesting mothers, because they have a common interest with their sons.

9    The time was thought that to allow a girl a high school education would ruin her morals, destroy her religion, impair her health . . . and take away her desire to be a good wife and mother. Such theories are long since exploded. As we have progressed in these matters, let us progress in reference to suffrage; let us show the saloon element, the gambling element, the selfish element (for these are the opponents of women's suffrage) that this great state of California is really a progressive state in every way.

1.  **Which sentence best reflects the author's position?**
    **A**  Women should be allowed to attend college.
    **B**  Women should be allowed to vote in elections.
    **C**  Women should be allowed to hold peaceful protests.
    **D**  Women should be allowed to hold government office.

2.  **Which statement is an opposing viewpoint cited by the author?**
    **F**  Women do not all want to vote.
    **G**  Women cannot vote in other countries.
    **H**  Women do not have the morals to vote.
    **J**  Women are not intelligent enough to vote.

3.  **Read this sentence from the text.**

    **In the penitentiaries in California we have about three thousand men and about thirty women.**

    **How does the author use this statement?**
    **A**  to refute the assertion that women are morally superior to men
    **B**  to support the assertion that women are morally superior to men
    **C**  to summarize the assertion that women are morally superior to men
    **D**  to acknowledge the assertion that women are morally superior to men

4.  **Read this sentence from the text.**

    **Women, being more faithful to duty, will exercise their right of franchise and do it cheerfully.**

    **What does the word franchise mean as it is used in the sentence?**
    **F**  the right for an individual to vote
    **G**  freedom from any type of restriction
    **H**  a team that belongs to a sports league
    **J**  a business that sells a company's goods

---

 **Test-Taking Tip**

Before writing a test essay, take a few minutes to plan your response. You might want to use a graphic organizer to organize your thoughts. Consider using a flow chart to explain steps in a process or a Venn diagram to compare and contrast ideas. A diagram that is used to visually represent causes and effects can also work for problems and solutions. Finally, concept webs are helpful for showing relationships among ideas.

---

## Analyzing Support for an Author's Position

To make their persuasive texts effective, authors provide evidence to support their position. They also offer evidence to refute opposing viewpoints. Without evidence, readers are not likely to be convinced that they should agree with the author or disagree with the opposing position.

**Directions:** Read the text. Then do Numbers 5–8.

## From the speech "We Shall Overcome"
### by Lyndon B. Johnson, March 15, 1965

1    Wednesday I will send to Congress a law designed to eliminate illegal barriers to the right to vote. . . . This bill will establish a simple, uniform standard which cannot be used, however ingenious the effort, to flout our Constitution.

2    It will provide for citizens to be registered by officials of the United States government if the state officials refuse to register them.

3    It will eliminate tedious, unnecessary lawsuits which delay the right to vote.

4    Finally, this legislation will ensure that properly registered individuals are not prohibited from voting.

5    I will welcome the suggestions from all the members of Congress—I have no doubt that I will get some—on ways and means to strengthen this law and to make it effective. But experience has plainly shown that this is the only path to carry out the command of the Constitution.

6    To those who seek to avoid action by their national government in their own communities, who want to and who seek to maintain purely local control over elections, the answer is simple:

7    Open your polling places to all your people. Allow men and women to register and vote whatever the color of their skin. Extend the rights of citizenship to every citizen of this land. . . .

8    There is no constitutional issue here. The command of the Constitution is plain.

9    There is no moral issue. It is wrong—deadly wrong—to deny any of your fellow Americans the right to vote in this country.

10    There is no issue of states' rights or national rights. There is only the struggle for human rights. . . .

11    The last time a president sent a civil rights bill to the Congress it contained a provision to protect voting rights in federal elections. That civil rights bill was passed after eight long months of debate. And when that bill came to my desk from the Congress for my signature, the heart of the voting provision had been eliminated.

12    This time, on this issue, there must be no delay, no hesitation and no compromise with our purpose. We cannot, we must not, refuse to protect the right of every American to vote in every election that he may desire to participate in. And we ought not and we cannot and we must not wait another eight months before we get a bill. We have already waited a hundred years and more, and the time for waiting is gone.

13    So I ask you to join me in working long hours—nights and weekends, if necessary—to pass this bill. And I don't make that request lightly. For from the window where I sit with the problems of our country I recognize that outside this chamber is the outraged conscience of a nation, the grave concern of many nations, and the harsh judgment of history on our acts. . . .

*(Continued on next page)*

14  But even if we pass this bill, the battle will not be over. What happened in Selma* is part of a far larger movement which reaches into every section and state of America. It is the effort of [African Americans] to secure for themselves the full blessings of American life.

15  Their cause must be our cause too. Because it is not just [African Americans], but really it is all of us, who must overcome the crippling legacy of bigotry and injustice.

16  And we shall overcome.

---

* Police in Selma, Alabama, physically attacked hundreds of civil-rights marchers.

**5.**  **What is Lyndon Johnson's position?**

   **A**  Congress must work harder.

   **B**  Congress must draft a new bill.

   **C**  Congress must guarantee states' rights.

   **D**  Congress must pass the voting rights bill.

**6.**  **Read this excerpt from the text.**

   **There is no issue of states' rights or national rights. There is only the struggle for human rights. . . .**

   **Which position is Johnson refuting?**

   **F**  States' rights take precedence over national rights.

   **G**  All people should have the right to vote in elections.

   **H**  The entire country agrees that changes should be made.

   **J**  The national government should determine election laws.

**7.**  **How does Johnson strengthen his position?**

   **A**  by refuting opposing viewpoints

   **B**  by creating opposing viewpoints

   **C**  by ignoring opposing viewpoints

   **D**  by supporting opposing viewpoints

**8.**  **Some opponents of Johnson in Congress felt that they should have an opportunity to revise his voting rights bill. In which paragraph does Johnson provide evidence that discredits the opposition?**

   **F**  paragraph 5

   **G**  paragraph 9

   **H**  paragraph 11

   **J**  paragraph 15

# Writing Practice

As you have learned, strong arguments acknowledge opposing viewpoints and use evidence or reasoning to refute them.

**Directions:** Write an argument about whether flag burning is protected under the First Amendment, based on the information in the following passages. In your argument, establish the significance of your claim, distinguish the claim from opposing claims, and create an organization that logically sequences your claim, counterclaims, reasons, and evidence. Cite evidence to support your position and to refute the opposing position.

*After a 1984 political demonstration in Dallas, Texas, Gregory Lee Johnson was convicted of burning the American flag. He appealed his conviction twice. The first time, the original ruling was upheld. However, in the second appeal, the appeals court overturned the original ruling. In 1989 the state of Texas took the case to the Supreme Court of the United States. The Supreme Court ruled that flag burning constitutes "protected speech" under the First Amendment, and therefore Johnson was not guilty of a crime. The following excerpts are the two arguments presented by the court. Justices William Brennan and Anthony Kennedy delivered the majority opinion. Chief Justice William Rehnquist and Justice John Paul Stevens delivered the dissenting, or opposing, opinion.*

## Argument: Burning the flag is protected speech.

[Justice Brennan:] After publicly burning an American flag as a means of political protest, Gregory Lee Johnson was convicted of desecrating a flag in violation of Texas law. This case presents the question [of] whether his conviction is consistent with the First Amendment. We hold that it is not.

While the Republican National Convention was taking place in Dallas in 1984, . . . Johnson participated in a political demonstration . . . to protest the policies of the Reagan administration and of certain Dallas-based corporations. The demonstrators marched through the Dallas streets, chanting political slogans and stopping at several corporate locations to stage "die-ins" intended to dramatize the consequences of nuclear war. On several occasions they spray-painted the walls of buildings and overturned potted plants, but Johnson himself took no part in such activities. He did, however, accept an American flag handed to him by a fellow protestor who had taken it from a flagpole outside one of the targeted buildings.

The demonstration ended in front of Dallas City Hall, where Johnson unfurled the American flag, doused it with kerosene, and set it on fire. . . . No one was physically injured or threatened with injury, though several witnesses testified that they had been seriously offended by the flag burning.

Of the approximately 100 demonstrators, Johnson alone was charged with a crime. . . .

The [appeals] court concluded that the state could not criminally sanction flag desecration in order to preserve the flag as a symbol of national unity. It also held that the statute did not meet the state's goal of preventing breaches of the peace. . . . Further, it stressed that another Texas statute prohibited breaches of the peace and could be used to prevent disturbances without punishing this flag desecration.

Held: Johnson's conviction for flag desecration is inconsistent with the First Amendment.

*(Continued on next page)*

(a) Under the circumstances, Johnson's burning of the flag constituted expressive conduct, permitting him to invoke the First Amendment. The state conceded that the conduct was expressive. . . . [T]he expressive, overtly political nature of the conduct was both intentional and overwhelmingly apparent. . . .

(b) . . . Expression may not be prohibited on the basis that an audience that takes serious offense to the expression may disturb the peace. . . . [T]he Government cannot assume that every expression of a provocative idea will incite a riot. . . . Johnson's expression of dissatisfaction with the federal government's policies also does not fall within the class of "fighting words." . . . Texas' interest in preserving the flag as a symbol of nationhood and national unity is related to expression in this case. . . .

(c) . . . The restriction on Johnson's political expression is content based. . . . [T]he Texas statute is not aimed at protecting the physical integrity of the flag in all circumstances, but is designed to protect it from intentional and knowing abuse that causes serious offense to others. It is therefore subject to "the most exacting scrutiny." . . . The government may not prohibit the verbal or nonverbal expression of an idea merely because society finds the idea offensive or disagreeable. . . . Nor may a state foster its own view of the flag by prohibiting expressive conduct relating to it, since the government may not permit designated symbols to be used to communicate a limited set of messages. Moreover, this Court will not create an exception to these principles protected by the First Amendment for the American flag alone. . . .

[Justice Kennedy:] Our colleagues in dissent advance powerful arguments why [Johnson] may be convicted for his expression. . . . [A]mong those who will be dismayed by our holding will be some who have had the singular honor of carrying the flag in battle. . . .

With all respect . . . , I do not believe the Constitution gives us the right to rule as the dissenting members of the Court urge, however painful this judgment is to announce. Though symbols often are what we ourselves make of them, the flag is constant in expressing beliefs Americans share, beliefs in law and peace and that freedom which sustains the human spirit. The case here today forces recognition of the costs to which those beliefs commit us. It is poignant but fundamental that the flag protects those who hold it in contempt. . . .

[T]he fact remains that [Johnson's] acts were speech, in both the technical and the fundamental meaning of the Constitution. So I agree with the Court that he must go free.

**Argument: Flag burning is not protected speech.**

[Justice Rehnquist:] For more than 200 years, the American flag has occupied a unique position as the symbol of our nation, a uniqueness that justifies a governmental prohibition against flag burning in the way . . . Johnson did here. . . .

Both Congress and the states have enacted numerous laws regulating misuse of the American flag. . . . [One law] provides that "Whoever knowingly casts contempt upon any flag of the United States by publicly mutilating, defacing, defiling, burning, or trampling upon it shall be fined not more than $1,000 or imprisoned for not more than one year, or both." . . .

The flag is not simply another "idea" or "point of view" competing for recognition in the marketplace of ideas. Millions and millions of Americans regard it with an almost mystical reverence, regardless of what sort of social, political, or philosophical beliefs they may have. I cannot agree that the First Amendment invalidates the Act of Congress, and the laws of 48 of the 50 states, which make criminal the public burning of the flag. . . .

*(Continued on next page)*

Here it may equally well be said that the public burning of the American flag by Johnson was no essential part of any exposition of ideas. . . . [At] the same time, it had a tendency to incite a breach of the peace. Johnson was free to make any verbal denunciation of the flag that he wished. [I]ndeed, he was free to burn the flag in private. He could publicly burn other symbols of the government or effigies of political leaders. He did lead a march through the streets of Dallas, and conducted a rally in front of the Dallas City Hall. He engaged in a "die-in" to protest nuclear weapons. He shouted out various slogans during the march. . . . For none of these acts was he arrested or prosecuted. [I]t was only when he proceeded to burn publicly an American flag stolen from its rightful owner that he violated the Texas statute. . . .

The uniquely deep awe and respect for our flag felt by virtually all of us are bundled off under the rubric of "designated symbols" . . . that the First Amendment prohibits the government from "establishing." But the government has not "established" this feeling; 200 years of history have done that. The government is simply recognizing as a fact the profound regard for the American flag created by that history when it enacts statutes prohibiting the disrespectful public burning of the flag.

[Justice Stevens:] A country's flag is a symbol of more than "nationhood and national unity." . . . It also signifies the ideas that characterize the society that has chosen that emblem as well as the special history that has animated the growth and power of those ideas. . . .

[The American flag] is more than a proud symbol of the courage, the determination, and the gifts of nature that transformed 13 fledgling colonies into a world power. It is a symbol of freedom, of equal opportunity, of religious tolerance, and of goodwill for other peoples who share our aspirations. The symbol carries its message to dissidents both at home and abroad who may have no interest at all in our national unity or survival. . . .

[S]anctioning the public desecration of the flag will tarnish its value. . . . That tarnish is not justified by the trivial burden on free expression occasioned by requiring that an available, alternative mode of expression . . . be employed.

The ideas of liberty and equality have been an irresistible force in motivating leaders like Patrick Henry, Susan B. Anthony, and Abraham Lincoln. . . . If those ideas are worth fighting for . . . it cannot be true that the flag that uniquely symbolizes their power is not itself worthy of protection from unnecessary desecration.

_____

_____

_____

_____

_____

_____

_____

_____

_____

_____

_____

_____

_____

_____

_____

_____

_____

_____

_____

_____

_____

_____

_____

_____

_____

_____

_____

_____

_____

_____

_____

_____

This lesson will help you practice analyzing the author's intention and effect in two texts. Use it with Core Lesson 5.5 *Analyze Author's Intention and Effect* to reinforce and apply your knowledge.

## Key Concept

Authors use several types of rhetorical devices to communicate their position and to achieve their goals for writing.

## Core Skills

- Determine Author's Purpose
- Determine Point of View

## Identifying Rhetorical Devices

Authors write with goals, or intentions, in mind. Among the many techniques they use are rhetorical devices, which help authors create desired effects on their audiences. Some common rhetorical devices are analogy, asking questions, enumeration, juxtaposition of opposites, qualification statements, repetition, and parallelism.

**Directions:** Read the text. Then do Numbers 1–4.

## From "Ghitza"

*by Konrad Bercovici*

That winter had been a very severe one in Romania. The Danube froze solid a week before Christmas and remained tight for five months. It was as if the blue waters were suddenly turned into steel. From across the river, from the Dobrudja, on sleds pulled by long-horned oxen, the Tartars brought barrels of frozen honey, quarters of killed lambs, poultry and game, and returned heavily laden with bags of flour and rolls of sole leather. The whole day long the crack of whips and the curses of the drivers rent the icy atmosphere. Whatever their destination, the carters were in a hurry to reach human habitation before nightfall—before the dreaded time when packs of wolves came out to prey for food.

In cold, clear nights, when even the wind was frozen still, the lugubrious howling of the wolf permitted no sleep. The indoor people spent the night praying for the lives and souls of the travellers.

All through the winter there was not one morning but some man or animal was found torn or eaten in our neighbourhood. The people of the village at first built fires on the shores to scare the beasts away, but they had to give it up because the thatched roofs of the huts in the village were set on fire in windy nights by flying sparks. The cold cowed the fiercest dogs. The wolves, crazed by hunger, grew more daring from day to day. They showed their heads even in daylight. When Baba Hana, the old . . . fortune-teller, ran into the school-house one morning and cried, "Wolf, wolf in the yard," the teacher was inclined to attribute her scare to a long drink the night before. But that very night, Stan, the horseshoer, who had returned late from the inn and had evidently not closed the door as he entered the smithy, was eaten up by the beasts. And the smithy stood in the centre of the village! A stone's throw from the inn, and the thatch-roofed school, and the red painted church!

1. **Read this sentence from the text.**

   **It was as if the blue waters were suddenly turned into steel.**

   **What type of rhetorical device is the author using in this sentence?**

   **A** analogy

   **B** enumeration

   **C** parallelism

   **D** repetition

2. **Read this sentence from the text.**

   **Whatever their destination, the carters were in a hurry to reach human habitation before nightfall—before the dreaded time when packs of wolves came out to prey for food.**

   **Which type of rhetorical device does this sentence contain?**

   **F** analogy

   **G** enumeration

   **H** qualifying statement

   **J** juxtaposition of opposites

3. **Which excerpt from the text is an example of enumeration?**

   **A** The Danube froze solid a week before Christmas and remained tight for five months.

   **B** In cold, clear nights, when even the wind was frozen still, the lugubrious howling of the wolf permitted no sleep.

   **C** The wolves, crazed by hunger, grew more daring from day to day.

   **D** A stone's throw from the inn, and the thatch-roofed school, and the red painted church!

4. **Read this sentence from the text.**

   **From across the river, from the Dobrudja, on sleds pulled by long-horned oxen, the Tartars brought barrels of frozen honey, quarters of killed lambs, poultry and game, and returned heavily laden with bags of flour and rolls of sole leather.**

   **Which definition fits the word <u>quarters</u> as it is used in this sentence?**

   **F** coins worth twenty-five cents

   **G** at close range or nearly in contact

   **H** lodgings for soldiers or crew members

   **J** one-fourth portions of slaughtered animals

## ✔ Test-Taking Tip

To familiarize yourself with the specifics of the test, consider using an online test-taking tutorial. Even if you will not be taking the test online, a tutorial provides helpful information. For example, you will learn what types of questions to expect and how to navigate through the test. Online tutorials also offer test-taking strategies and information about how to keep track of remaining time and monitor your progress.

# Identifying an Author's Intention and Effect

Authors write for a purpose: to entertain, to inform, or to persuade. Authors also write with an intention, which combines purpose and point of view. The author's intention is what he or she hopes to accomplish with the written work. The author uses rhetorical devices to produce the desired effect.

**Directions:** Read the text. Then do Numbers 5–8.

## From *Narrative of the Life of Frederick Douglass an American Slave*

### by Frederick Douglass

There were no beds given the slaves, unless one coarse blanket be considered such, and none but the men and women had these. This, however, is not considered a very great privation. They find less difficulty from the want of beds, than from the want of time to sleep; for when their day's work in the field is done, the most of them having their washing, mending, and cooking to do, and having few or none of the ordinary facilities for doing either of these, very many of their sleeping hours are consumed in preparing for the field the coming day; and when this is done, old and young, male and female, married and single, drop down side by side, on one common bed—the cold, damp floor—each covering himself or herself with their miserable blankets; and here they sleep till they are summoned to the field by the driver's horn. At the sound of this, all must rise, and be off to the field.

There must be no halting; every one must be at his or her post; and woe betides them who hear not this morning summons to the field; for if they are not awakened by the sense of hearing, they are by the sense of feeling: no age nor sex finds any favor. Mr. Severe, the overseer, used to stand by the door of the quarter, armed with a large hickory stick and heavy cowskin, ready to whip any one who was so unfortunate as not to hear, or, from any other cause, was prevented from being ready to start for the field at the sound of the horn.

Mr. Severe was rightly named: he was a cruel man. I have seen him whip a woman, causing the blood to run half an hour at the time; and this, too, in the midst of her crying children, pleading for their mother's release. He seemed to take pleasure in manifesting his fiendish barbarity. Added to his cruelty, he was a profane swearer. It was enough to chill the blood and stiffen the hair of an ordinary man to hear him talk. Scarce a sentence escaped him but that was commenced or concluded by some horrid oath. The field was the place to witness his cruelty and profanity. His presence made it both the field of blood and of blasphemy. From the rising till the going down of the sun, he was cursing, raving, cutting, and slashing among the slaves of the field, in the most frightful manner. His career was short. He died very soon after I went to Colonel Lloyd's; and he died as he lived, uttering, with his dying groans, bitter curses and horrid oaths. His death was regarded by the slaves as the result of a merciful providence.

5. **Based on the rhetorical devices he used, Frederick Douglass' intention was likely**

   A   to clarify what it is like to work on a farm

   B   to entertain readers with a tale from his childhood

   C   to convey how unfairly he and other slaves were treated

   D   to convince readers that Mr. Severe's death was deserved

6. **Which sentence best describes the effect of rhetoric in the narrative?**

   F   It inspires people to make changes in their daily lives.

   G   It evokes an emotional response to the treatment of the slaves.

   H   It prompts people to be skeptical about the experiences of slaves.

   J   It stimulates a discussion about life in the rural south in the 1800s.

7. **Read this excerpt from the text.**

   **. . . and when this is done, old and young, male and female, married and single, drop down side by side . . .**

   **In this excerpt, which rhetorical device does the author use?**

   A   analogy

   B   enumeration

   C   asking questions

   D   qualifying statement

8. **Which excerpt from the text does not convey the author's intention?**

   F   There were no beds given the slaves . . .

   G   . . . the cold, damp floor . . .

   H   . . . ready to whip any one . . .

   J   His career was short.

## Language Practice

A participle is a verb that acts as an adjective. It modifies nouns and pronouns and comes in two forms: present, ending with -*ing*, and past, ending with -*ed*. Not all verbs with these endings are participles. When you use participles, make sure you use the correct form.

**Directions:** For Numbers 9 through 12, read the questions and choose the best answers.

9. **Which version of the sentence is grammatically correct?**

   A   While he was drinking a cup of steamed coffee and read the morning paper, Nestor heard a barking dog.

   B   While he was drinking a cup of steamed coffee and reading the morning paper, Nestor heard a barked dog.

   C   While he was drinking a cup of steaming coffee and reading the morning paper, Nestor heard a barked dog.

   D   While he was drinking a cup of steaming coffee and reading the morning paper, Nestor heard a barking dog.

**10.** **In which version of the sentence are participles in the correct form?**

   **F** Peered out the window, he saw his beagle dashed after a sped mail truck.

   **G** Peered out the window, he saw his beagle dashing after a speeding mail truck.

   **H** Peering out the window, he saw his beagle dashed after a speeding mail truck.

   **J** Peering out the window, he saw his beagle dashing after a speeding mail truck.

**11.** **Which version of the sentence includes grammatically correct participles?**

   **A** Alarmed, Nestor rushing outside and called to the panted dog, "Peppy! Here, boy!"

   **B** Alarmed, Nestor rushed outside and called to the panting dog, "Peppy! Here, boy!"

   **C** Alarming, Nestor rushed outside and called to the panting dog, "Peppy! Here, boy!"

   **D** Alarming, Nestor rushing outside and calling to the panted dog, "Peppy! Here, boy!"

**12.** **In which version of the sentence are the participles grammatically correct?**

   **F** Ignored Nestor and gained on the truck, Peppy continued pursued the truck.

   **G** Ignoring Nestor and gained on the truck, Peppy continued pursuing the truck.

   **H** Ignoring Nestor and gaining on the truck, Peppy continued pursuing the truck.

   **J** Ignored Nestor and gaining on the truck, Peppy continued pursuing the truck.

## Writing Practice

Have you ever read something that had a dramatic effect on you? Perhaps it helped you see an issue in a new way, or maybe a particular description evoked an emotional response. A writer's intention and use of rhetorical devices might create these effects. When you are reading, it is helpful to think critically about the devices the writer uses to achieve his or her goals.

**Directions:** Write an explanatory text analyzing the excerpt from *Narrative of the Life of Frederick Douglass an American Slave* (page 135). Summarize the excerpt, and explain Douglass' intention and effect clearly and accurately. Describe the rhetorical devices that Douglass used, and explain how those devices helped him achieve his goals. Support your ideas with effectively selected details and examples.

_____

_____

_____

_____

_____

_____

_____

This lesson will help you practice identifying argument development in two texts. Use it with Core Lesson 6.1 *Identify Argument Development* to reinforce and apply your knowledge.

## Key Concept

The purpose of an argument is to persuade the reader that a claim is reasonable. A well-developed argument includes reasons and evidence that support the writer's claim.

## Core Skills

- Understand the Relationship among Ideas
- Analyze Text Structure to Evaluate an Argument

## Developing an Argument

An argument starts with a claim, or a statement of the author's opinion or position on a topic. The author wants to persuade readers to believe or act on the claim. In a good argument, a claim is supported by evidence such as reasons, facts, and examples. The conclusion of an argument may restate the author's claim, summarize the evidence, or call upon the reader to take action.

**Directions:** Read the text. Then do Numbers 1–5.

## From *Common Sense*

### by Thomas Paine

*Thomas Paine, a British American political activist and revolutionary, published the booklet* Common Sense *in 1776. In it, he spoke against the authority of the British government and the king, whom he felt oppressed the people in the American colonies. He also believed that the constitution of England encouraged oppression by the king, rather than freeing the people from tyranny. The king could override elected officials and often did.* Common Sense *was the first publication to encourage colonists in America to declare independence. The "peers" referred to in the passage are nobility, who inherited their positions, while people in the commons were elected.*

I offer a few remarks on the so much boasted constitution of England. That it was noble for the dark and slavish times in which it was erected, is granted. When the world was overrun with tyranny the least remove therefrom was a glorious rescue. But that it is imperfect, subject to convulsions, and incapable of producing what it seems to promise, is easily demonstrated. . . .

I know it is difficult to get over local or long standing prejudices, yet if we will suffer ourselves to examine the component parts of the English constitution, we shall find them to be the base remains of two ancient tyrannies, compounded with some new republican materials.

FIRST—The remains of monarchial tyranny in the person of the king.

SECONDLY—The remains of aristocratical tyranny in the persons of the peers.

THIRDLY—The new republican materials in the persons of the commons, on whose virtue depends the freedom of England.

The two first, by being hereditary, are independent of the people; wherefore in a CONSTITUTIONAL SENSE they contribute nothing towards the freedom of the state.

To say that the constitution of England is a UNION of three powers reciprocally CHECKING each other, is farcical, either the words have no meaning, or they are flat contradictions.

To say that the commons is a check upon the king, presupposes two things:

*(Continued on next page)*

FIRST—That the king is not to be trusted without being looked after, or in other words, that a thirst for absolute power is the natural disease of monarchy.

SECONDLY—That the commons, by being appointed for that purpose, are either wiser or more worthy of confidence than the crown.

But as the same constitution which gives the commons a power to check the king by withholding the supplies, gives afterwards the king a power to check the commons, by empowering him to reject their other bills; it again supposes that the king is wiser than those whom it has already supposed to be wiser than him. A mere absurdity!

1. **Which statement best expresses one of Thomas Paine's main claims in this passage?**

   **A** Members of the peers are part of the old tyranny.

   **B** The king can reject bills that the commons passes.

   **C** Members of the commons are elected by the people.

   **D** England's constitutional process does not encourage liberty.

2. **Read this sentence from the text.**

   **To say that the constitution of England is a UNION of three powers reciprocally CHECKING each other, is farcical; either the words have no meaning, or they are flat contradictions.**

   **What does the word checking mean as it is used in this sentence?**

   **F** holding accountable

   **G** investigating something

   **H** comparing to an original source

   **J** inspecting for satisfactory conditions

3. **Which phrase best describes the quality of the evidence that Paine presents to support his argument?**

   **A** relevant to the claim

   **B** irrelevant to the claim

   **C** contradictory to the claim

   **D** insufficient to support the claim

4. **Which statement related to the claim that the constitution of England is absurd is a fact?**

   **F** The king should be looked after by the commons.

   **G** The king has the power to reject bills passed by the commons.

   **H** The members of the peers and the king are part of an ancient tyranny.

   **J** The members of the commons are wiser and more reliable than the king.

5. **Which type of conclusion does Paine use at the end this passage?**

   **A** one new idea

   **B** a call to action

   **C** a restatement of ideas

   **D** ideas that extend the argument

# Analyzing Argument Development

Whether an author's claim is implied or clearly laid out in the text, you can gain a better understanding of the author's claim when you analyze the author's argument. When an argument is well structured, the relationship between ideas is clear and readers can easily understand the author's point of view.

**Directions:** Read the text. Then do Numbers 6–11.

## From "The Woman and the Right to Vote"

*by Rafael Palma*

Female suffrage is a reform demanded by the social conditions of our times, by the high culture of woman, and by the aspiration of all classes of society to . . . work for [common] interests. . . .

. . . [W]henever an attempt is made to introduce a social reform . . . , there is never a lack of opposition. . . . As was to be expected, the eternal calamity howlers and false prophets of evil raise their [prophetic] voices . . . in protest against female suffrage. [These people invoke] the sanctity of the home and the necessity of perpetuating customs. . . .

Frankly speaking, I have no patience with people who voice such objections. . . . [N]ot so very long ago, the same apprehension and fears were felt with regard to higher education for our women. . . . We are now able to observe the results. [If] these results are . . . detrimental to the social and political welfare of the country, it is our duty to undo what we have done. . . .

Fortunately, nobody would think of such a thing. . . . Education has not atrophied or impaired any of the fundamental faculties of woman. On the contrary, it has enhanced and enriched them. . . . Thank God, people are no longer ready to cast ridicule upon what some used to consider the foolish presumption of women to know as much as the men. This is doubtless due to the fact that the disastrous results predicted by . . . the terrible prophets of failure have not materialized.

Very well. If you allow the instruction and education of woman in all the branches of science, you must allow woman to take on her place not only in domestic life, but also in social and public life. Instruction and education have a twofold purpose; individually, they redeem the human intellect from the perils of ignorance, and socially they prepare man and woman for the proper performance of their duties of citizenship. A person is not educated exclusively for his or her own good, but principally to be useful and of service to the others. Nothing is more dangerous to society than the educated man who thinks only of himself, because his education enables him to do more harm and to sacrifice everybody else to his convenience or personal ambition. The real object of education is public service, that is, to utilize the knowledge one has acquired for the benefit and improvement of the society in which one is living.

In societies, therefore, where woman is admitted to all the professions and where no source of knowledge is barred to her, woman must necessarily and logically be allowed to take a part in the public life, otherwise, her education would be incomplete or society would commit an injustice towards her, giving her the means to educate herself and then depriving her of the necessary power to use that education for the benefit of society and collective progress.

6. **What is the claim made in this passage?**

   F  Women are entitled to the right to vote.

   G  Women are admitted to all the professions.

   H  Women participate in all aspects of education.

   J  Women participate in many aspects of public life.

7. **How does the author feel about people who protest against women's right to vote?**

   A  He thinks they are correct.

   B  He thinks they are doing their duty.

   C  He thinks they have no reason to protest.

   D  He thinks they should be better educated.

8. **What type of evidence does the author cite to support his claim that women should have a role in public life?**

   F  fact about women's suffrage

   G  his personal opinion about women

   H  example of women's success in education

   J  expert opinion about women's intelligence

9. **Which statement best describes how Palma builds his argument?**

   A  He states his claim and supports it with his opinion on the topic.

   B  He states his claim and supports it with facts, reasons, and examples.

   C  He states his claim and supports it with experts' opinions on the topic.

   D  He states his claim and supports it with examples of ways to gain the vote.

10. **Which sentence best describes the way the author connects his ideas in this passage?**

    F  He connects his ideas logically.

    G  He connects his ideas chronologically.

    H  He connects his ideas through comparison and contrast.

    J  He connects his ideas in the form of a question and answer.

11. **Which sentence best states the author's conclusion?**

    A  A woman is not educated solely for her own good.

    B  A woman has access to all sources of knowledge and all professions.

    C  It is logical and necessary for women to participate in public life by voting.

    D  It is not necessary to perpetuate customs that have been observed for many years.

# Language Practice

The way that words or phrases are used in a text often depends on where and when the text was written. Spelling, grammar, and expressions change from one region to another. For instance, some words are spelled differently in British English than in American English, such as *colour* and *color*.

Usage also evolves over time, due to changes in the world or to gradual shifts in meaning. For example, when we hear the word *scroll*, we think of moving through text on a computer screen rather than of rolled sheets of parchment. Words also change meaning as a result of linguistic fashion. *Bad*, for instance, may mean "not good," but it may also mean "really good." In rare cases, usage changes as a result of social upheaval or public discussion.

A dictionary will usually tell you if a spelling or an expression is out of date or associated with a particular geographical area.

**Directions:** Read this excerpt from William Shakespeare's play *Two Gentlemen of Verona*. Then do Numbers 12 and 13.

Love is your master, for he masters you:

And he that is so yoked by a fool,

Methinks, should not be chronicled for wise. . . .

But wherefore [why] waste I time to counsel thee,

That art a votary [devotee, devout worshipper] to fond desire?

12. **Which of these is the best definition of the word fond as it is used in the context of this excerpt?**

   **F** affectionate

   **G** dear

   **H** foolish

   **J** tender

13. **Which of the following best describes the usage of fond?**

   **A** Fond has a different meaning in Britain than it does in the United States.

   **B** This meaning of fond is archaic; today, it is generally understood differently.

   **C** The meaning of fond as Shakespeare uses it has become socially controversial.

   **D** Shakespeare uses fond in much the same way as we use it in the United States today.

**Directions** Read this paragraph from a story. Then do Numbers 14 and 15.

The other day, my friend Mary, who comes from Pennsylvania, was telling a group of us about her aunt. "She's so nebby! She always has to know every little detail about my life," Mary said. "It's an invasion of privacy." Mary was surprised when Rick, who's from California, asked her what *nebby* means.

14. **Which is the best definition of the word nebby as used in this paragraph?**

   **F** abusive

   **G** aggressive

   **H** friendly

   **J** nosy

**15. Which of the following best describes the usage of nebby?**

   **A**  Nebby is regional dialect.

   **B**  People no longer use the word nebby.

   **C**  Nebby is offensive to some groups, so it is no longer used.

   **D**  The writer's friend Mary probably invented the word nebby.

---

### ✓ Test-Taking Tip

To answer test questions based on a reading passage, you should eliminate information that is not necessary for answering questions. One way to do this is to read through the passage, taking notes of important information, and then review the questions to see what information is covered and what is not.

---

## Writing Practice

People develop arguments for a wide range of reasons. However, all good arguments share common traits. First, they state a claim clearly. Then they support that claim with facts and evidence.

**Directions:** The following passages contain arguments for and against a legislative initiative. Read the passages, and then write an argument for or against the initiative. State your claim clearly. Include facts, valid reasoning, and examples from the passages as relevant and sufficient evidence to support your argument. Provide a concluding statement that follows from and supports the argument presented.

A 2013 ballot measure proposed a change to consumer food labels in Washington state. Initiative Measure 522 would require labels identifying many raw agricultural products and processed foods as genetically modified. The following excerpts appeared in a Washington voters' pamphlet.

## Argument for Initiative Measure 522

**Right to Know**

In America, we have a right to know important information about the food we eat and feed our families—such as sugar and sodium levels, whether flavors are natural or artificial, the country of origin, and if fish are wild or farm-raised.

We also should have a right to choose whether we want to buy and eat genetically engineered food. Labels matter. They ensure transparency and preserve the freedom to make our own decisions about the food we eat. I-522 is a step in the right direction.

US companies already label genetically engineered foods for markets in the 64 countries that require labeling, including some of Washington's largest trading partners. Genetically engineered crops, such as wheat, have contaminated conventional crops in the Northwest. Some countries suspended imports from our farmers, putting our economy at risk. Separation and labeling, from the seed level up through the supply chain, helps protect exports to countries that require labeling. . . .

*(Continued on next page)*

**Labels Let You Decide**

Voting *Yes on I-522* is an important step for more information about your food. You should have the freedom to decide what to eat. Your food decisions should be up to you—not corporations, the government, or special interests. Labels let you decide. Vote for the right to know what's in your food.

**Rebuttal of Argument Against**

Powerful chemical corporations that genetically engineer food oppose labeling because they care about their profits, not our right to know. The truth: labels ensure transparency.

The government has conducted no independent safety tests and the Washington State Nurses Association endorses labeling to trace health issues. Labeling is easy, and it gives us the freedom to decide what to buy. Foods are relabeled frequently. Adding words to a label doesn't increase costs. Trust yourself to decide.

# Argument Against Initiative Measure 522

**I-522 makes no sense.**

For decades, agricultural biotechnology has helped improve food crops so they resist disease, require fewer pesticides or are more nutritious. Today, 70–80% of grocery products include ingredients from these foods, and they're deemed safe by the FDA and major scientific and medical organizations. Yet I-522 would require thousands of these products to have special, new labels—only for Washington—while giving special exemptions to thousands of others, even when they contain "genetically engineered" (GE) ingredients.

I-522 requires fruits, vegetables and grain-based products to be labeled, but exempts meat and dairy products from animals fed GE grains. It mandates special labels and signs in supermarkets, but exempts restaurants from providing information about GE ingredients in their foods. Foods from foreign countries would be exempt if manufacturers simply *claim* they're exempt. So I-522 wouldn't even give consumers a reliable way of knowing which foods contain GE ingredients.

**Higher taxpayer costs, more state bureaucracy and lawsuits.**

I-522 would require the state to monitor labels on thousands of products in thousands of stores—costing taxpayers millions. . . . And studies show I-522's Washington-only labeling requirements would hurt local farmers and increase an average family's food costs by hundreds of dollars per year.

Washington scientists, farmers and food producers urge *no* on 522.

**Rebuttal of Argument For**

Existing food labels already give consumers the option to choose foods without GE ingredients by choosing products labeled "certified organic." I-522's complicated, poorly written regulations would put Washington farmers and food producers at a competitive disadvantage, not protect them. I-522 would not protect our export markets or provide consumers with reliable information about our food. But it would increase grocery prices for Washington families and cost taxpayers millions. Vote *no* on this costly, unnecessary measure.

_____

_____

_____

_____

This lesson will help you practice identifying supporting evidence in two texts. Use it with Core Lesson 6.2 *Identify Supporting Evidence* to reinforce and apply your knowledge.

### Key Concept

Authors use various types of reasoning in developing an argument. Some types of reasoning are useful, but others are ineffective.

### Core Skills

• Evaluate Arguments
• Cite Specific Evidence

## Supporting Evidence

Authors making a claim in an argument must support that claim with evidence such as facts, reasons, and examples. Authors use this supporting evidence to back up their claim and to persuade you, the reader, that the claim is reasonable. The evidence presented must be logical, and it must be connected to the claim. Emotional appeals and faulty logic do not qualify as supporting evidence.

**Directions:** Read the text. Then do Numbers 1–5.

## From "The One Man Power"

*from* The New York Times, *January 5, 1860*

Mayor Wood, in his eagerness to impress the public with the belief that he cannot justly be held responsible for defects or malfeasances in the city government, overlooks or misrepresents one point of considerable importance. He states that there is no general supervision confided to the mayor;—these are his words:

"While the Common Council, with the mayor, can enact an ordinance, the administrative authority is not thus defined. This is diffused and uncertain. It is disseminated among several independent departments. There is no general head; there is no chief executive. Instead of one, there are eight coordinate executives, separate and independent of each other, the mayor having no supervisory control. These departments constitute the whole administrative municipal government of the corporation."

This is an entire mistake. The charter makes the heads of nearly all the departments directly responsible to the mayor. The comptroller and corporation counsel are, it is true, elected by the people, and are not accountable to the executive; but the Croton Aqueduct board, the street commissioner, the city inspector, and the four superintendents of bureaux under him, are all appointed by the mayor and aldermen, and may at any time be removed by the mayor and board for cause. Any malfeasance or neglect of duty on the part of either of those officers, entitles the mayor instantly to supersede them. What more does Mayor Wood desire? What greater power is necessary to enable him to enforce proper vigilance and energy in the business of these departments? In speaking of the street inspector the mayor says:

"The mayor, being without power, should not be held accountable by the public. If nuisances abound and the streets remain filthy, it will be unjust to lay the responsibility at his door. Until he has power to appoint and remove the subordinates upon whom it is incumbent to perform these duties, he should be relieved from any censure which attaches to the neglect. It is well for the public and myself to have an understanding upon the subject at the commencement of my administration."

*(Continued on next page)*

"The public and myself" should have an accurate understanding of the subject, if they have any at all: —yet the mayor's words convey an impression in regard to the matter which is not correct. In the same paragraph the mayor says: "The city inspector and the superintendents under him are appointed and removed in the same manner as the street commissioner"; and in regard to that officer, he says:

"Like the officers of the Croton board, he derives his appointment, in the first instance, from the mayor and aldermen, but with a tenure of two years, unless sooner removed for cause, which removal requires the sanction of a majority of all the members elected to the Board of Aldermen."

His own admissions thus completely contradict his assertion that the mayor is without power, and should therefore be without responsibility. He has power in every case of misconduct to remove the offender from office, and to demand the concurrence of the Board of Aldermen. Does he doubt the disposition of that board to second promptly any effort he may make to remedy evils or punish mal-practices on the part of city officers? If so, he can very easily throw upon them the responsibility which he deprecates so much. Let him remove an officer for misconduct, and show clear cause for the proceeding, and he will be sustained by the public, whether the board second his action or not. But the fact that he is not arbitrary and absolute, —that others share the power of punishment which is placed in his hands, cannot relieve him from the just responsibility which belongs to his office.

1. **Which claim does the author make in this passage about the mayor?**
   **A** The mayor is shirking his responsibilities.
   **B** The mayor is taking on too much responsibility.
   **C** The mayor has no real power over city employees.
   **D** The mayor is not responsible for removing officers.

2. **How does the mayor describe his role in city government?**
   **F** He is responsible for removing officers for misconduct.
   **G** He has supervisory power over members of city government.
   **H** He cannot ignore his duty to evaluate the work of appointed officials.
   **J** He is not responsible for removing officers for misconduct in city government.

3. **Which statement includes logical evidence used to support the author's claim?**
   **A** The mayor does not have the responsibility to supervise city executives.
   **B** The mayor has the responsibility to help the public understand how power is distributed in the city.
   **C** The mayor does not have power to control all city offices, so he should not be held accountable for all city services.
   **D** The mayor has the power to remove an offender from office and to demand that the Board of Aldermen agrees with his decision to do so.

4. **How would the mayor's statements be described?**
   **F** They are false.
   **G** They are authoritative.
   **H** They are contradictory.
   **J** They are based on truth.

5. **Which word best describes the mayor's logic in explaining his lack of responsibility?**
   **A** connected
   **B** faulty
   **C** sound
   **D** supporting

## Connecting Claims and Evidence

When you are reading an argument, use reasoning to evaluate the author's argument and to determine whether the argument is valid. If the reasoning is logical and you can cite specific evidence that supports and connects directly to the author's claim, then you can safely say that the argument is valid and reasonable.

**Directions:** Read the text. Then do Numbers 6–10.

# From the "Checkers" speech
### *by Richard M. Nixon, September 23, 1952*

My fellow Americans,

I come before you tonight as a candidate for the vice presidency and as a man whose honesty and integrity has been questioned. . . .

I am sure that you have read the charges, and you have heard it, that I, Senator Nixon, took $18,000 from a group of my supporters.

. . . [L]et me say this: Not a cent of the $18,000 or any other money of that type ever went to me for my personal use. Every penny of it was used to pay for political expenses that I did not think should be charged to the taxpayers of the United States.

It was not a secret fund. . . .

I just don't believe in that, and I can say that never, while I have been in the Senate of the United States, as far as the people that contributed to this fund are concerned, have I made a telephone call to an agency, nor have I gone down to an agency on their behalf.

And the records will show that, the records which are in the hands of the administration.

Let me tell you in just a word how a senate office operates. First of all, the senator gets $15,000 a year in salary. He gets enough money to pay for one trip a year, a round trip, that is, for himself, and his family between his home and Washington, D.C., and then he gets an allowance to handle the people that work in his office to handle his mail.

And the allowance for my state of California is enough to hire 13 people. And let me say, incidentally, that this allowance is not paid to the senator.

It is paid directly to the individuals that the senator puts on his payroll, but all of these people and all of these allowances are for strictly official business; business, for example, when a constituent writes in and wants you to go down to the Veterans Administration and get some information about his GI policy—items of that type, for example. But there are other expenses that are not covered by the government. And I think I can best discuss those expenses by asking you some questions.

Do you think that when I or any other senator makes a political speech and has it printed, we should charge the printing of that speech and the mailing of that speech to the taxpayers?

Do you think, for example, when I or any other senator makes a trip to his home state to make a purely political speech that the cost of that trip, we should charge it to the taxpayers?

Do you think when a senator makes political broadcasts or political television broadcasts, radio or television that the expense of those broadcasts should be charged to the taxpayers?

. . . The answer is no. The taxpayers should not be required to finance items which are not official business but which are primarily political business.

*(Continued on next page)*

Well, then the question arises, you say, "Well, how do you pay for these and how can you do it legally?" And there are several ways that it can be done, incidentally, and it is done legally in the United States Senate and in the Congress.

The first way is to be a rich man. So I couldn't use that.

Another way that is used is to put your wife on the payroll. Let me say, incidentally, that my opponent, my opposite number for the vice presidency on the Democratic ticket, does have his wife on the payroll and has had her on his payroll for the past ten years. Now let me just say this: That is his business, and I am not critical of him for doing that. You will have to pass judgment on that particular point, but I have never done that for this reason:

I have found that there are so many deserving stenographers and secretaries in Washington that needed the work that I just didn't feel it was right to put my wife on the payroll. . . .

What are the other ways that these finances can be taken care of? Some who are lawyers, and I happen to be a lawyer, continue to practice law, but I haven't been able to do that. . . .

And so I felt that the best way to handle these necessary political expenses of getting my message to the American people and the speeches I made—the speeches I had printed for the most part concerned this one message of exposing this administration, the Communism in it, the corruption in it—the only way I could do that was to accept the aid which people in my home state of California, who contributed to my campaign and who continued to make these contributions after I was elected, were glad to make.

And let me say that I am proud of the fact that not one of them has ever asked me for a special favor. I am proud of the fact that not one of them has ever asked me to vote on a bill other than my own conscience would dictate. And I am proud of the fact that the taxpayers by subterfuge or otherwise have never paid one dime for expenses which I thought were political and should not be charged [to] the taxpayers.

**6.** **Which claim is made by Richard Nixon in this speech?**

   **F**  He hired his wife to manage his political expenses.

   **G**  He did not use money from supporters for personal expenses.

   **H**  He received money from the government for political expenses.

   **J**  He did not receive money from supporters for political expenses.

**7.** **Read this sentence from the text.**

   **The taxpayers should not be required to finance items which are not official business but which are primarily political business.**

   **Which type of evidence is this statement?**

   **A**  example

   **B**  verifiable fact

   **C**  emotional appeal

   **D**  supporting reason

8. **Read this sentence from the text.**

> The taxpayers should not be required to finance items which are not official business but which are primarily political business.

**What does the word <u>finance</u> mean as it is used in this sentence?**

F   manage large amounts of money

G   provide funds for someone or for a venture

H   raise the funds to contribute support for a project

J   donate resources and monetary affairs of a government or organization

9. **What does Nixon provide as evidence to support his claim that he used the money given to him for political expenses?**

A   broadcasts

B   letters

C   records

D   speeches

10. **The fact that Nixon does not have proof that he avoided giving special favors for contributions makes his argument**

F   faulty

G   logical

H   reasonable

J   valid

## Test-Taking Tip

When a test includes questions related to a passage, it is often helpful to read the questions before reading the passage. You can jot down notes and key words to help you identify the information that you'll need to look for in the passage. Then as you read the passage, keep the questions in mind and look for the information that you need to answer them correctly.

## Language Practice

Hyphens have two main functions. The first is to indicate that a word continues on the next line. The hyphen belongs between syllables or between the two parts of an already hyphenated word. However, a word should not be broken where only one letter would appear alone at the end of a line or if one or two letters would appear alone at the beginning of a line (for example, *lovely*). In this case, the options are to hyphenate elsewhere or to place the entire word on the new line.

The second use of hyphens is to join one or more words that form a compound. Hyphens are commonly used in the following situations:

- between two words functioning as a single adjective when they appear before a noun (but not after the noun), such as *friendly-looking dog*
- in compound numbers, such as *twenty-one*
- with certain prefixes, such as *ex-*, *self-*, and *all-*
- with the suffix *-elect*

*(Continued on next page)*

- to avoid confusion about the meaning of a word, such as *ten-year-old children* compared to *ten year-old children*
- to avoid an awkward combination of letters, such as *co-opt* and *pre-eminent*
- between a prefix and a capitalized word or between a prefix and a number, such as *pro-Kennedy* and *pre-1800*
- certain compound nouns, such as brother-in-law

Note, however, that not all compounds are hyphenated. They may also be written as one word or as two words without a hyphen. If you are unsure whether a compound should be hyphenated or where to hyphenate a word split between lines, check a dictionary.

**Directions:** For Numbers 11 through 14, read the question and choose the best answer.

11. **Which of the following is correct hyphenation if the word *originally* has to be split between lines?**

    A  o-riginally

    B  origi-nally

    C  origina-lly

    D  original-ly

12. **Which of the following sentences uses hyphenation(s) correctly?**

    F  Green and Union were two-way streets.

    G  Green and Union were two way-streets.

    H  Green and Union were two-way-streets.

    J  Green-and-Union were two way streets.

13. **Which of the following sentences uses hyphenation(s) correctly?**

    A  Mayor-Chung decided to change them in the mid 1990s.

    B  Mayor Chung decided to change them in the-mid 1990s.

    C  Mayor Chung decided to change them in the-mid-1990s.

    D  Mayor Chung decided to change them in the mid-1990s.

14. **Which of the following sentences uses hyphenation(s) correctly?**

    F  Mayor elect-Garcia has some creative ideas on the subject.

    G  Mayor-elect Garcia has some creative ideas on the subject.

    H  Mayor-elect-Garcia has some creative ideas on the subject.

    J  Mayor elect Garcia has some creative-ideas on the subject.

## Writing Practice

Many people have said or done things that others disagree with. For example, Nixon firmly believed that he had spent taxpayer money and political contributions wisely, but some people criticized his behavior. Similarly, the author of "The One Man Power" criticizes the behavior of New York City's mayor. The author argues that the mayor should take responsibility for corruption in city government.

**Directions:** Reread the passage "The One Man Power" on pages 147 and 148 with this question in mind: Do you agree that a government official—whether a mayor, a governor, or a president—should be held accountable for corruption? Then write an argument, supporting your claim with valid reasoning, significant and relevant facts, and examples from the text.

This lesson will help you practice evaluating the relevance and sufficiency of supporting evidence in two texts. Use it with Core Lesson 6.3 *Evaluate Relevance and Sufficiency* to reinforce and apply your knowledge.

| **Key Concept** | **Core Skills** |
| --- | --- |
| To create a reasonable argument, an author must provide relevant and sufficient evidence for his or her claim. | • Identify Relevant Information<br>• Evaluate Arguments |

## Building a Case

To build an effective argument, writers must support their claim with evidence that is relevant not only to the claim but also to the audience's interests and needs. Writers must also provide more than one piece of evidence to build a convincing argument. The validity of the argument depends on the relevancy and sufficiency of the evidence.

**Directions:** Read the text. Then do Number 1–6.

# Corporate Memo on Sick-Leave Legislation

In response to the current influenza outbreak, the New York City Council is fast-tracking a piece of legislation. If passed, this would place statutory standards on the administration of corporate sick-leave policies. In a nutshell, it would require all New York City employers to provide the following:

- 10 paid sick days a year for full-time employees, and
- 5 paid sick days a year for employees working between 20 and 32 hours per week.

We strongly encourage employees to oppose this legislation. We have always acknowledged the importance of employee health. We also realize that our employees are more productive when their salary and position in the workforce are protected. Our current policy of granting sick leave on a documented, case-by-case basis is efficient and effective. It provides protection for our employees, their families, and society as a whole:

- It helps to maintain workplace health, in support of CDC guidelines. These guidelines suggest that people infected with influenza remain isolated for at least 24 hours after their fever breaks.
- It helps to maintain a healthy school environment for the children of our employees by allowing parents to remain home while their children are contagious.

Current law does not require employers to provide sick leave, paid or unpaid, under any circumstances. If, however, a company is held to a specific number of sick days, it is likewise obliged to compensate employees for their unused sick days. This amount must be paid yearly or when an employee leaves the company.

(continued)

Our current policy, then, is a vital tool for maintaining our bottom line. This, in turn, translates into benefits and job security for you, the employee.

- According to a March 2010 Department of Labor Statistics report, the cost of sick leave to a business or agency can average 81 cents per hour per employee. We are a mid-sized company. We employ approximately 1,200 full-time and part-time workers. Using the DLS report as a guide, let's consider some figures.

One full-time employee works 260 days a year. At 8 hours per workday, an individual works 2,080 hours per year. Multiply that by the number of employees (1,200), and there are 2,496,000 work hours per year in our company. Finally, multiply the number of work hours by the per-hour cost of sick leave ($.81), and you get $2,021,760 per year.

This is an unacceptable level of expense. It would force overall cost reduction. This cost reduction would most likely be administered through layoffs and reduced employee salaries. As an employee, voter, and citizen, this concerns you directly. Phone your city representative to protest this intrusion into the private sector—and remind him or her that you vote!

1. **Which statement provides evidence to support the claim that employees should oppose mandatory paid sick leave?**
   A  Employees should support their company's position.
   B  The company cannot afford mandatory paid sick leave.
   C  The mandatory sick-leave legislation is in response to the influenza outbreak.
   D  The New York City council is trying to pass legislation for mandatory paid sick leave.

2. **Which piece of evidence supports the claim that the company "always acknowledged the importance of employee health"?**
   F  "Current law does not require employers to provide sick leave," but this company does provide it.
   G  The cost of sick leave to a business or agency can average "81 cents per hour per employee."
   H  A company that provides a number of paid sick days is expected to "compensate employees for their unused sick days."
   J  The company recognizes that "employees are more productive when their salary and position in the workforce are protected."

3. **Which statement is directly relevant to the audience?**
   A  We have always acknowledged the importance of employee health.
   B  Our current policy, then, is a vital tool for maintaining our bottom line.
   C  This, in turn, translates into benefits and job security for you, the employee.
   D  We employ approximately 1,200 full-time and part-time workers.

4. **The financial information in the memo is relevant to the claim because it shows how the new law would**
   F  negatively affect employees' job security
   G  improve the company's health-care policy
   H  prevent the company from giving its CEO a raise
   J  ensure that employees do not lose income when they are sick

**5.** Which type of evidence does the author provide to support the claim that legislated sick leave would cost the company a lot of money?

**A** verifiable but faulty

**B** biased and repetitive

**C** relevant and sufficient

**D** valid but contradictory

**6.** The author links the evidence to the claim at the end of the passage by stating that

**F** the city leaders have doubts about the proposed legislation

**G** the company's management is going to oppose the legislation

**H** the employees should oppose the legislation out of loyalty to the company

**J** the employees are directly affected by this legislation and should oppose it

## Evaluating Evidence in Various Texts

When you evaluate the evidence in a text, you look for appropriate evidence that supports the author's claim and is relevant to the topic and the audience's interests. You should also check for sufficient evidence, in both strength and amount, to support the claim.

**Directions:** Read the text. Then do Numbers 7–12.

## From "Address Before a Joint Session of the Congress Reporting on the State of the Union"

*by Ronald Reagan*

Today marks my first State of the Union address to you. . . .

When I visited this Chamber last year as a newcomer to Washington, critical of past policies . . . , I proposed a new spirit of partnership between this Congress and this administration and between Washington and our State and local governments. In forging this new partnership for America, we could achieve the oldest hopes of our Republic—prosperity for our nation, peace for the world, and the blessings of individual liberty for our children and, someday, for all of humanity.

It's my duty to report to you tonight on the progress that we have made. . . .

Seldom have the stakes been higher for America. . . . The situation at this time last year was truly ominous.

The last decade has seen a series of recessions. There was a recession in 1970, in 1974, and again in the spring of 1980. Each time, unemployment increased and inflation soon turned up again. . . .

Late in 1981 we sank into the present recession, largely because continued high interest rates hurt the auto industry and construction. And there was a drop in productivity, and the already high unemployment increased.

This time, however, things are different. We have an economic program in place, completely different from the artificial quick fixes of the past. It calls for a reduction of the rate of increase in government spending. . . . But reduced spending alone isn't enough. We've just implemented the first and smallest phase of a 3-year tax-rate reduction designed to stimulate the economy and create jobs. . . .

*(Continued on next page)*

I will seek no tax increases this year. . . . I promise to bring the American people—to bring their tax rates down and to keep them down, to provide them incentives to rebuild our economy, to save, to invest in America's future. . . . Seize these new opportunities to produce, to save, to invest, and together we'll make this economy a mighty engine of freedom, hope, and prosperity again.

Now, the budget deficit this year will exceed our earlier expectations. The recession did that. It lowered revenues and increased costs. To some extent, we're also victims of our own success. We've brought inflation down faster than we thought we could. . . . [W]e've deprived government of those hidden revenues that occur when inflation pushes people into higher income tax brackets. . . .

We must cut out more nonessential government spending and rout out more waste. . . .

The budget plan I submit to you on February 8th will realize major savings by dismantling the Departments of Energy and Education. . . . We'll continue to redirect our resources to our two highest budget priorities—a strong national defense to keep America free and at peace and a reliable safety net of social programs for those who have contributed and those who are in need. . . .

Our faith in the American people is reflected in another major endeavor. Our private sector initiatives task force is seeking out successful community models of school, church, business, union, foundation, and civic programs that help community needs. Such groups are almost invariably far more efficient than government in running social programs.

We're not asking them to replace discarded and often discredited government programs dollar for dollar, service for service. We just want to help them perform the good works they choose and help others to profit by their example. Three hundred and eighty-five thousand corporations and private organizations are already working on social programs ranging from drug rehabilitation to job training, and thousands more Americans have written us asking how they can help. The volunteer spirit is still alive and well in America. . . .

Our foreign policy is a policy of strength, fairness, and balance. By restoring America's military credibility, by pursuing peace at the negotiating table wherever both sides are willing to sit down in good faith, and by regaining the respect of America's allies and adversaries alike, we have strengthened our country's position as a force for peace and progress in the world. . . .

We have made pledges of a new frankness in our public statements and worldwide broadcasts. In the face of a climate of falsehood and misinformation, we've promised the world a season of truth—the truth of our great civilized ideas: individual liberty, representative government, the rule of law under God. We've never needed walls or minefields or barbed wire to keep our people in. Nor do we declare martial law to keep our people from voting for the kind of government they want. . . .

A hundred and twenty years ago, the greatest of all our Presidents delivered his second State of the Union message in this Chamber. "We cannot escape history," Abraham Lincoln warned. "We of this Congress and this administration will be remembered in spite of ourselves." The "trial through which we pass will light us down, in honor or dishonor, to the latest [last] generation."

Well, that President and that Congress did not fail the American people. Together they weathered the storm and preserved the Union. Let it be said of us that we, too, did not fail; that we, too, worked together to bring America through difficult times. Let us so conduct ourselves that two centuries from now, another Congress and another President, meeting in this Chamber as we are meeting, will speak of us with pride, saying that we met the test and preserved for them in their day the sacred flame of liberty—this last, best hope of man on Earth.

7. **How does President Reagan use Abraham Lincoln's words to support his claim that the country needs to work together to bring the United States through difficult times?**

   **A** as relevant evidence

   **B** as sufficient evidence

   **C** as an additional claim

   **D** as opposition to a claim

8. **In which sentence does President Reagan present evidence to support his claim that government programs can be cut?**

   **F** [Volunteer] groups are almost invariably far more efficient than government in running social programs.

   **G** We just want to help [private sector groups] perform the good works they choose and help others to profit by their example.

   **H** [W]e have strengthened our country's position as a force for peace and progress in the world.

   **J** [We do not] declare martial law to keep our people from voting for the kind of government they want.

9. **Read this sentence from the text.**

   **The budget plan I submit to you on February 8th will realize major savings by dismantling the Departments of Energy and Education.**

   **What does the word dismantling mean as it is used in this sentence?**

   **A** eliminating

   **B** improving

   **C** rebuilding

   **D** restructuring

10. **Which statement is relevant evidence to support President Reagan's claim that the government will do its part to turn around the recession?**

    **F** He has promised the country a season of truth.

    **G** He will not declare martial law to change voting.

    **H** He will not raise taxes to pay for the new budget.

    **J** He believes our foreign policy is fair, strong, and balanced.

11. **President Reagan's argument is supported by several pieces of evidence related to his claim, but the lack of specific examples makes the evidence**

    **A** insufficient

    **B** irrelevant

    **C** relevant

    **D** sufficient

12. **Which phrase best describes the evidence that the recession caused the budget deficit?**

    **F** connected but faulty

    **G** interesting but biased

    **H** factual but not verifiable

    **J** relevant but not sufficient

**Test-Taking Tip**

When you take a test that involves reading a text, scan the text for features such as headings and lists. As you scan, look in the text features and the text for words that you associate with the topic and words that are frequently repeated. These steps will help activate your prior knowledge about the topic and make it easier for you to answer questions about the text.

## Writing Practice

As you have learned, an effective argument includes relevant and sufficient evidence. In the company memo on pages 154 and 155, company leaders urge employees to oppose legislation to standardize the number of employee sick days and provide evidence in support of their position. Some might argue that it is unethical to pressure employees in this way. If you were the CEO of a company in this situation, what would you do? Would you take similar steps? Why or why not?

**Directions:** Reread "Corporate Memo on Sick-Leave Legislation" on pages 154 and 155. Write an argument introducing a precise and knowledgeable claim stating whether you would take similar actions. Create an organization that logically sequences the claim, any counterclaims, reasons, and evidence. Use valid reasoning and relevant and sufficient evidence from the memo to support your position.

This lesson will help you practice evaluating validity and reasoning in arguments in two texts. Use it with Core Lesson 6.4 *Evaluate Validity and Reasoning* to reinforce and apply your knowledge.

## Key Concept

Readers can use logical tests to determine whether the reasoning authors use in their arguments is valid.

## Core Skills

- Cite Specific Evidence
- Evaluate Arguments

## Understanding Validity and Reasoning

An argument's validity depends on whether the argument is logical and factually reliable. An argument is valid when it is supported with sound, or sensible, evidence. An argument is reasonable when each piece of evidence is connected to the claim and to other pieces of evidence. An argument is invalid if the author exhibits bias or presents contradictory evidence.

**Directions:** Read the text. Then do Numbers 1–4.

## From "Argument Against Women's Suffrage"

*by J.B. Sanford, Chairman of California Democratic Caucus*

Suffrage is not a right. It is a privilege that may or may not be granted. Politics is no place for a woman, consequently the privilege should not be granted to her. The mother's influence is needed in the home. She can do little good by gadding the street and neglecting her children. Let her teach her daughters that modesty, patience and gentleness are the charms of woman. Let her teach her sons that an honest conscience is every man's first political law; that no splendor can rob him nor no force justify the surrender of the simplest right of a free and independent citizen. The mothers of this country can shape the destinies of the nation by keeping in their places and attending to those duties that God Almighty intended for them. The kindly, gentle influence of the mother in the home and the dignified influence of the teacher in the school will far outweigh all the influence of all the mannish female politicians on earth.

The courageous, chivalrous, and manly men and the womanly women, the real mothers and homebuilders of the country, are opposed to this innovation in American political life. There was a bill (the Sanford bill) before the last legislature which proposed to leave the equal suffrage question to women to decide first before the men should vote on it. This bill was defeated by the suffragettes because they knew that the women would vote down the amendment by a vote of ten to one. Do women have to vote in order to receive the protection of men? Why, men have gone to war, endured every privation, and death itself in defense of woman. To man, woman is the dearest creature on earth, and there is no extreme to which he would not go for his mother or sister. By keeping woman in her exalted position man can be induced to do more for her than he could by having the mix up in affairs that will cause him to lose respect and regard for her. Woman does not have to vote to secure her rights. Man will go to any extreme to protect and elevate her now. As long as woman is woman and keeps her place she will get more protection and more consideration than man gets. When she abdicates her throne she throws down the scepter of her power and loses her influence.

Woman suffrage has been proven a failure in states that have tried it. It is wrong. California should profit by the mistakes of other states. Not one reform has equal suffrage effected.

1. **Read this sentence from the text.**

   There was a bill (the Sanford bill) before the last legislature which proposed to leave the equal suffrage question to women to decide first before the men should vote on it.

   **What does the word <u>suffrage</u> mean as it is used in this sentence?**

   **A**  the right to vote

   **B**  the right to go to war

   **C**  the securing of rights

   **D**  the right to be a citizen

2. **Which idea from this passage is a verifiable fact?**

   **F**  Women should keep their place in the home.

   **G**  Women do not have to vote to secure their rights.

   **H**  The Sanford bill was defeated by the suffragettes.

   **J**  Men can protect women if women keep their exalted position.

3. **The author of this passage uses evidence to support his claim that is**

   **A**  reasonable and logically sound

   **B**  unreasonable but logically sound

   **C**  reasonable but not logically sound

   **D**  unreasonable and not logically sound

4. **Which phrase <u>best</u> describes the author's argument as a whole?**

   **F**  biased but logical

   **G**  biased and invalid

   **H**  reasonable and valid

   **J**  logical but unreasonable

## Evaluating Validity and Reasoning in Texts

To evaluate the validity of an argument, check whether the evidence is accurate and connected to the claim. To evaluate an argument's reasoning, make sure the evidence relates to the claim and is linked to other evidence in a logical way. The argument's reasoning is not sound if the evidence does not support the claim.

**Directions:** Read the text. Then do Numbers 5–9.

## From "Remarks by the President at Campaign Event—Stamford, CT"

### *by Barack Obama*

We are here to build an economy where work pays off so that no matter what you look like or where you come from, you can make it here if you try. . . .

We've got the best workers in the world. We've got the best entrepreneurs in the world. We have the best scientists and the best researchers in the world. We have the best universities and the best colleges in the world. We are a young nation, and we've got the greatest diversity of talent and ingenuity from every corner of the globe. . . . [N]o matter what the naysayers may say, no matter how dark the picture they try to paint, there's not another country on Earth that wouldn't gladly trade places with the United States of America. . . .

So what's standing in our way right now is not the lack of technical solutions to the deficit or to education or to energy. What's standing in our way is . . . the uncompromising view that says we should be going back to the old, top-down economics that got us into this mess in the first place. . . .

And I don't exaggerate when it comes to how my opponent and his allies in Congress view this economy. They believe . . . that if we give more tax breaks to some of the wealthiest Americans, and we get rid of regulations . . . that somehow prosperity will rain down on everybody. . . .

So you're talking about each year, a tax cut that's equivalent of our defense budget for the next 10 years. . . . Governor Romney's plan would effectively raise taxes on middle-class families with children by an average of $2,000—to pay for this tax cut. . . . He'd ask the middle class to pay more in taxes so that he could give another $250,000 tax cut to people making more than $3 million a year. . . . It's like Robin Hood in reverse. . . .

They have tried to sell us this trickle-down, tax cut fairy dust before. . . . It didn't work then; it won't work now. It's not a plan to create jobs. It's not a plan to reduce our deficit. And it is not a plan to move our economy forward.

We need tax cuts for working Americans. We need tax cuts for families who are trying to raise kids, and keep them healthy, and send them to college, and keep a roof over their heads.

So that's the choice in this election. That's what this is about. That's why I'm running for a second term as President of the United States. . . .

Four years ago, I promised to cut middle-class taxes—that's exactly what I've done, by a total of about $3,600 for the typical family. . . .

[W]hen a construction worker has got some money in his pocket, he goes out and buys a new car. When a teacher is getting paid a decent wage, that means they can maybe take their family to a restaurant once in a while. And when the middle class is doing well, then business is doing well, and those at the top do well. Everybody does well. That's what we believe in—an economy that grows from the middle class out and the bottom up. That's the choice in this election. . . .

*(Continued on next page)*

And over the course of the next three months, the other side is going to spend more money than we have ever seen on ads that basically say the same thing you've been hearing for months. They know their economics theory won't sell, so their ads are going to say the same thing over and over again, which is: The economy is not where it needs to be and it's Obama's fault. . . .

Their strategists admit it. They say . . . we're not going to put out any plans. We're just going to see if this works. . . .

They don't have that plan. I do. . . .

And if you still believe in me, and you're willing to stand with me, and knock on some doors for me, make some phone calls with me, work hard and organize and mobilize with me for the next three months, we will finish what we started in 2008, and we will show the world why the United States of America is the greatest nation on Earth.

5. **Which piece of evidence is a verifiable fact?**
   **A** The United States is the best country on Earth.
   **B** The United States has the best workers in the world.
   **C** Obama cut taxes by about $3,600 for the typical middle-class family.
   **D** Every country in the world would want to trade places with the United States.

6. **Obama gives Romney's tax plan as an example to**
   **F** support the idea that trickle-down economics always works
   **G** refute the idea that trickle-down economics does not always work
   **H** support the idea that trickle-down economics can sometimes work
   **J** support the idea that trickle-down economics does not work at all

7. **The evidence about middle-class families helping the economy when they have more income is logically related to the idea that**
   **A** giving the rich a tax cut will help the economy
   **B** raising taxes on everyone will help the economy
   **C** raising taxes on the middle class will not help the economy
   **D** lowering taxes on the middle class will not help the economy

8. **Which phrase best describes the evidence presented to support Obama's claim?**
   **F** faulty reasoning but valid evidence
   **G** sound reasoning and valid evidence
   **H** sound reasoning but invalid evidence
   **J** faulty reasoning and invalid evidence

9. **Which of these sentences most strongly supports Obama's claim?**
   **A** The opponent spends money on ads that repeat the same message.
   **B** The opponent does not have a solid economic plan, but Obama does.
   **C** The opponent says that problems with the economy are Obama's fault.
   **D** The opponent wants to cut Americans' taxes in order to stimulate the economy.

## Test-Taking Tip

When you take a test, first answer questions that are easy for you. This approach increases your chances of completing the greatest number of items. Avoid getting stuck on a question. If you can't answer a question quickly, move on. Then go back to the more challenging questions if you have time.

## Language Practice

Verbs may be active or passive. If the subject of the sentence performs the action, the verb is active. If the subject receives the action, the verb is passive. A passive verb includes a form of the verb *to be* and the past participle of the main verb.

**Directions:** Read the excerpt from a draft of an informative text. Then do Numbers 10 through 13.

Origami is the art of folding paper. Although the origin of origami is unknown, it is assumed by experts that this art form was begun in Japan. Objects such as animals and flowers are common shapes formed by people. In Japan, paper is folded into embellishments attached by people to gifts. Origami is not difficult to learn. Many instructional books and videos have been created.

10. **Which version of the first underlined sentence contains only active verbs?**

   F  Although the origin of origami is unknown, experts assume that this art form began in Japan.

   G  Although we do not know the origin of origami, experts assume that this art form began in Japan.

   H  Although the origin of origami is unknown, it is assumed by experts that this art form began in Japan.

   J  Although the origin of origami is unknown, it is assumed by experts that this art form was begun in Japan.

11. **Which version of the second underlined sentence contains the correct active verb form?**

   A  Commonly formed objects are animals and flowers.

   B  Commonly formed by people are objects such as animals and flowers.

   C  Objects such as animals and flowers are common shapes that people form.

   D  Objects such as animals and flowers are common shapes formed by people.

12. **Which version of the third underlined sentence contains one passive verb and one active verb?**

   F  In Japan, people fold paper into embellishments for gifts.

   G  In Japan, people fold paper into embellishments they attach to gifts.

   H  In Japan, paper is folded into embellishments that people attach to gifts.

   J  In Japan, paper is folded into embellishments attached by people to gifts.

13. **Which version of the fourth underlined sentence contains the correct passive verb form?**

   A  Many instructional books and videos have been created.

   B  Created have been many instructional books and videos.

   C  Experts have done the creation of many instructional books and videos.

   D  Authors and producers have created many instructional books and videos.

# Writing Practice

A valid argument is logical and factually reliable, and it is supported with relevant evidence connected to the claim and to other pieces of evidence. An invalid argument is biased or contains contradictory evidence.

**Directions:** Write an argument explaining why you agree or disagree with the position of J.B. Sanford or Barack Obama. Paraphrase Sanford's arguments in "Argument Against Women's Suffrage" (page 160) or Obama's arguments in "Remarks by the President at Campaign Event" (pages 162–163). Then support your analysis with relevant and sufficient evidence from the text. State whether the author's claim is valid, and explain why or why not. Note whether the author provides relevant evidence, and identify any fallacious reasoning.

This lesson will help you practice evaluating logic and identifying hidden assumptions in two texts. Use it with Core Lesson 6.5 *Evaluate Logic and Identify Hidden Assumptions* to reinforce and apply your knowledge.

| Key Concept | Core Skills |
|---|---|
| Authors may support their claims with arguments based on logical reasoning. | • Identify Stated Assumptions<br>• Infer Hidden Assumptions |

## Evaluating Arguments Founded on Logical Reasoning

Typically, it is important to cite supporting evidence such as facts, examples, and expert opinions when writing an argument. However, if evidence is not available or appropriate, writers must base their arguments on logical reasoning instead. The writer starts by making an assumption and then builds the argument using the assumption as the basis for a series of deductions.

**Directions:** Read the text. Then do Numbers 1–5.

## Overcoming Obesity

Doctors say that obesity causes or aggravates diseases such as diabetes, high blood pressure, and heart disease. In fact, about 90 percent of the type II diabetes cases worldwide are caused by excessive weight. The causes of obesity are too varied for doctors to be able to suggest a simple solution to the problem.

According to the U.S. Centers for Disease Control and Prevention, "Overweight and obesity are both labels for ranges of weight that are greater than what is generally considered healthy for a given height." In medical terms, obesity means having a body-mass index (BMI) of 30 or higher. BMI is an estimate of total body fat. It is based on a calculation using a person's height and weight.

Despite the many negative effects of obesity, about 34 percent of adults and 17 percent of children 2 to 19 years old in the United States are obese. Obesity is also a problem in most other industrialized countries.

Some studies support an explanation of body weight called the "set-point theory." According to the set-point theory, a person's genes determine his or her preferred weight. The brain adjusts a person's metabolism and eating behavior to maintain weight at this genetically determined level. No one has proved the set-point theory. However, doctors have observed that most people's bodies resist a weight that is lower than the "normal" weight for that person.

Some people believe that the set-point theory helps explain why people find it difficult to maintain weight loss. These people are fighting against their bodies' set points. To weigh less than their set points, they must constantly exercise and limit food intake.

There is evidence that environmental factors have a strong influence on weight gain and obesity. Researchers have found that obesity affects people in wealthier industrial countries more than people in poorer countries. Because there is a large food supply in industrial nations, the people there tend to eat more high-calorie, processed foods. Because they have access to transportation and do less manual labor, they have lower levels of physical activity.

Doctors believe that many weight-loss programs are mostly ineffective. As many as 95 out of 100 people who lose weight on a specific program will gain back the weight within five years. Because body weight is the result of genes, environment, metabolism, behavior, and socioeconomic status, there is no one solution for weight loss.

1. **What is the claim in this passage?**
   A that a person's BMI determines whether or not he or she is obese
   B that people in wealthy countries have a higher risk for being obese
   C that 95 percent of people who lose weight on a diet will gain it back
   D that the causes of obesity are too varied to suggest a simple solution

2. **Which statement is an assumption made in the passage?**
   F Obesity is a medical problem that needs to be solved.
   G BMI is based on a calculation using height and weight.
   H A person's genes determine his or her preferred weight.
   J People in industrialized countries have lower levels of physical activity.

3. **What purpose does the explanation of the set-point theory serve?**
   A It is a fact.
   B It is a claim.
   C It is a deduction.
   D It is an assumption.

4. **Read this sentence from the text.**

   **To weigh less than their set points, they must constantly exercise and limit food intake.**

   **Which definition fits the word __intake__ as it is used in this sentence?**
   F a shaft that serves to ventilate
   G a quantity of something taken in
   H a contraction or narrowing of fabric
   J an opening through which fluid flows

5. **To support the claim, the author of this passage gives information about studies on obesity and**
   A lists specific plans for further studies
   B criticizes methods used by the studies
   C formulates deductions from the results
   D expresses disagreements about the results

## Evaluating Arguments Based on Hidden Assumptions

The assumption on which a writer bases an argument might be unstated, or hidden. If the reasoning in the argument depends on the reader accepting an idea that is not explicitly stated, then this idea is the hidden assumption. The validity of this supposition affects the validity of the argument as a whole. It can be challenging to find this assumption.

**Directions:** Read the text. Then do Numbers 6–10.

## From *The Family Shakespeare*
### by Thomas Bowdler

[T]he works of the poet may be considered in a very different light from those of the painter and the statuary. Shak[e]speare, inimitable Shak[e]speare, will remain the subject of admiration as long as taste and literature shall exist. . . . [H]is writings will be handed down to posterity in their native beauty, although the present attempt to add to his fame should prove entirely abortive. Here, then, is the great difference. If the endeavor to improve the picture or the statue should be unsuccessful, the beauty of the original would be destroyed, and the injury be irreparable. In such a case, let the artist refrain from using the chisel or the pencil. [But] with the works of the poet no such danger occurs . . . [T]he critic need not be afraid of employing his pen, for the original will continue unimpaired. . . . That Shak[e]speare is the first of dramatic writers will be denied by few. I doubt whether it will be denied by any who have really studied his works, and compared the beauties which they contain with the very finest productions either of our own or of former ages. It must, however, be acknowledged, by his warmest admirers, that some defects are to be found in the writings of our immortal bard. The language is not always faultless. Many words and expressions occur which are of so indecent a nature as to render it highly desirable that they should be erased. Of these, the greater part are evidently introduced to gratify the bad taste of the age in which he lived. [T]he rest may perhaps be ascribed to his own unbridled fancy. But neither the vicious taste of the age, nor the brilliant effusions of wit, can afford an excuse for profaneness or obscenity. . . . [I]f these could be obliterated, the transcendent genius of the poet would undoubtedly shine with more unclouded lustre. To banish every thing of this nature from the writings of Shak[e]speare is the object of the present undertaking. My earnest wish is to render his plays unsullied by any scene, by any speech, or if possible, by any word that can give pain to the most chaste, or offence to the most religious of his readers.

6. **What is the author's claim in this passage?**
   F  Families should read Shakespeare's plays.
   G  Shakespeare is a widely admired dramatic writer.
   H  Shakespeare wrote for the tastes and language of his age.
   J  The language in Shakespeare's works should be cleaned up.

7. **What is a hidden assumption in this passage?**
   A  Shakespeare compares favorably with modern productions of plays.
   B  Words that may offend readers lower the artistic quality of literature.
   C  Shakespeare's works would be more beautiful without obscene words.
   D  Critics can change words in a passage and not damage the original work.

8. **Which assumption do you have to accept to evaluate the author's argument as valid?**
   F  Changing a painting or a sculpture damages the work.
   G  Changing a painting or a sculpture does not damage the work.
   H  Changing the words in a work of literature damages the work.
   J  Changing the words in a work of literature does not damage the work.

9. **Which statement is based on an invalid assumption?**

    A  Shakespeare's plays are among the finest in dramatic literature.

    B  Shakespeare's genius would shine more if his works were censored.

    C  Shakespeare's works should be read by everyone who loves literature.

    D  Shakespeare's words fit with the language of his times and his culture.

10. **The idea that Shakespeare's use of obscene language is a defect in his writing is**

    F  the author's personal opinion

    G  a common observation among writers

    H  factual evidence presented to support the claim

    J  an expert opinion the author quotes as evidence

 **Test-Taking Tip**

After answering a question on a test, before you move on to another question, reread the question and your answer together. Make sure that you have correctly understood the question and answer choices and that you selected the answer you intended to select.

## Language Practice

A shift is a sudden change in grammar that can confuse the reader—for instance, when the verb tense suddenly changes for no reason. Shifts in the voice or mood of a verb may also be confusing. Therefore, when a sentence contains more than one verb, the verbs should generally be in the same voice and mood.

If the first verb is in active voice, any other verbs in a sentence should also be active.

  Example:  Juan took his sister to the gym, where she ran on the treadmill.

Likewise, if the first verb is passive, any other verbs should be passive, too.

  Example:  The decision was made by the appeals court to uphold the ruling made by the lower court.

If both verbs relate to the same subject, it may be best to express the second verb as a participle.

  Example:  Caroline hurries to class by running to make it on time.

In some cases, though, in order to keep the same subject in the sentence, it may be necessary to change from one voice to the other.

  Example:  The kitten that got stuck in the tree was rescued soon enough.

Similarly, if the first verb in the sentence is in one mood, the second should also be in that mood. For example, if the first verb in a sentence is in the subjunctive or imperative mood, the second should not be indicative.

  Incorrect:  Turn right on Main Street, and then you should turn left on Elm.

  Correct:  Turn right on Main Street, and then turn left on Elm.

**Directions:** Read the draft of a blog. Then do Numbers 11 through 14.

My favorite local restaurant is Spanish, and you can eat tapas there. Tapas are small portions of different foods, and they serve them hot or cold. One of my favorites is Spanish tortilla. If you were to order tortilla, you will be surprised. It's not a type of bread, but a type of omelet. Of course, you can easily make tortilla at home. First, sauté some peppers, onions, and garlic in olive oil; then, you just pour in beaten eggs. Turn down the heat and let the tortilla cook till the eggs are firm.

11. **Which version of the first underlined sentence best expresses the idea and avoids an inappropriate shift in voice?**

    A  My favorite local restaurant is Spanish and serves tapas.

    B  My favorite local restaurant is Spanish, and tapas are served there.

    C  My favorite local restaurant is Spanish, and you can eat tapas there.

    D  My favorite local restaurant is Spanish, and you should eat tapas there.

12. **Which version of the second underlined sentence best expresses the idea and avoids an inappropriate shift in voice?**

    F  Tapas are small portions of different hot or cold foods.

    G  Tapas are small portions of different foods and can be served hot or cold.

    H  Tapas are small portions of different foods, and they serve them hot or cold.

    J  Tapas are small portions of different foods, and tapas can be either hot or cold.

13. **Which version of the third underlined sentence best expresses the idea and avoids an inappropriate shift in mood?**

    A  If you were to order tortilla, it surprises you.

    B  If you were to order tortilla, it will surprise you.

    C  If you were to order tortilla, you will be surprised.

    D  If you were to order tortilla, you would be surprised.

14. **Which version of the fourth underlined sentence best expresses the idea and avoids an inappropriate shift in voice or mood?**

    F  First, you sauté some peppers, onions, and garlic in olive oil; then pour in beaten eggs.

    G  First, sauté some peppers, onions, and garlic in olive oil; then just pour in beaten eggs.

    H  First, sauté some peppers, onions, and garlic in olive oil; then beaten eggs are poured in.

    J  First, sauté some peppers, onions, and garlic in olive oil; then you just pour in beaten eggs.

# Writing Practice

Many arguments rest on hidden assumptions. This often happens when the writer or speaker believes that the audience understands and agrees with the assumption. Think about political campaign speeches. Candidates often talk about how their policies will not involve raising taxes. The underlying, unstated assumption is that no one wants to pay higher taxes.

**Directions:** Write an explanatory text stating the underlying assumption in the following speech. Effectively select and cite details that helped you determine this assumption. Then evaluate the speech, assessing the validity of the reasoning and the relevance and sufficiency of the evidence.

## From "Our Agenda Is America's Agenda"
### by Elizabeth Warren

*Elizabeth Warren is a senator from Massachusetts. She gave this speech to a convention of union members in 2013.*

. . . But let's be clear, we have always had to run uphill. We have had to fight for what we've achieved. Powerful interests have done everything they can to block reform. They attacked Social Security and Medicare. They attacked pensions and public employees. They attacked bank regulation and consumer protection.

The powerful interests have attacked so many of the basic foundations that built a strong middle class—and too many times, they have prevailed.

Even today, our work is uphill. The powerful interests fight us on every battlefield they can.

Look at the increasing corporate capture of the federal courts.

According to a recent study, the five conservative justices currently sitting on the Supreme Court are in the top ten most pro-corporate justices in a half century—and Justices Alito and Roberts are numbers one and two—the most anti-consumer in this entire time. The Chamber of Commerce is now a major player in the Supreme Court, and its win rate has risen to 70% of all cases it supports. Follow this pro-corporate trend to its logical conclusion, and sooner or later you'll end up with a Supreme Court that functions as a wholly owned subsidiary of big business.

Look at where we are on the "Too Big to Fail" problem.

Five years ago, experts said the banks had to be bailed out because there was too much concentration in banking and one failure would bring down the entire economy. Now the four biggest banks are 30% larger than they were five years ago. The five largest banks now hold more than half of all banking assets in the country. Because investors know they are too big to fail, those big banks get cheaper borrowing, which, according to one study, adds up to an annual $83 billion subsidy from taxpayers—another benefit of being Too Big to Fail.

What about reform? The Dodd-Frank [Wall Street Reform and Consumer Protection] Act was an incredibly important achievement. [However,] since it passed, the big banks and their army of lobbyists have fought every step of the way to delay, water down, block, or strike down regulations. When a new approach is proposed—like my bill with John McCain, Angus King, and Maria Cantwell to bring back Glass-Steagall [the Banking Act of 1933]—you know what happens—they throw everything they've got against it.

One more: take a look at what's happening with trade deals.

*(Continued on next page)*

For big corporations, trade agreement time is like Christmas morning. They can get special gifts they could never pass through Congress out in public. Because it's a trade deal, the negotiations are secret and the big corporations can do their work behind closed doors. We've seen what happens here at home when our trading partners around the world are allowed to ignore workers' rights, wages, and environmental rules. From what I hear, Wall Street, pharmaceuticals, telecom, big polluters, and outsourcers are all salivating at the chance to rig the upcoming trade deals in their favor.

Why are trade deals secret? I've heard people actually say that they have to be secret because if the American people knew what was going on, they would be opposed. Think about that. I believe that if people would be opposed to a particular trade agreement, then that trade agreement should not happen.

Finally, look what is happening in our states. Republican governors in Indiana and Michigan push for so-called right-to-work laws, and in Wisconsin Scott Walker and the legislature he controls have declared war on working families by ripping the guts out of collective-bargaining agreements.

The fight continues to rage, and the powerful interests continue to be guided by their age-old principle: "I've got mine, the rest of you are on your own."

But we're guided by principle too. It's a simple idea, and all of you know it as an old labor idea—we all do better when we work together and invest in our future.

We know that the economy grows when hard-working families can improve their lives. We know that the country gets stronger when we invest in helping people succeed. We know that our lives improve when we care for our neighbors.

And we know that even though pundits and big corporate lobbyists in Washington might need to be dragged kicking and screaming—we know that America agrees with us.

On almost every issue of economic concern, our values are America's values, and our agenda is America's agenda. . . .

_____

_____

_____

_____

_____

_____

_____

_____

_____

_____

This lesson will help you practice comparing the formats of two similar texts. Use it with Core Lesson 7.1 *Compare Similar Topics in Different Formats* to reinforce and apply your knowledge.

## Key Concept

Different writers can present similar information in different formats. Each format fits the message the writer wants to convey.

## Core Skills

- Compare Two Texts on Similar Topics
- Compare Texts in Different Formats
- Compare Fictional and Nonfictional Accounts of the Same Event

## Comparing Texts on Similar Topics

Two texts about the same topic can be presented in different ways. The texts might have different formats; for example, a scientific article and an advertisement could both present facts about a new medication. The texts could be influenced by the context, or the circumstances in which the author wrote. A description of an event written at the time when the event occurred would probably differ from a description written later for a history book. Format and context affect a reader's understanding of a text.

**Directions:** Read the texts. Then do Numbers 1–4.

# From "In Mammoth Cave"

### *by John Burroughs*

Some idea of the impression which Mammoth Cave makes upon the senses, irrespective even of sight, may be had from the fact that blind people go there to see it, and are greatly struck with it. . . . The blind seem as much impressed by it as those who have their sight. When the guide pauses at the more interesting point, or lights the scene up with a great torch . . . and points out the more striking features, the blind exclaim, "How wonderful! How beautiful!" They can feel it, if they cannot see it. They get some idea of the spaciousness when words are uttered. The voice goes forth in these colossal chambers like a bird. When no word is spoken, the silence is of a kind never experienced on the surface of the earth. . . . This, and the absolute darkness, to a person with eyes makes him feel as if he were face to face with the primordial nothingness. . . .

Here in the loose soil are ruts worn by cart-wheels in 1812, when, during the war with Great Britain, the earth was searched to make saltpetre. The guide kicks corn-cobs out of the dust where the oxen were fed at noon, and they look nearly as fresh as ever they did. In those frail corn-cobs and in those wheel-tracks, as if the carts had but just gone along, one seemed to come very near to the youth of the century, almost to overtake it.

Probably the prettiest thing they have to show you in Mammoth Cave is the "Star Chamber." . . . The guide takes your lantern from you and leaves you seated upon a bench by the wayside, in the profound cosmic darkness. He retreats down a side alley that seems to go down to a lower level, and at a certain point shades his lamp with his hat, so that the light falls upon the ceiling over your head. You look up, and the first thought is that there is an opening just there that permits you to look forth upon the midnight skies. You see the darker horizon line where the sky ends and the mountains begin. The sky is blue-black and is thickly studded with stars—rather small stars, but apparently genuine. At one point a long luminous streak simulates exactly the form and effect of a comet.

*(Continued on next page)*

As you gaze, the guide slowly moves his hat, and a black cloud gradually creeps over the sky, and all is blackness again. Then you hear footsteps retreating and dying away in the distance. Presently all is still, save the ringing in your own ears. Then after a few moments, during which you have sat in silence like that of the interstellar spaces, you hear over your left shoulder a distant flapping of wings, followed by the crowing of a cock. You turn your head in that direction and behold a faint dawn breaking on the horizon. It slowly increases till you hear footsteps approaching, and your dusky companion, playing the part of Apollo with lamp in hand, ushers in the light of day. It is rather theatrical, but a very pleasant diversion nevertheless.

## Adapted from "Mammoth Cave National Park"

### by the National Park Service

Mammoth Cave National Park was established in 1941. It preserves and protects the world's longest known cave system, along with a portion of the Green River valley and much of south central Kentucky. More than 400 miles of its caves have been explored to date.

Study has shown the park to be far more complex than first imagined, and not simply because of its labyrinthine underground. The area sustains a broad diversity of plant and animal life, in myriad specialized and interconnected ecosystems. More than 70 threatened, endangered, or state-listed species make their homes there. The Federal Endangered Species Act of 1973 gives park officials the means to ensure the survival of these species.

The cave system ecosystem ranks among the most diverse in the world, hosting more than 130 varieties of animal. These species are almost equally divided among the three classes of cave life: troglobites, which need a cave environment to survive; troglophiles, which can survive in or out of caves; and trogloxenes, which use caves primarily for refuge.

Even if one does not consider the abundance of life underground, the Mammoth Cave area merits its National Park status due solely to the extraordinary density and variety of its plant life. While . . . Great Smoky Mountains National Park has approximately 1,500 flowering species in its more than 500,000 acres, Mammoth Cave National Park supports more than 1,300 species within only one-tenth of that acreage.

The park is open to visitors year-round. Most of its resources and facilities are available free of charge. The following fees are charged for cave tours, camping, and selected picnic shelters.

| Cave Tour Fees | | | |
|---|---|---|---|
| Cave Tour | Adults | Youth* | Seniors |
| Mammoth Passage Tour | $5.00 | $3.50 | $2.50 |
| Historic Tour | $12.00 | $8.00 | $6.00 |
| Grand Avenue Tour | $24.00 | $18.00 | $12.00 |
| Great Onyx Tour | $15.00 | $11.00 | $7.50 |
| Violet City Lantern Tour | $15.00 | $11.00 | $7.50 |
| River Styx Tour | $13.00 | $9.00 | $6.50 |
| Star Chamber Tour | $12.00 | $8.00 | $6.00 |
| Wild Cave Tour | $48.00 | n/a | $24.00 |
| Introduction to Caving | $23.00 | $18.00 | $11.50 |
| Trog | n/a | $14.00 | n/a |
| *Youth is 6–12 years of age. | | | |

| Campground and Picnic Shelter Fees | |
|---|---|
| Campsite/ Picnic Area | Fee Senior discounts in ( ) |
| Mammoth Cave Campground | $17.00 ($8.50) |
| Maple Springs Group Camp | $30.00 |
| Houchins Ferry Campground | $12.00 ($6.00) |
| Open-Air Picnic Shelter | $25.00/day; limited availability |
| Enclosed Picnic Shelter | $50.00/day; one shelter, available Sat/Sun March 1– Memorial Day; daily Memorial Day–Labor Day; Sat/Sun Labor Day–November 30 |

1. **Which statement is true about both passages?**
   A  The topic is the same.
   B  The genre is the same.
   C  The format is the same.
   D  The narrator is the same.

2. **Which fact about passage 1 <u>most</u> affects your understanding of the passage?**
   F  It is a work of nonfiction.
   G  It was written by a nature essayist.
   H  It is an excerpt from a longer work.
   J  It was written in the late 19th century.

3. **Who is the intended audience for passage 2?**
   A  families
   B  historians
   C  park visitors
   D  conservationists

4. **How do the main purposes of the two passages differ?**
   F  Passage 1 was written to inform; passage 2 was written to entertain.
   G  Passage 1 was written to entertain; passage 2 was written to inform.
   H  Passage 1 was written to persuade; passage 2 was written to entertain.
   J  Passage 1 was written to entertain; passage 2 was written to persuade.

## Comparing Fiction and Nonfiction

It is not always easy to distinguish fiction from nonfiction. A fictional tale may be rooted in fact, and a nonfiction text may describe an amazing event that is difficult to believe. By studying a text's characteristics, you can identify it as fiction or nonfiction. Pay particular attention to the text's context, purpose, and tone.

**Directions:** Read the texts. Then do Numbers 5–9.

*The Spanish Inquisition was a religious court established in 1478. Its main purpose was to find and punish people who did not agree with the Catholic church. Today many of the methods used as punishment would be considered torture. The following passages are both about the Spanish Inquisition.*

## From "Records of the Spanish Inquisition"
### *translated by Andrew Dickson White*

There were three sorts of persons distinguished by the Tribunal as suspected of heresy [belief disagreeing with a particular religion, in this case Catholicism]: those who were lightly suspected, those who were seriously suspected, and those who were violently suspected.

*(continued on next page)*

There were three methods of torture; the cord, fire, and water. In the first method, they tied the hands behind the back of the patient by means of a cord which passed through a pulley attached to the roof, and the executioners drew him up as high as possible. After suspending him for some time, the cord was loosened, and he fell within six inches of the ground. This terrible shock dislocated all the joints and cut the flesh even to the sinews. The process was renewed every hour and left the patient without strength or motion. It was not until after the physician had declared that the sufferer could no longer endure the torture without dying, that the Inquisitors sent him back to prison.

The second was performed by means of water. The executioners stretched the victim over a wooden instrument like a spout . . . without any bottom but a stick passing across it. The body falling backwards, came to such a position that the feet were higher than the head. In this cruel position the executioners passed into the throat a piece of fine linen, wet, a part of which covered the nostrils. They then turned water into the mouth and nose and left it to filter so slowly that one hour at least was consumed before the sufferer had swallowed a drop, although it trickled without interruption. Thus the patient found no interval for respiration.

If by this second torment they could obtain no confession, the inquisitors resorted to fire. For this purpose the executioners tied the hands and feet in such a manner that the sufferer could not change his position. They then rubbed the feet with oil and lard, and other penetrating matter, and placed them before the fire, until the flesh was so roasted that the bones and sinews appeared in every part.

# From "The Pit and the Pendulum"

### by Edgar Allan Poe

Unreal!—Even while I breathed there came to my nostrils the breath of the vapour of heated iron! A suffocating odour pervaded the prison! A deeper glow settled each moment in the eyes that glared at my agonies! A richer tint of crimson diffused itself over the pictured horrors of blood. . . . I gasped for breath! There could be no doubt of the design of my tormentors—oh! . . . most demoniac of men! Yet, for a wild moment, did my spirit refuse to comprehend the meaning of what I saw. At length it forced—it wrestled its way into my soul—it burned itself in upon my shuddering reason.—Oh! for a voice to speak!—oh! horror!—oh! any horror but this! With a shriek, I rushed from the margin, and buried my face in my hands—weeping bitterly. . . .

"Death," I said, "any death but that of the pit!" Fool! Might I have not known that into the pit it was the object of the burning iron to urge me? Could I . . . withstand its pressure? And now, flatter and flatter grew the lozenge. . . . Its centre, and of course, its greatest width, came just over the yawning gulf. I shrank back—but the closing walls pressed me resistlessly onward. At length for my seared and writhing body there was no longer an inch of foothold on the firm floor of the prison. I struggled no more, but the agony of my soul found vent in one loud, long, and final scream of despair. I felt that I tottered upon the brink—I averted my eyes—

There was a discordant hum of human voices! There was a loud blast as of many trumpets! There was a harsh grating as of a thousand thunders! The fiery walls rushed back! An outstretched arm caught my own as I fell, fainting, into the abyss. It was that of General Lasalle. The French army had entered Toledo. The Inquisition was in the hands of its enemies.

**5.** **What is the topic of both of these passages?**

  **A**  the methods of torture used in the Spanish Inquisition

  **B**  the events that led to the end of the Spanish Inquisition

  **C**  the key players in the creation of the Spanish Inquisition

  **D**  the purposes behind the formation of the Spanish Inquisition

**6.** **How do the authors' approaches to the subject differ?**

  **F**  White criticizes the methods used by the inquisitors; Poe shows sympathy for the accused.

  **G**  White details the torture experienced by one man; Poe writes about the experiences of many.

  **H**  White gives a factual account of torture methods; Poe focuses on the terror felt by a prisoner.

  **J**  White writes from the point of view of the inquisitor; Poe writes from the point of view of the accused.

**7.** **What is the main purpose of passage 1?**

  **A**  to help

  **B**  to inform

  **C**  to entertain

  **D**  to persuade

**8.** **Read this sentence from passage 1.**

  The executioners stretched the victim over a wooden instrument like a spout . . . without any bottom but a stick passing across it.

  **What does the word <u>instrument</u> mean as it is used in this sentence?**

  **F**  a tool or implement

  **G**  a device used for measuring

  **H**  a device used to produce music

  **J**  a means of getting something done

**9.** **What is the genre of "The Pit and the Pendulum"?**

  **A**  essay

  **B**  fiction

  **C**  memoir

  **D**  nonfiction

### Test-Taking Tip

If you are not happy with your score on one or more subject-area tests, consider retaking those tests. You can retake each test twice. You will be at an advantage the second time around because you can focus your studying, and you'll be familiar with the test's format.

# Writing Practice

As you have learned, authors may address the same topic in different ways.

**Directions:** Write an explanatory text in which you compare and contrast the two passages about Mammoth Cave on pages 174 and 175. Provide an analysis of the similarities and differences between the two passages' formats, context, and content. Organize ideas and information including formatting when it is useful in aiding comprehension. Then consider significant and relevant details from both passages to draw a conclusion about the subject.

_____

_____

_____

_____

_____

_____

_____

_____

_____

_____

_____

_____

_____

_____

_____

_____

_____

_____

This lesson will help you practice comparing two texts from similar genres. Use it with Core Lesson 7.2 *Compare Similar Genres* to reinforce and apply your knowledge.

## Key Concept

Authors may use similar genres to address common themes or ideas.

## Core Skills

- Determine Genre
- Compare Similar Genres

## Identifying Genre

A genre is a category of writing that has specific characteristics. Identifying the differences in genres helps the reader understand the differences in the authors' purposes for writing.

**Directions:** Read the two texts. Then do Numbers 1–4.

## From *The Book of Tea*
### *by Kakuzo Okakura*

Tea began as a medicine and grew into a beverage. In China, in the eighth century, it entered the realm of poetry as one of the polite amusements. The fifteenth century saw Japan ennoble it into a religion of aestheticism—Teaism. Teaism is a cult founded on the adoration of the beautiful among the sordid facts of everyday existence. It inculcates purity and harmony, the mystery of mutual charity, the romanticism of the social order. It is essentially a worship of the Imperfect, as it is a tender attempt to accomplish something possible in this impossible thing we know as life. . . .

The long isolation of Japan from the rest of the world, so conducive to introspection, has been highly favorable to the development of Teaism. Our home and habits, costume and cuisine, porcelain, lacquer, painting—our very literature—all have been subject to its influence. No student of Japanese culture could ever ignore its presence. It has permeated the elegance of noble boudoirs, and entered the abode of the humble. Our peasants have learned to arrange flowers, our meanest laborer to offer his salutation to the rocks and waters. In our common parlance we speak of the man "with no tea" in him, when he is insusceptible to the serio-comic interests of the personal drama. Again we stigmatize the untamed aesthete who, regardless of the mundane tragedy, runs riot in the springtide of emancipated emotions, as one "with too much tea" in him.

The outsider may indeed wonder at this seeming much ado about nothing. What a tempest in a tea-cup! he will say. But when we consider how small after all the cup of human enjoyment is, how soon overflowed with tears, how easily drained to the dregs in our quenchless thirst for infinity, we shall not blame ourselves for making so much of the tea-cup. Mankind has done worse. . . .

Those who cannot feel the littleness of great things in themselves are apt to overlook the greatness of little things in others. The average Westerner, in his sleek complacency, will see in the tea ceremony but another instance of the thousand and one oddities which constitute the quaintness and childishness of the East to him. He was wont to regard Japan as barbarous while she indulged in the gentle arts of peace: he calls her civilized since she began to commit wholesale slaughter on Manchurian battlefields. Much comment has been given lately to the Code of the Samurai—the Art of Death which makes our soldiers exult in self-sacrifice; but scarcely any attention has been drawn to Teaism, which represents so much of our Art of Life.

# From "A History of Japanese Americans in California"

*by the National Park Service*

One of the first groups of settlers that came from Japan to the United States, the Wakamatsu Tea and Silk Farm Colony under the leadership of John Schnell, arrived at Cold Hill, El Dorado County, in June 1869. Additional colonists arrived in the fall of 1869. These first immigrants brought mulberry trees, silk cocoons, tea plants, bamboo roots, and other agricultural products. The U.S. Census of 1870 showed 55 Japanese in the United States; 33 were in California, with 22 living at Gold Hill. Within a few years of the colony's founding, the colonists had dispersed, their agricultural venture a failure.

The 1880 Census showed 86 Japanese in California, with a total of 148 in the United States. Possibly these were students, or Japanese who had illegally left their country, since Japanese laborers were not allowed to leave their country until after 1884 when an agreement was signed between the Japanese government and Hawaiian sugar plantations to allow labor immigration. From Hawaii, many Japanese continued on to the United States mainland. . . .

Laborers for the Hawaiian sugar plantations were carefully chosen. . . . [A] systematic method of recruiting workers from specific regions in Japan was established. Natives from Hiroshima, Kumamoto, Yamaguchi, and Fukushima were sought for their supposed expertise in agriculture, for their hard work, and for their willingness to travel. . . .

Except for a temporary suspension of immigration to Hawaii in 1900, the flow of immigration from Japan remained relatively unaffected until 1907–08, when agitation from white supremacist organizations, labor unions, and politicians resulted in the "Gentlemen's Agreement," curtailing further immigration of laborers from Japan. A provision in the Gentlemen's Agreement, however, permitted wives and children of laborers, as well as laborers who had already been in the United States, to continue to enter the country. Until that time, Japanese immigrants had been primarily male. The 1900 Census indicates that only 410 of 24,326 Japanese were female. From 1908 to 1924, Japanese women continued to immigrate to the United States, some as "picture brides."

In Japan . . . go-betweens arranged marriages between compatible males and females. . . . [A]n exchange of photographs became a first step in this long process. Entering the bride's name in the groom's family registry legally constituted marriage. Those Japanese males who could afford the cost of traveling to Japan returned there to be married. Others resorted to long-distance . . .marriages. . . . [T]he bride would immigrate to the United States as the wife of a laborer. . . . For wives who entered after 1910, the first glimpse of the United States was the Detention Barracks at Angel Island in San Francisco Bay. New immigrants were processed there, and given medical exams. As a result, this was the place where most "picture brides" saw their new husbands for the first time.

1. **Which genres are used in these two passages?**
   A Passage 1 is a folktale, and passage 2 is an essay.
   B Passage 1 is autobiography, and passage 2 is biography.
   C Passage 1 is an essay, and passage 2 is a historical article.
   D Passage 1 is biography, and passage 2 is historical fiction.

2. **What is the main purpose of both passages?**
   F to support readers learning Japanese
   G to inform readers about Japanese culture
   H to entertain readers with Japanese literature
   J to persuade readers to meet Japanese people

3. **What is the main difference in literary technique between the two passages?**

   **A** Passage 1 is about Teaism in Japan; passage 2 is about immigrants.

   **B** Passage 1 contains a plot; passage 2 contains only facts and figures.

   **C** Passage 1 begins in the 8th century; passage 2 begins in the 19th century.

   **D** Passage 1 includes vivid descriptions; passage 2 relies on facts and figures.

4. **How does the portrayal of the Japanese differ in these two passages?**

   **F** Passage 1 depicts the Japanese as hard working; Passage 2 depicts the Japanese as lazy.

   **G** Passage 1 shows the refinement of Japanese culture; Passage 2 shows the plight of Japanese laborers in America.

   **H** Passage 1 emphasizes the woman's place in Japan; Passage 2 highlights the lack of Japanese women in America at the turn of the 20th century.

   **J** Passage 1 depicts Japanese culture as more advanced than other cultures; Passage 2 depicts Japanese culture as less advanced than American culture.

## Comparing Texts from Similar Genres

Some nonfiction texts—such as memoirs, biographies, or letters—are narratives. They tell the story of a person, event, time, or place. As you compare narrative texts of similar genres, pay attention to text features, literary techniques, tone, and the author's attitude toward the topic.

**Directions:** Read the two texts. Then do Numbers 5–8.

## From *Down the Yellowstone*
### *by Lewis R. Freeman*

As we edged our way out to a better position, the sun rose and threw a series of three rainbows in the mist clouds as they floated up out of the shadowed depths. The lowest and clearest of these semicircles of irised spray seemed to spring from a patch of bright saffron sand, where it was laid bare by the melting snow. Now I know where the story of the gold at the end of the rainbow came from.

Carr and I tried to come through from the canyon by moonlight last night and had rather a bad time of it. First a fog obscured the moon. Then we tried to take a shortcut by following the telephone line, got lost in the dark, and stayed lost till the moon set and made it darker still. In cutting across the hills to get back into Hayden Valley, Carr fell over a snow bank and landed right in the middle of the road. . . .

After a while we were lost again, this time in a level space bounded on four sides by a winding creek. I know it was on four sides of the place, for we carefully walked off toward each point of the compass in rotation, and each time landed in the creek. We finally escaped by wading. How we got in without wading will always be a mystery. . . .

We passed the famous and only Mud Geyser an hour before daybreak. Things were in a bad way with him, judging from the noise. . . . Carr said it reminded him of something between a mad bull buffalo and a boatload of seasick tourists when the summer wind stirs up the lake. But Carr was too tired and disgusted to be elegant. Indeed, we were both pretty well played out. Personally, I felt just about like the Mud Geyser sounded.

# From *Letters to a Friend*

*by John Muir*

November 1st [1868]

I was extremely glad to receive yet one more of your ever welcome letters. . . . I am not surprised to hear of your leaving Madison and am anxious to know where your lot will be cast. . . . If you make your home in California, I know from experience how keenly you will feel the absence of the special flowers you love. . . . [However,] I think that you will find in California just what you desire in climate and scenery, for both are so varied.

March is the springtime of the plains, April the summer, and May the autumn. The other months are dry and wet winter. . . . I rode across the seasons in going to the Yosemite last spring. I started from the Joaquin in the last week of May. All the plain flowers, so lately fresh in the power of full beauty, were dead. Their parched leaves crisped and fell to powder. . . .

After riding for two days in this autumn I found summer again in the higher foothills. Flower petals were spread confidingly open, the grasses waved their branches all bright and gay in the colors of healthy prime, and the winds and streams were cool. Forty or fifty miles further into the mountains, I came to spring. The leaves on the oak were small and drooping, and they still retained their first tintings of crimson and purple, and the wrinkles of their bud folds were distinct as if newly opened. . . .

A few miles farther "onward and upward" I found the edge of winter. Scarce a grass could be seen. . . . Soon my horse was plunging in snow ten feet in depth, the sky became darker and more terrible, many-voiced mountain winds swept the pines, speaking the dread language of the cold north. . . .

Descending these higher mountains towards the Yosemite, the snow gradually disappeared from the pines and the sky . . . and violets appeared again, and I once more found spring in the grand valley. Thus meet and blend the seasons of these mountains and plains, beautiful in their joinings as those of lake and land or of the bands of the rainbow. . . .

Ever yours most cordially,

J.M.

5. **The genre of passage 1 is memoir. What is the genre of passage 2?**
   **A** autobiography
   **B** biography
   **C** essay
   **D** letter

6. **How do the attitudes of the authors differ?**
   **F** Lewis is amused; Muir is amazed.
   **G** Lewis is disgusted; Muir is fearful.
   **H** Lewis is awestruck; Muir is amused.
   **J** Lewis is surprised; Muir is awestruck.

**7. Read this sentence from passage 2.**

> If you make your home in California, I know from experience how keenly you will feel the absence of the special flowers you love. . . .

**What does the word <u>keenly</u> mean as it is used in this sentence?**

**A** cleverly

**B** intensely

**C** sensitively

**D** sharply

**8. Which characteristic do the two texts share?**

**F** Both passages convey a serious tone.

**G** Both passages are told in the first person.

**H** Both passages directly address the readers.

**J** Both passages include a date and signature.

 **Test-Taking Tip**

Essays written for tests are graded by a human. Therefore, keep your reader in mind as you write. Engage the reader with clear explanations, lively descriptions, and specific details. Reread your essay to check for correct grammar and punctuation. Practice the rules of grammar and punctuation ahead of time so you and your reader can focus on the content of your essay.

## Writing Practice

Autobiographies and memoirs are about the life of the author. The author chooses literary techniques and a tone that will convey his or her attitude, or point of view, toward the subject matter.

**Directions:** Reread the excerpts from *Down the Yellowstone* on page 182 and *Letters to a Friend* on page 183. Analyze the literary techniques and tone of each passage. Then write an explanatory text comparing and contrasting the authors' attitudes toward their experiences in nature, clearly identifying the relationship among ideas, concepts, and information.

_____

_____

_____

_____

_____

_____

This lesson will help you practice analyzing opposing arguments expressed in two texts. Use it with Core Lesson 7.3 *Analyze Two Arguments* to reinforce and apply your knowledge.

<table>
<tr><td>

## Key Concept

In order to choose which side of an argument to support, a reader must evaluate the evidence and logic used by each side.

</td><td>

## Core Skills

- Compare Arguments
- Evaluate Evidence in Opposing Arguments

</td></tr>
</table>

## Comparing and Contrasting Two Arguments

For every argument in favor of an opinion, there is likely an argument that disputes that opinion, or argues against it. When reading an argument, begin by identifying the claim. Then analyze the evidence to determine whether the claim is valid and well supported.

**Directions** Read the two texts. Then do Numbers 1–6.

## From "The Doctrine of Evolution: Its Basis and Its Scope"

*by Henry Edward Crampton*

1    Not very long before birth the human embryo is strikingly similar to the embryo of the ape; still earlier, it presents an appearance very like that of the embryos of other mammals lower in the scale, like the cat and the rabbit. . . . Indeed, as we trace back the still earlier history, more and more characters are found which are the common properties of wider and wider arrays of organisms. [A]t one time the embryo exhibits gill-slits in the sides of its throat which in all essential respects are just like those of the embryos of birds and reptiles and amphibian. . . . Can we reasonably regard these resemblances as indications of anything else but a community of ancestry of the forms that exhibit them?

2    Yet a still more wonderful fact is revealed by the study of the very earliest stages of individual development. The human embryo begins its very existence as a single cell,—nothing more and nothing less. . . . I do not think we could ask nature for more complete proof that human beings have evolved from one-cell ancestors as simple as modern protozoa. . . . They at least are real and not the logical deductions of reason. . . .

3    And now . . . we may look to nature for fossil evidence regarding the ancestry of our species. Much is known about the remains of many kinds of men who lived in prehistoric times, but we need consider here only one form which lived long before the glacial period in the so-called Tertiary times. In 1894 a scientist named Dubois discovered in Java some of the remains of an animal which was partly ape and partly man. So well did these remains exhibit the characters of Haeckel's hypothetical ape-man, *Pithecanthropus*, that the name fitted the creature like a glove. Specifically, the cranium presents an arch which is intermediate between that of the average ape and of the lowest human beings. It possessed protruding brows like those of the gorilla. The estimated brain capacity was about one thousand cubic centimeters, four hundred more than that of any known ape, and much less than the [human average]. Even without other characters, these would indicate that the animal was actually a "missing link" in the scientific sense,—that is, a form which is near the common progenitors of the modern species of apes and of man. . . . So *Pithecanthropus* is a part of the chain leading to man, not far from the place where the human line sprang from a lower primate ancestor. . . .

*(Continued on next page)*

4    The foregoing facts illustrate the conclusive evidence brought forward by science that human evolution in physical respects is true. Even if we wished to do so, we cannot do away with the facts of structure and development and fossil history, nor is there any other explanation more reasonable than evolution for these facts.

# From "At the Deathbed of Darwinism"
### by Eberhard Dennert

1    [I]t would be indeed strange, if no honest man could be found to tell . . . the truth regarding Darwinism. This has occurred sooner than I dared to hope. This chapter can announce the glad tidings that even in "social-democratic science" Darwinism is doomed to decay. Much printer's ink will, of course, be yet wasted before it will be so entirely dead as to be no longer available as a weapon against Christianity; but a beginning at least has been made.

2    In the December [issue] of the ninth year of the *Sozialistische Monatshefte*, a social-democratic writer, Curt Grottewitz, undertakes to bring out an article on "Darwinian Myths." It is stated there that Darwin had a few eminent followers, but that the educated world took no notice of their work; that now, however, they seemed to be attracting more attention. "There is no doubt that a number of Darwinian views, which are still prevalent to-day, have sunk to the level of untenable myths. . . ." . . .

3    Grottewitz very frankly continues: "The difficulty with the Darwinian doctrines consists in the fact that they are incapable of being strictly and irrefutably demonstrated. The origin of one species from another, the conservation of useful forms, the existence of countless intermediary links, are all assumptions, which could never be supported by concrete cases found in actual experience." Some are said to be well established indirectly by proofs drawn from probabilities, while others are proved to be absolutely untenable. Among the latter Grottewitz includes "[natural] selection," which is indeed a monstrous figment of the imagination. There was moreover really no reason for adhering to it so long. It is eminently untrue, that the biological research of the last few years proved for the *first* time the untenableness of this doctrine, as Grottewitz seems to think. Clear thinkers recognized its untenableness long ago. . . .

4    It is certainly a very peculiar phenomenon; for decades we behold a doctrine reverently re-echoed; thoughtful investigators expose its folly, but still the worship continues.

1.   **What is the claim of Crampton's argument?**
     A   Human embryos are similar to ape embryos.
     B   Human beings have evolved over the centuries.
     C   Fossils show the evolution of humans over time.
     D   Humans are physically similar to other types of primates.

2.   **Which type of evidence is Crampton's argument about evolution based on?**
     F   facts
     G   hearsay
     H   logic
     J   opinion

3.  **Read this sentence from the text.**

    **Not very long before birth the human embryo is strikingly similar to the embryo of the ape; still earlier, it presents an appearance very like that of the embryos of other mammals lower in the scale, like the cat and the rabbit.**

    **What does the word <u>scale</u> mean as it is used in this sentence?**

    **A** an indication of distance on a map

    **B** a graduated series or range of values

    **C** a thin plate covering the skin of a fish

    **D** a series of tests used to rate performance

4.  **Which additional claim would Crampton be most likely to make?**

    **F** Humans were created in God's image.

    **G** Fossils are not sufficient proof of evolution.

    **H** Unused traits disappear as a species evolves.

    **J** There is no relation between human and monkey.

5.  **What is the claim of Dennert's argument?**

    **A** Natural selection is impossible.

    **B** Darwinism damages Christianity.

    **C** Darwinism is not widely accepted.

    **D** Scientific evidence does not prove evolution.

6.  **Which statement describes Dennert's view of the theory of evolution?**

    **F** He disputes it.

    **G** He supports it.

    **H** He questions it.

    **J** He understands it.

## Analyzing Evidence in Two Arguments

When readers compare opposing arguments, they must carefully evaluate the evidence provided by each author and decide whether that evidence is relevant, accurate, sufficient, credible, and logical and whether the claim is well supported.

**Directions** Reread the two texts. Then do Numbers 7–10.

7.  **How does the *Pithecanthropus* support Crampton's argument?**

    **A** The *Pithecanthropus* is not the "missing link."

    **B** It proves that humans are more highly evolved than other primates.

    **C** It supports the claim of a physiological relationship between humans and apes.

    **D** It shows that other well-regarded scientists supported Darwin's theory of evolution.

8.  **Which type of evidence does Crampton use to support his argument?**

    **F** opinion

    **G** biblical support

    **H** witness statements

    **J** scientific research and analysis

9. **Which type of evidence does Dennert use to support his argument?**

   A logic

   B opinion

   C record of events

   D scientific research

10. **What evidence in Crampton's argument refutes the claim of Dennert's argument?**

   F A "missing link" between ape and human once existed.

   G Humans and apes are primates with similar structures.

   H Cats and rabbits are on the lower end of the evolutionary scale.

   J Amphibians, reptiles, and birds have similar embryonic structures.

---

 **Test-Taking Tip**

How much should you write on a writing test? You should write as much as you need to clearly respond to the prompt and provide supporting evidence. If you do not have much to say about the topic, do not try to stretch your material. Adding extraneous or irrelevant information just to make your essay longer can actually harm your overall score.

---

## Writing Practice

To make an informed decision about an issue, it is important to examine opposing arguments. Compare them, evaluating the evidence in each for accuracy, relevance, and sufficiency. Once you have analyzed the two arguments, you can decide whether to support either side.

**Directions:** Analyze the claims on both sides of the issue of raising the minimum wage in the following passages. Then write an argument to support one side of the debate in which you argue either for or against raising the minimum wage. Be sure to use valid reasoning and relevant and sufficient evidence from both texts. Provide a concluding statement that follows from and supports the argument presented.

## From "Minimum Wage Increase Is Bad Economic Policy"
### by Senate Republican Policy Committee, May 7, 2013

**Harmful to Young Workers**

Democrats have portrayed the minimum wage as a way to improve the quality of life for the working poor. However, independent studies have repeatedly disproved this theory.

Despite the claim that raising the minimum wage will benefit working families, U.S. Department of Labor [statistics show that] minimum wage workers [are] young. About half of all workers paid the federal minimum wage or less are less than 25 years old. Among employed teenagers paid by the hour, 21 percent earned the minimum wage or less. [This compares] with three percent of workers age 25 and over.

Many beneficiaries of minimum wage laws report family incomes that are twice the poverty level. According to Census Bureau data, the average family income of a beneficiary from the last increase in the federal minimum wage was more than $47,000 a year. It is estimated that just 11 percent of workers paid the minimum wage are actually the working poor.

*(Continued on next page)*

Another concern is that raising the minimum wage could hurt opportunities for teens to land their first job—and with it the chance to learn valuable life and work skills. . . . Teens are typically entry-level workers with limited job skills. They learn the importance of meeting deadlines, how to report to a manager, and how to get along with coworkers and customers. [Young] workers . . . acquire skills that can put them on a path for future success and salaries above the minimum wage.

Proponents of increasing the minimum wage argue that minimum wage employees are dependent on government policies to receive a wage increase. . . .

According to research using more than two decades of Current Population Survey data, the majority of minimum wage workers earn a pay increase their first year on the job.

Also, employers report that when their costs are arbitrarily increased, such as with minimum wage hikes, they become . . . less likely to take a chance on young workers. This delays the opportunity for young workers to gain important on-the-job training. . . .

**Harmful to All Workers**

If the government mandates that certain workers be paid a higher wage, employers make adjustments to pay for the added costs. Currently, the majority of minimum wage workers are employed in the leisure and hospitality industry. [These] establishments typically [have] thin profit margins. Common adjustments include reduced hiring, cutting employee work hours, reducing benefits, and charging higher prices.

Any increase in salaries for minimum wage workers will be at least partly offset by the higher prices they have to pay as consumers. The higher prices will be felt especially by lower wage workers, as poorer people typically spend a larger share of their income than more affluent people do. . . .

Minimum wages stifle job opportunities for low-skill workers, youth, and minorities—which would be particularly damaging in today's sluggish economy.

# From "The President's Plan to Reward Work by Raising the Minimum Wage"

*from The White House, February 13, 2013*

The President believes that no one who works full time should have to raise their family in poverty. But right now, a full-time minimum wage worker makes $14,500 a year. [This salary] leaves too many families struggling to make ends meet. . . . [A] family of four with a minimum wage worker still [lives] below the poverty line. That's why the President is calling on Congress to raise the Federal minimum wage for working Americans in stages to $9 in 2015 and index it to inflation thereafter. . . .

**Rewarding Work and Ensuring a Decent Living for Working Families**

- **Raising wages for over 15 million workers:** The minimum wage has a substantial impact on the wages of low-income workers. Raising the minimum wage to $9 would directly boost the wages of about 15 million workers by the end of 2015. [It] . . . would [also] raise wages for millions more by causing a ripple effect of employers choosing to raise wages for workers above the minimum wage.

- **Reducing poverty and inequality, and helping more families realize the American Dream:** A higher minimum wage will allow more families a shot at the American Dream. [It will] lift . . . many out of poverty. . . . [Roughly] 10 to 20 percent of the increase in income inequality since 1980 . . . can be traced to the erosion of the minimum wage adjusted for inflation. . . .

*(Continued on next page)*

- **Indexing the minimum wage to inflation would help lower-income workers keep up in the future:** Indexing the minimum wage to inflation would ensure that working families can keep up with expenses and will not suffer if Congress fails to act. Indexing would prevent a repeat of the 34 percent decline in the real value of the minimum wage from 1978 to 1989 and the 19 percent decline . . . from 1998 to 2006.

**A Stronger Middle Class Is a Key to a Stronger Economy**

- **Leading economists say that a higher minimum wage would help the economy:** A recent letter by leading economists . . . argued that "[L]ow-wage workers spend their additional earnings potentially raising demand and job growth. Therefore, pursuing a higher minimum wage at this juncture will not only provide raises for low-wage workers but would provide some help on the jobs front as well."

- **Raising the minimum wage will boost wages without jeopardizing jobs while improving turnover and productivity:** A range of economic studies show that modestly raising the minimum wage increases earnings and reduces poverty without measurably reducing employment. . . . [In] fact, employers may see a more stable workforce due to reduced turnover and increased productivity. . . .

**Helping Parents Make Ends Meet**

- **Raising the minimum wage mostly benefits adults, and especially working women:** Around 60 percent of workers benefiting from a higher minimum wage are women, and few are teenagers—less than 20 percent.

- **Raising the minimum wage helps parents:** The average worker who would benefit from a rise in the minimum wage . . . brought home 46 percent of his or her household's total wage and salary income in 2011, according to the Current Population Survey.

- **For a working family earning $20,000–$30,000, the extra $3,500 per year from raising the minimum wage would cover:**
  - the family's spending on groceries for a year, or
  - the family's spending on utilities for a year, or
  - the family's spending on gasoline and clothing for a year, or
  - six months of housing.

_____

_____

_____

_____

_____

_____

_____

_____

This lesson will help you practice evaluating the impact of genre and format. Use it with Core Lesson 7.4 *Evaluate the Impact of Genre and Format* to reinforce and apply your knowledge.

## Key Concept

By comparing genres that present similar ideas, readers can identify differences in scope, impact, purpose, and intended audience.

## Core Skills

- Compare Text and Image
- Compare Textual Genres

## Comparing Textual and Visual Genres

The genre and the format that writers choose depend in part on their purpose. Writers, as well as visual artists, consider the impact, or effect, that they want to have on their audience. The same topic presented as text or in a visual format can affect readers in different ways.

**Directions:** Read the texts. Then do Numbers 1–4.

# From "Niagara, June 10, 1843" from *At Home and Abroad; or, Things and Thoughts in America and Europe*

### *by Margaret Fuller Ossoli*

The whirlpool I like very much. It is seen to advantage after the great falls; it is so sternly solemn. The river cannot look more imperturbable, almost sullen in its marble green, than it does just below the great fall. But the slight circles that mark the hidden vortex seem to whisper mysteries the thundering voice above could not proclaim—a meaning as untold as ever. . . .

It is fearful, too, to know . . . that whatever has been swallowed by the cataract is like to rise suddenly to light here, whether uprooted tree, or body of man or bird.

The rapids enchanted me far beyond what I expected. They are so swift that they cease to seem so; you can think only of their beauty. The fountain beyond the Moss Islands I discovered for myself. [I] thought it for some time an accidental beauty which it would not do to leave, lest I might never see it again. After I found it permanent, I returned many times to watch the play of its crest. In the little waterfall beyond, Nature seems, as she often does, to have made a study for some larger design. She delights in this—a sketch within a sketch, a dream within a dream. Wherever we see it, the lines of the great buttress in the fragment of stone, the hues of the waterfall copied in the flowers that star its bordering mosses, we are delighted; for all the lineaments become fluent, and we mold the scene in congenial thought with its genius.

People complain of the buildings at Niagara, and fear to see it further deformed. I cannot sympathize with such an apprehension. The spectacle is capable of swallowing up all such objects; they are not seen in the great whole, more than an earthworm in a wide field.

And now farewell, Niagara. . . . I will be here again beneath some flooding July moon and sun. Owing to the absence of light, I have seen the rainbow only two or three times by day, the lunar bow not at all. However, the imperial presence needs not its crown, though illustrated by it.

# From "Niagara Falls Geology Facts & Figures"

*by Niagara Parks*

- The Niagara River is about 36 miles in length and is the natural outlet from Lake Erie to Lake Ontario. . . .

- More than 6 million cubic feet of water go over the crestline of the Falls every minute during peak daytime tourist hours. . . .

- The rapids above the Falls reach a maximum speed of 25 mph, with the fastest speeds occurring at the Falls themselves (recorded up to 68 mph). The water through the Whirlpool Rapids below the Falls reaches 30 mph, and at Devil's Hole Rapids, 22 mph.

- . . . The huge volume of water rushing from the Falls is crushed into the narrow Great Gorge, creating the Whirlpool Rapids that stretch for 1 mile. The water surface here drops 50 feet and the rushing waters can reach speeds as high as 30 feet per second.

- The whirlpool is a basin 1,700 feet long by 1,200 feet wide, with depths up to 125 feet. This is the elbow, where the river makes a sharp right-angled turn. . . .

- When the Niagara River is at full flow, the waters travel over the rapids and enter the pool, then travel counter-clockwise around the pool past the natural outlet. Pressure builds up . . . and this pressure forces the water under the incoming stream. The swirling waters create a vortex, or whirlpool. . . .

- The [green] color [of the water] comes from . . . dissolved salts and "rock flour," very finely ground rock. [These are] picked up primarily from the limestone bed. [They] probably also [come] from the shales and sandstones under the limestone cap at the falls.

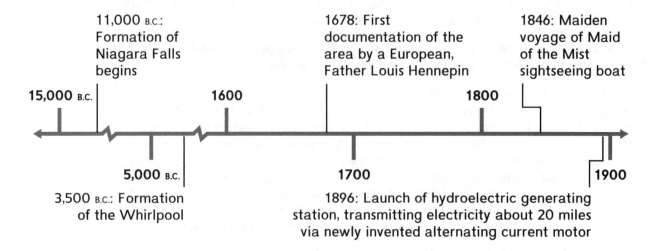

1. **"Niagara, June 10, 1843," "Niagara Falls Geology Facts & Figures," and the time line share the same**

   **A** format

   **B** genre

   **C** speaker

   **D** topic

2. **Read this sentence from "Niagara, June 10, 1843."**

   **I cannot sympathize with such an apprehension.**

   **What does the word <u>apprehension</u> mean as it is used in the sentence?**

   **F** capture

   **G** comprehension

   **H** concern

   **J** understanding

3. **Which statement <u>best</u> describes the impact of "Niagara, June 10, 1843" on readers?**

   **A** Readers are informed about the history of Niagara Falls.

   **B** Readers understand the author's feelings about Niagara Falls.

   **C** Readers can recall features of Niagara Falls and statistics about the falls.

   **D** Readers are persuaded that buildings should be constructed at Niagara Falls.

4. **Which statement <u>best</u> describes how the time line compares to "Niagara, June 10, 1843"?**

   **F** The time line gives interesting facts about the water at Niagara Falls; whereas, the passage explains the best sites to visit there.

   **G** The time line organizes the events of a person's visit to Niagara in a visual way; whereas, the passage describes the events on the trip.

   **H** The time line visually organizes information about the history of Niagara Falls; whereas, the passage describes the history in more detail.

   **J** The time line visually organizes information about the history of Niagara Falls; whereas, the passage describes a person's visit to the falls.

## Evaluating Differences between Genres

When considering differences between genres, readers can compare the unique characteristics of each genre. They can also determine the intended audience for a piece of writing. Finally, they can study the scope of the information presented; some texts cover a broad range of information about a topic, while other texts limit the range to one specific event or idea.

**Directions:** Read the texts. Then do Numbers 5–8.

## From "Evacuating Yourself and Your Family"
### *by the Federal Emergency Management Agency*

Evacuations are more common than many people realize. Fires and floods cause evacuations most frequently across the U.S. and almost every year, people along coastlines evacuate as hurricanes approach. . . .

In some circumstances, local officials . . . require mandatory evacuations. In others, evacuations are advised or households decide to evacuate to avoid situations they believe are potentially dangerous. When community evacuations become necessary local officials provide information to the public through the media. In some circumstances, other warning methods, such as sirens, text alerts, emails or telephone calls are used. . . .

If the event is a weather condition, such as a hurricane, you might have a day or two to get ready. However, many disasters allow no time for people to gather even the most basic necessities, which is why planning ahead is essential.

Plan how you will assemble your family and supplies and anticipate where you will go for different situations. Choose several destinations in different directions so you have options in an emergency and know the evacuation routes to get to those destinations. Follow these guidelines for evacuation:

- Plan places where your family will meet, both within and outside of your immediate neighborhood. . . .

- If you have a car, keep a full tank of gas in it if an evacuation seems likely. . . . Gas stations may be closed during emergencies and unable to pump gas during power outages. Plan to take one car per family to reduce congestion and delay.

- Become familiar with alternate routes . . . out of your area. . . .

- Leave early enough to avoid being trapped by severe weather.

- Follow recommended evacuation routes. Do not take shortcuts; they may be blocked.

- Be alert for road hazards such as washed-out roads . . . and downed power lines. . . .

- Take your emergency supply kit unless . . . it has been contaminated.

- Listen to a battery-powered radio and follow local evacuation instructions.

- Take your pets with you, but understand that only service animals may be permitted in public shelters. Plan how you will care for your pets in an emergency.

# From "The Story of an Eye-Witness"

### by Jack London

The earthquake in San Francisco shook down hundreds of thousands of dollars' worth of walls and chimneys. But the conflagration that followed burned up hundreds of millions of dollars' worth of property. There is no estimating within hundreds of millions the actual damage wrought.

Not in history has a modern imperial city been so completely destroyed. San Francisco is gone. Nothing remains of it but memories and a fringe of dwelling houses on its outskirts. Its industrial section is wiped out. Its business section is wiped out. Its social and residential section is wiped out. The factories and warehouses, the great stores and newspaper buildings, the hotels and the palaces . . . are all gone. . . . Within an hour after the earthquake shock, the smoke of San Francisco's burning was a lurid tower visible a hundred miles away. And for three days and nights this lurid tower swayed in the sky, reddening the sun, darkening the day, and filling the land with smoke.

On Wednesday morning at a quarter past five came the earthquake. A minute later the flames were leaping upward. In a dozen different quarters south of Market Street, in the working-class ghetto, and in the factories, fires started. There was no opposing the flames. There was no organization, no communication. All the cunning adjustments of a twentieth-century city had been smashed by the earthquake. The streets were humped into ridges and depressions and piled with the debris of fallen walls. The steel rails were twisted into perpendicular and horizontal angles. The telephone and telegraph systems were disrupted. And the great water mains had burst.

By Wednesday afternoon . . . half the heart of the city was gone. . . . East, west, north, and south, strong winds were blowing upon the doomed city. The heated air rising made an enormous suck. Thus did the fire of itself build its own colossal chimney through the atmosphere. . . .

San Francisco . . . is like the crater of a volcano, around which are camped tens of thousands of refugees. . . . All the surrounding cities and towns are jammed with the homeless ones, where they are being cared for by the relief committees. The refugees were carried free by the railroads to any point they wished to go, and it is estimated that over one hundred thousand people have left. . . . The government has the situation in hand, and, thanks to the immediate relief given by the whole United States, there is not the slightest possibility of a famine. The bankers and business men have already set about making preparations to rebuild San Francisco.

5. **Which characteristic applies only to passage 2?**
   A  facts
   B  information
   C  practical advice
   D  vivid descriptions

6. **Which conclusion could the reader draw about the intended audience of passage 1?**
   F  The audience is people who want to learn more about the weather.
   G  The audience is people who have already experienced a natural disaster.
   H  The audience is people who might need to prepare for a natural disaster.
   J  The audience is people who work for the Federal Emergency Management Agency.

**7.** **How does the genre support the author's purpose for writing "The Story of an Eye-Witness"?**

  **A**  It allows the reader to understand key concepts about earthquakes.

  **B**  It allows the author to persuade readers to prepare for earthquakes.

  **C**  It allows the author to use details that appeal to readers' emotions.

  **D**  It allows the reader to keep track of the account's sequence of events.

**8.** **When comparing the passages, the scope of passage 1 is**

  **F**  equal to the scope of passage 2

  **G**  superior to the scope of passage 2

  **H**  broader than the scope of passage 2

  **J**  narrower than the scope of passage 2

---

 **Test-Taking Tip**

As you plan to write an essay on a test, ask yourself, "What is my purpose for writing?" and "Who is my intended audience?" The purpose and the audience will influence your choice of genre and format.

---

## Language Practice

In addition to tense, every main verb in a sentence is also characterized by its mood. Depending on its function, a verb may be in one of three moods: indicative, imperative, or subjunctive.

The most common is the indicative mood, which is used to ask and tell about facts and opinions. The imperative mood is also common. It is used to express advice, commands, requests, and instructions. Imperatives have no stated subject; the subject "you" is implied.

The least common verb mood is the subjunctive, which expresses situations that are not factual, such as wishes and hypothetical states. The subjunctive mood is also used to make requests or give advice indirectly. Each purpose takes a different form. When stating a wish or hypothetical situation in the present, use the past tense of the verb; sometimes, you can create the subjunctive by adding a past-tense modal, like *would* or *could*, before the main verb. You should note that the present subjunctive of the verb *be* is always *were*, even after a first- or third-person singular subject (for example, "I wish I were older"). To state a wish or hypothetical situation in the past, the subjunctive is formed by using the past perfect tense of the verb. The past subjunctive of *be*, for example, is *had been*.

To form the subjunctive when indirectly making a request or giving advice, use the simple, uninflected form of the verb. Here's an example: "The doctor advised that my wife drink more fluids and get plenty of rest."

**Directions:** Read the excerpt from a draft of an essay. Then do Numbers 9 through 14.

My friend Kathy wishes that she lives in England—not the England of today, but Edwardian England, the England of the early 1900s! We talked about this fantasy of hers recently. "What do you think?" she asked me. "Before you answer, you watch the latest *Masterpiece* series. I recommend that everyone watches it to get a realistic impression of Edwardian life." I would tell her what I thought: "If I went to England, I'd want to fly there and rent a car when I arrived."

9. **Which version of the first underlined sentence forms the present subjunctive mood correctly to express a situation that is not factual?**

   A  My friend Kathy wishes that she lives in England.

   B  My friend Kathy wishes that she lived in England.

   C  My friend Kathy wishes that she had lived in England.

   D  My friend Kathy wishes that she would live in England.

10. **Read this excerpt from the text.**

    **"What do you think?"**

    **What is the mood of the verb in this excerpt?**

    F  imperative

    G  indicative

    H  subjunctive (indirect request)

    J  subjunctive (non-factual situation)

11. **Which version of the second underlined sentence forms the imperative mood correctly?**

    A  Before you answer, watch the latest *Masterpiece* series.

    B  Before you answer, you watch the latest *Masterpiece* series.

    C  Before you answer, you watched the latest *Masterpiece* series.

    D  Before you answer, you would watch the latest *Masterpiece* series.

12. **Which version of the third underlined sentence forms the subjunctive mood correctly to give advice indirectly?**

    F  I recommend that everyone watch it to get a realistic impression of Edwardian life.

    G  I recommend that everyone watches it to get a realistic impression of Edwardian life.

    H  I recommend that everyone watched it to get a realistic impression of Edwardian life.

    J  I recommend that everyone would watch it to get a realistic impression of Edwardian life.

13. **Which version of the fourth underlined sentence forms the indicative mood correctly?**

    A  I tell her what I thought.

    B  I told her what I thought.

    C  I could tell her what I thought.

    D  I would tell her what I thought.

14. **Read this excerpt from the text.**

    **I would tell her what I thought: "If I went to England, I'd want to fly there and rent a car when I arrived."**

    **What is the mood of the main verbs in the conditional statement after the colon?**

    F  imperative

    G  indicative

    H  subjunctive (indirect advice)

    J  subjunctive (non-factual situation)

## Writing Practice

When natural disasters occur or are predicted, government officials may enforce mandatory evacuations of homes and businesses in affected areas. Do you think the government has the right to enforce evacuations? Why or why not?

**Directions:** Write an argument to support your claim in an analysis of "Evacuating Yourself and Your Family" on page 196 and "The Story of an Eye-Witness," on page 197 using valid reasoning and relevant and sufficient evidence. Then explain which passage was more helpful in supporting your opinion, and why.

_____

_____

_____

_____

_____

_____

_____

_____

_____

_____

_____

_____

_____

_____

_____

_____

_____

_____

_____

_____

# Lesson 1.1

## Main Idea in Informational Text, p. 2

1. **A** The heading above each section explains what the section is about. This helps you identify the main idea of the section. The title provides information about what the entire passage is about, but the title does not focus on specific sections. The first and last sentences provide details, not the main idea of the section.

2. **G** Answer G is the only detail that is about starting work.

3. **D** Answer D tells the main idea of the section. The other sentences are not related to rates.

4. **J** The "Change orders" section explains how change orders need to be used when the scope of work changes. This includes adding work to the project. The other sections are about other aspects of the PT system.

5. **A** The main idea tells what the passage is about. The paragraphs in the memo outline the various procedures that employees must implement when using the new purchasing system.

6. **F** The topic sentence is presented at the start of the passage so employees will know what the remaining text is about. The topic sentence is not the least important information. Reading the topic sentence does not eliminate the need to read the details in the rest of the passage.

## Main Idea in Literary Text, p. 3

7. **D** Answer D explains the main idea of the excerpt. The other sentences do not reflect the details in the passage.

8. **G** The lack of imagination makes the man ill-equipped for the harsh environment. The other details are not about his shortcomings.

9. **C** Answer C explains the main idea of the paragraph. The other sentences are details or untrue statements.

10. **G** The excerpt is about how instinct is more important than knowledge in severe cold.

11. **B**

12. **F** There is no topic sentence in this passage. However, the author uses details to imply the main idea.

## Language Practice, p. 5

13. **A**

14. **H**

15. **B**

16. **J**

## Writing Practice, p. 7

Make sure your explanatory text clearly and concisely summarizes the main idea of the excerpt and includes effectively selected supporting details. Your supporting details should support the main idea.

> Answers will vary. Sample answer: The excerpt from "The Souls of Black Folk" describes the difficulties of growing up as an African American in a world where white people had all the advantages and privileges. W.E.B. DuBois describes the moment when, as a young boy, "the shadow swept across me"—the moment he realized that the color of his skin made him different from others—"or like, mayhap, in heart and life and longing, but shut out from their world by a vast veil." He explains how he tried to fight the shadow and reach the "blue sky"—that is, a sense of self-esteem and contentment—by besting his white peers in assorted ways: "That sky was bluest when I could beat my mates at examination-time, or beat them at a foot-race, or even beat their stringy heads." Ultimately, his boyhood efforts brought only temporary satisfaction. As he got older, Dubois realized more and more acutely that true equality was out of his reach. He writes that "the words I longed for, and all their dazzling opportunities, were theirs, not mine." He felt a sense of hopelessness as "the shades of the prison-house closed round about" him and his fellow "sons of the night." The passage is filled with a sense of outrage and disillusionment as Dubois battles the harshly unfair society into which he was born.

# Lesson 1.2

## Identifying Supporting Details, p. 10

1.  **D**  Supporting details may include facts, examples, reasons, and descriptions. The information about mythology and the calendar are facts that help support the main idea that Greeks and Romans contributed to the culture of the surrounding areas.

2.  **F**  Answer F supports the main idea that Greeks and Romans contributed to the culture of surrounding areas. It provides examples—traditions and technology—of what they contributed to other cultures. The other answers give information about Greeks and Romans, but they do not link this information to the surrounding cultures.

3.  **C**  The main idea of paragraph 4 is that mythology had an important role in Greek and Roman culture. Answer C is the only detail that supports this main idea. The other answers give details about the Romans and culture, but they do not mention mythology or the Greek or Roman gods.

4.  **F**  Paragraph 2 contains details about cultural development in ancient Greece. This includes supporting details about citizen participation in the Greek government.

5.  **C**  Answer C is a supporting detail describing government structure. The other answers do not relate to the structure of Roman society. Answer A is a detail about myths, answer B is about athletics, and answer D is about the Roman calendar.

## Using Details to Make Generalizations, p. 13

6.  **H**  Answer H is supported by the detail: "There are many different kinds of marshes, ranging from prairie potholes to the Everglades, coastal to inland, freshwater to saltwater." Answer F is incorrect because marshes have an abundance of plant life. The paragraph does not mention anything about marshes being fragile, so answer G is incorrect. Answer J is unrelated to the paragraph and factually inaccurate.

7.  **B**  Answer B describes one way that marshes help decontaminate water. Answer A describes the types of marshes, answer C describes the location of marshes, and answer D describes threats to the marshes.

8.  **H**  Answer H lists various kinds of plants and animals found in a marsh. Answers F, G, and J describe the makeup of marshes and threats to marshes, but they do not support a generalization about the ecosystem.

9.  **A**

## Language Practice, p. 14

10. **F**
11. **B**
12. **H**
13. **D**

## Writing Practice, p. 15

Make sure your informative text has a clearly stated main idea and significant and relevant supporting details from the passage.

Answers will vary. Sample answer: Our daily lives would be dramatically different—and not for the better—without the foundations laid by the ancient Greeks and Romans. Let us start with our physical health. The ancient Greeks and Romans held physical fitness in very high regard; it was just as important as the quest for knowledge and wisdom. To celebrate physical achievement, the Greeks invented the Olympic Games, which are more popular today than ever. At the same time, Greek scholars and philosophers such as Socrates and Aristotle developed ideas that are still relevant today. Then there is government. The ancient Greeks helped shape our modern democracy by promoting the role of citizens in government. The Romans, for their part, introduced the Julian calendar—the same calendar (with a few modifications) that is hanging on your wall today.

# Lesson 1.3

### Direct and Implied Main Ideas, p. 17

1. **C** Since the writer does not directly state the main idea, the reader must infer the main idea by studying the detail in the passage.

2. **J** The entire passage is about the changes in US policies. The other answer choices are supporting details.

3. **A** The main idea of the first paragraph is stated explicitly in the first sentence of the paragraph. The other choices are supporting details.

4. **J** The main idea of paragraphs 7 and 8 is that the United States expanded its borders to the Pacific coast through a war with Mexico. This supports the inference that the United States expanded its boundaries through a war with another country.

### Implied Main Ideas and Supporting Details, p. 19

5. **A** Details in this passage help you determine the main idea of a story.

6. **J** The main idea is not directly stated. Instead, readers must identify the implied main idea by figuring out how the supporting details are related.

7. **B** The main idea of the passage is that "Things are not always the way we see them." This is suggested when the boy realizes that his own house has golden windows when he looks at it from a distance.

8. **H** The girl's comment supports the main idea that "Things aren't always the way we see them."

9. **B**

### Language Practice, p. 21

10. **J**

11. **D**

12. **G**

13. **C**

### Writing Practice, p. 22

Make sure your explanatory text clearly states the main idea of "The Golden Windows" and cites story details that help develop the idea.

Answers will vary. Sample answer:

Early in the story, the author describes the boy standing at the top of a hill looking at a house at the top of another hill, miles away. One day, the boy's father gives him a day off and tells him to "try to learn some good thing." The boy sets out to find the house with the golden windows, only to discover that the house is a simple farmhouse, just like his own, with windows of glass rather than gold. A woman who lives at the farm tells him that she comes from a poor farming family with regular glass windows. The woman's daughter then points out another house, miles away that appears to have gold and diamond windows. It's the boy's own house, with the setting sun shining on it. When he returns to his humble home, his family greets him with warmth and affection.

"The Golden Windows" does not state the main idea directly at any point in the story. But the author uses the story details to gradually uncover the story's message: Things are not always as they appear to be, and love is the most valuable thing.

When the boy's father gives him a day off and tells him to "try to learn some good thing," readers get a clue that the boy is about to discover something important. The woman living in the house that the boy believes has golden windows tells the boy, "We are poor farming people and are not likely to have gold about our windows; but glass is better to see through." This helps convey the idea that things are not always as they appear. The woman's daughter describes the boy's own windows of "clear gold and diamonds." This also hints at the idea that things are not what they appear to be, since the boy also has regular glass windows. When the boy returns and tells his father that their house "has windows of gold and diamond," the writer conveys the idea that the farm is a place of great value because it is full of love.

# Lesson 1.4

### Summarizing Key Information, p. 24

1. **C** The main idea of this passage is that the clothing worn by slaves was uncomfortable and sometimes painful. The discomfort and pain of the clothing is not complete enough to be a summary or paraphrase of the passage, and it is too general to be a detail.

2. **H** The passage describes the uncomfortable clothing worn by slaves; answer H best paraphrases the main idea. The clothing was described as uncomfortable and painful, not luxurious. Though the clothing may have been simple, practical, and durable, this is not the focus of the main idea. The passage does not explain any relationship between clothes and a slave's life.

3. **D** The main idea of the passage is that the clothing was uncomfortable. Answer D is the only detail that conveys that the clothing felt uncomfortable. The other answers are part of the passage but are not closely related to the main idea, so they would not be included in the summary.

4. **H** Answer choice H describes how painful the new flax shirts were to wear. This detail supports the main idea that the clothing was uncomfortable. None of the other choices support the main idea that the clothing was uncomfortable.

5. **D**

### Summarizing a Text, p. 26

6. **G** The statement retells the key points of the first paragraph. The statement does not critique, quote from, or constitute a supporting detail of the first paragraph.

7. **C** The text describes precautions that travelers should take when traveling during hurricane season. Answer C is the best summary of the main idea. The other answers are details that are included in the paragraph but do not express the main idea.

8. **J** The main idea is to be prepared when traveling. Answer J is an important detail about how to be prepared. The other answer options do not relate specifically to being prepared while traveling during the upcoming hurricane season.

9. **A** Answer choice A best summarizes all the details in the paragraph. The other choices paraphrase only one detail each or contain inaccurate information.

10. **J** This passage includes the boldfaced headings, "Travel Alert" and "Hurricane Season." These headings tell you what the most important information to include in a summary would be. The passage does not contain italicized text. The date of the alert and paragraph breaks do not need to be included in a summary.

11. **C** Included in these statements are the main idea ("During hurricane season, travelers should be prepared for emergencies") and summary details. There are two statements which do not meet that criteria: "It is likely that 13 to 20 named storms will occur this season" is too small a detail to include in a summary, and the passage does not contain information about NOAA recommending against travel. Option C does not include those responses.

### Writing Practice, p. 28

Make sure your explanatory text states the main idea and the most significant and relevant supporting details and explains whether the excerpt is effective in conveying the author's ideas.

> Answers will vary. Sample answer: In the excerpt from *Up From Slavery*, Booker T. Washington writes about the horribly uncomfortable clothes slaves were forced to wear. He writes about wearing wooden shoes that "were very inconvenient, since there was no yielding to the natural pressure of the foot." Worse still were the shirts, which were made from the "cheapest and roughest" flax. Washington writes that he can imagine no torture—"except, perhaps, the pulling of a tooth"—that would be worse than wearing one of these shirts for the first time. It felt, he says, like "a hundred small pin-points."

Finally, he describes the great kindness of his older brother, who offered to wear a new flax shirt for him until it was "broken in." Washington vividly conveys the pain and humiliation slaves suffered in even the smallest aspects of daily life, and through his details he gives a larger sense of what it was like to *be* a slave.

# Lesson 1.5

## Using Fictional Elements to Determine Theme, p. 29

**1. A** The theme is the central message of the passage. The slow and steady work of Measuring-Worm expresses the story's theme of perseverance leading to success.

**2. J** In the story, Measuring-Worm slowly creeps up the cliff over the course of a year and is the only one who is successful in rescuing the boys. The passage is about persistence, not about working together, judging appearances, or being strong.

**3. D** The perseverance of Measuring-Worm is an important detail in identifying the theme. The other sentences describe different things that happen in the story, but they do not directly relate to the central theme.

**4. F**

## Synthesizing Multiple Main Ideas to Determine Theme, p. 31

**5. D** The story is told from the narrator's point of view, allowing the reader to learn lessons from both characters. When these lessons are synthesized, they reveal the theme. The story is not told from the perspective of the king, patriot, or Great Head Factotum.

**6. G** The story is a satire, which uses humor to help readers understand culture. The use of the term *patriot* highlights the man's dishonesty and disloyalty. The other sentences provide details about the main character but do not help identify the theme.

**7. D** In the short story, the patriot is dishonest in his words and actions. These actions reveal the theme. The other statements do not describe the theme.

**8. H** The theme of the story is implied and can be found by synthesizing the information from the characterization of the king and the patriot, the language used in the dialog, and the outcome of the interaction between the characters.

## Writing Practice, p. 32

Make sure you explain your ideas clearly and effectively select details from the story to support your analysis of how literary elements contribute to the text's theme

Answers may vary. Sample answer: The literary elements of plot, characterization, and setting contribute to the theme of "Legend of Tu-Tok-A-Nu'-La (El Capitan)." Synthesizing, or putting together, these elements allows the reader to fully understand the theme.

The plot of the story is that a group of animals attempt to rescue two boys who have fallen asleep on a boulder that has grown as high as the clouds. The animals try, one at a time, to jump to the top of the boulder. Each animal jumps higher than the one before, but not even the largest or most nimble animal can jump high enough. Finally, tiny Measuring-Worm retrieves the boys by slowly creeping his way to the top. The theme of the fable is that a slow, concentrated effort gets the job done better than a fast, incomplete effort.

The plot plays a large role in conveying the theme of the fable. The central conflict—the boys are stuck and need to be rescued—drives the actions of the animals. In turn, the resolution of the conflict spells out the theme. The author does not have to state that Measuring-Worm has the most successful approach to solving the problem. Instead, Measuring-Worm's actions embody the theme of perseverance. At the end of the story, the narrator mentions that the rock is named after Measuring-Worm. This fact highlights Measuring-Worm as the hero of the story.

Characterization also communicates the theme. Each of the larger animals "leap[s] as high as he could" but falls short of the goal. While well meaning, these animals lack the initiative and dedication of Measuring-Worm. The contrast in size between the worm and the other animals further emphasizes the degree of perseverance shown by Measuring-Worm.

Like the plot and characterization, the setting is crucial to the theme of this story. In fact, the story could not take place anywhere else. Without the enormous boulder, the conflict, and thus the plot, would not exist.

Examining each literary element individually gives the reader a good idea of the story's theme, but analyzing the elements together leaves no doubt in the reader's mind.

# Lesson 2.1

## Sequence of Time, p. 34

1. **B** The words *When* and *But today* help you understand that picking out a pair of athletic shoes was easier before there were so many brands and styles.

2. **G** The word *finally* is used to tell you that style and special features are the last things to consider when you are looking for shoes to purchase.

3. **D** *When* and *while* both mean "at the same time."

4. **H**

5. **C** According to the passage, deciding what kind of shoes you need should be the first step.

## Sequence in a Process, p. 36

6. **H** The sequence described in that section is a process.

7. **C** Each section of the text explains a process, and in both cases they are explained in chronological order. The sections themselves are also arranged in chronological order.

8. **J** The only feature used in this passage to show the organization of the text is boldfaced headings. The two questions in these headings help the reader understand the order of events.

9. **A** The passage explains that scientists use seismic surveys to find the right places to drill wells. Then they study rock samples and take measurements. Because the process described in the section is in chronological order, this means that studying samples and taking measurements takes place after seismic surveys are completed.

## Language Practice, p. 37

10. **J**

11. **A**

12. **H**

13. **C**

## Writing Practice, p. 38

Make sure that your informative text uses signal words, transitions, key terms, and text features like headings to reinforce the sequence of events.

Answers will vary. Sample answer:

**The Titanic Sinks**

The *Titanic* collided with an iceberg at about 10:25 on the night of April 14. After the collision, the crew sent out calls for help. The message was received by at least three ships. Thirty minutes later, the crew reported that the ship was sinking. The Marconi station contacted the Allan liner *Virginian*, which started heading to the *Titanic's* location.

After reporting that the ship was sinking, *Titanic* crew members reported putting women and children into lifeboats. Other members of the crew sent distress signals at the same time. Finally, the *Virginian* heard some blurred signals at 12:27 the morning of April 15, which then suddenly ended.

**Rescuers Locate the Wreckage**

At daybreak on April 15, the Cunarder *Carpathia* reached the position of the *Titanic* where it sank. It had drifted about 34 miles south of the collision. The crew found lifeboats with about 655 surviving passengers and the wreckage of the ship.

Then the *Carpathia* took on the survivors and sailed for New York. Another ship, the Leyland liner *California* remained at the wreckage to search the scene. By 11:00 on the night of April 15, no other ships in the area found signs of any other survivors.

# Lesson 2.2

## Inferring a Writer's Meaning, p. 41

**1. B** From Dick Baker's speech and dress, you can figure out that he is a simple man who is not well educated. The reference to his heart being finer than gold is a metaphor that means Baker is kindhearted. The other statements do not describe Dick Baker.

**2. J** The narrator seems to doubt that Tom Quartz is so special. The narrator does not imply that he agrees with Dick Baker or that he thinks Jim is not as smart as the cat. Dogs are never mentioned.

**3. C** The actions of the cat—laying low, observing the miners, sleeping on the miners' coats—are normal actions for cats. However, the cat's owner sees the cat's behavior as "superintending" (acting like a supervisor), and he interprets the cat's behavior as humanlike. Most people would not consider these actions supernatural, impressive, or like a circus animal.

**4. H** Dick Baker says the cat "never *could* altogether understand that eternal sinkin' of a shaft an' never pannin' out anything." The reader can infer that the cat does not think mining underground is a worthwhile activity. There is no mention that the cat is interested in quartz or prefers digging deep.

**5. A** Dick Baker describes the event in a way that is entertaining. He does not express sadness, satisfaction, or fear.

## Citing Evidence, p. 44

**6. G** The impenetrable darkness and the mist covering the hills are examples used to support the idea that this is a night when one ought to be indoors. These descriptions are not inferences made by readers. The "darkness [was] impenetrable" is an opinion, and "raw mist [was] enveloping hill and valley" is a fact about the weather.

**7. D**

**8. H** The narrator's description of his feelings is the best evidence to support the inference that he feels uneasy in the house. The other excerpts do not express discomfort or tension.

**9. C** Because the man leaving the house mentions that others are expected, readers can logically infer that guests have been invited. Because the house is furnished, a reader would not infer that the house has never been lived in. There is no evidence that the man is the butler. Finally, the narrator seems intrigued and has no intention of leaving immediately.

## Writing Practice, p. 46

Make sure your explanatory text includes specific details from "An Open Door" that clearly show relationships between setting, characters, and plot, as well as the inferences you drew from these connections.

> Answers will vary. Sample answer: The excerpt from "An Open Door" follows a young traveler as he seeks shelter on a dark, eerie night. The author describes it as a night of "impenetrable darkness," with a "raw mist" that makes travel "anything but desirable." Darkness is often associated with danger, so the night seems dangerous. The main character is "young, untrammelled, and naturally

indifferent to danger." He tends to seek "the strange, the unknown, and sometimes the terrible." Therefore, the character and the setting are closely linked because the man seems to be seeking out danger in this environment. As the plot develops, it is clear that the main character is walking into a strange and unknown situation, one that is as cloaked in mist as the night itself. Details such as "confused wanderings through tangled hedges" help readers infer that the main character's mind will be confused and tangled by events to come. When the main character encounters a stranger, the stranger is soon "swallowed" by the misty night, adding to the air of mystery and foreboding and connecting the stranger to the night itself. Finally, the main character arrives at a well-lit and well-furnished house, yet the place makes him uneasy because of its solitude. From this accumulation of details, the reader can infer that trouble lies within the walls of this house. Trouble seems inevitable because of the connections of darkness, danger, and mystery the author establishes between the story's setting, characters, and events.

# Lesson 2.3

### Identifying Literary Elements, p. 48

1. **B** The nephew calls Scrooge dismal and morose, so Scrooge is in a bad mood. Answers C and D describe the nephew, not Scrooge. The clerk, the nephew, and the people outside are cold, but Scrooge is not described this way.

2. **H** The phrases describe the story's setting, specifically the weather of the place where the story takes place. The phrases do not describe the narrative, the characters, or the theme.

3. **B** The text does not tell us that Scrooge walked outside in the fog; he is already working when this passage begins. The plot does include choices A, C, and D.

4. **J** Characterization is the writer's way of helping the reader visualize a character. Answer J is a description of Scrooge's nephew. The other choices do not describe characters.

### Analyzing Relationships in Text, p. 50

5. **D** The room can be considered the setting, and the observations made about the room relate directly to the plot. The other choices do not specifically relate the setting to the overall plot of the mystery story.

6. **F** In the story, the tavern owner shows the rooms to Coroner Golden and the deputy sheriff, who are investigating an incident involving a young woman. Choices G and H would have happened prior to the event in the passage, and Choice J is a fact that is not proved in the passage.

7. **C** The text explains that the tavern is old and that the owner does not want to change the tavern. Choice A is incorrect because the owner loves the place, and no information is given about changing the owner's mood or his life.

8. **G** The wallpaper in the room (setting), which is not the same color or pattern that a witness reported, ties the story to its setting. The gables, Jake's sleeping in room 3, and the closeness of the tavern to Danton do not tie the plot to the setting.

9. **B**

10. **H** The deputy sheriff has some suspicions, but he also makes careful observations before coming to any conclusions. The other choices are important ideas, but they are not a theme in this story.

### Writing Practice, p. 52

Make sure your explanatory text clearly describes how setting, characters, and plot interact in the excerpt and indicates how these relationships, as well as the story's meaning, would change if any of the text elements were different. Remember to use text details to support your ideas.

> Answers will vary. Sample answer: *A Christmas Carol* is set on a cold, bleak Christmas Eve, with dense fog creeping through "every chink and keyhole." This dismal setting matches the mood of Ebenezer Scrooge, a cold-hearted figure who won't spare even a coal for his clerk's fire. The setting also elicits sympathy for Scrooge's clerk, who not only is forced to work on Christmas Eve but also must try to "warm himself at a candle." If the story were instead set on a sunny morning in spring, this appropriately chilly mood would vanish, and the author would have to find other ways to

portray Scrooge's cold nature and his clerk's sad plight. The story's plot also illuminates Scrooge's nature: When Scrooge's nephew arrives with good cheer and a warm greeting, as befits Christmas Eve, Scrooge gruffly replies, "Bah" and "Humbug!" and remarks that his nephew has little reason to be merry, given that he is "poor enough." This plot element reinforces the idea that Scrooge is not only grouchy but also overly concerned with money, and it contrasts his unhappy wealth with his nephew's good nature, despite his poverty. If, instead, Scrooge had merely left his office without this visit from his nephew, we would lack important information about his character and the story's theme.

# Lesson 2.4

### Interpreting Implied Relationships between Ideas, p. 54

1. **D**  The similar sentence structure in paragraphs 2 and 3 with the word *unstable* and then *stable*, is a clue that the author is contrasting cold and warm air masses, or showing how they are different. Comparing would show how the two types of air masses are alike, and the author does not explain how one air mass becomes another, so the other choices are incorrect.

2. **J**  The fact that the weather in central Canada is cold and dry is implied. The reader must infer this idea based on explicit details. The other answer options are explicit in the text and do not have to be inferred.

3. **A**  The text does not explicitly say that cold air masses produce more rain. However, because they can produce heavy loads of precipitation; whereas, warm air masses produce just drizzle, this is a reasonable inference. Gusty, nonsteady winds do not occur with warm air masses, so choice B is incorrect. Drizzle, a kind of rain, occurs with some warm air masses, so choice C is incorrect. The text explicitly states that puffy clouds occur when cold and warm air masses meet, so choice D would not need to be inferred.

4. **J**  The text explicitly says that the Coriolis Effect is a force that affects all wind and water currents, so a reader can infer that hurricanes as well as tornadoes have a counterclockwise spin. For that reason, choice G is incorrect. Because tornadoes take place over land in central states, choices F and H are also incorrect.

### Citing Evidence of Implied Relationships, p. 56

5. **B**  This statement helps the reader predict that the Supreme Court will overturn DOMA. The text cites the many laws and regulations that do not apply to same-sex spouses to show that the law does not treat all people equally. Therefore, it does not imply that DOMA will be upheld. The Supreme Court was not considering a case about government-integrity rules, so choices C and D are not reasonable inferences.

6. **H**  The idea that DOMA is in violation of the Fifth Amendment is the strongest evidence that the court's decision is based on existing legislation. None of the other answers mention existing laws or regulations.

7. **B**  The logical conclusion of these two sentences is that DOMA diminishes the dignity and integrity of some couples. Couples of the opposite sex are not deprived of anything under the law, so the rights and responsibilities and dignity and integrity of all or opposite-sex couples are not diminished.

8. **H**  The text emphasizes that DOMA asks the federal government to deny rights already recognized by the state. This idea could be applied to other decisions made by the court. The other answer choices are not related to rights granted by the state or federal government.

9. **D**

### Writing Practice, p. 58

Make sure you include a summary and an explanation of the implicit relationships among the text's ideas. Also make sure you effectively select and cite specific details, and include an explanation of how the details helped you make inferences.

> Answers may vary. Sample answer: The passage explains, in a cause-and-effect structure, that scientists have definitively detected water vapor on the dwarf planet Ceres, using far-infrared

technology from the Herschel space observatory. The author notes that this discovery proves the theory that Ceres has both an icy surface and an atmosphere. Scientists think the water vapor is a result of the ice warming when Ceres' orbit is near the sun. According to the passage, more will be learned when NASA's Dawn mission lands a spacecraft on Ceres in 2015. Dawn will provide context for the discovery, as well as additional geological and chemical details.

Numerous implicit relationships in the text allowed me to infer the cause-and-effect structure, beginning with an explanation of what scientists believe causes Ceres' water vapor: "Plumes of water vapor are thought to shoot up . . . when portions of its icy surface warm slightly." This cause-and-effect relationship is confirmed later in the passage, when the author writes that "a portion of its [Ceres'] icy surface becomes warm enough to cause water vapor to escape." The cause of the warming is explained as Ceres' proximity to the sun during part of the dwarf planet's orbit. The author frames the discovery itself as the result of "Herschel's far-infrared vision" which revealed "a clear spectral signature of the water vapor." The author notes that the Dawn mission (cause) will show "the processes that drive the outgassing activity" (effect). Even the description of Ceres' reclassification is presented in a cause-and-effect relationship. The use of the word *because* was a clue to the structure: "For the last century, Ceres was known as the largest asteroid. . . . But [it was] reclassified . . . as a dwarf planet because of its large size."

# Lesson 2.5

## Examining Complex Literary Texts, p. 61

1. **A** The title and the first sentence of the last paragraph indicate that the narrator is talking about a cat. In other paragraphs, he begins by using the first person and mentions his childhood and his marriage, so the reader also knows that the author is also talking about his life. The other choices do not cover what the passage is mainly about.

2. **H** The following phrases support this answer: "perhaps, some intellect . . . will reduce my phantasm [fantasy/nightmare] to the commonplace [ordinary]"; "nothing more than an ordinary succession of very natural causes and effects." Because the narrator states that he is telling the story "without comment," it is unlikely he is trying to persuade readers. He also says that readers might find the events less terrifying than he does. Finally, he is not concerned with readers understanding why he has written his account—rather, he wonders if readers will understand the events themselves.

3. **C** The main idea is that the narrator married someone who also loved animals, and together they adopted many different types of pets. The narrator does not say that his wife had pets before their marriage. Nor does he say that she was agreeable; he says the pets are agreeable. In addition, he states that his wife procured (got) pets for him, not that she allowed him to do so.

4. **F**

## Understanding Complex Informational Texts, p. 63

5. **A** From the title and the end of the second paragraph, we understand that Obama is concerned with the affordability, or cost, of higher education. The other choices are not the theme of this speech.

6. **J** The difference between the rise in tuition costs and the rise in income is the strongest evidence that tuition is not affordable. The other choices are mentioned in the speech as problems, but they do not support as strongly the idea that tuition is unaffordable.

7. **D** By visualizing a student writing a large check, a reader could imagine and understand the burden of repaying the student loan. Picturing an unemployment line would help a reader understand unemployment, but not the cost of tuition. The other choices would not help the reader better understand the problem either.

8. **G** The text in this section lays out the different steps taken by the government to protect students from being exploited by lenders and to help them to obtain and repay loans. The other choices mention one step or another, but not the entire process.

9. **B** The text tells us that Obama is glad that changes have been made, but is not satisfied that the problem of tuition affordability has been resolved. The other choices are explicit details from the text, but they do not state the conclusion.

**10.** J

**11.** C

**12.** J

**13.** A

## Writing Practice, p. 65

In your informative text, make sure you clearly state the main idea and note the most important details. In addition, include an explanation of how the details helped you determine the main idea and an analysis of how the main idea is developed throughout the passage.

> Answers will vary. Sample answer: The main idea of the text is that even though nitrogen and phosphorous are found naturally in the environment and are necessary for supporting aquatic ecosystems, an overabundance of these nutrients—nutrient pollution—caused by human activity has created environmental, health, and economic problems. For example, nutrient pollution causes the overgrowth of algae, known as algal blooms. Algal blooms affect water quality, restrict oxygen available to fish, and increase toxins and bacteria. As a result, fish can become sick or die, and humans can get sick by eating contaminated fish or by otherwise coming in contact with the water. Nutrient pollution in drinking water is another cause of concern. Humans, particularly infants, can suffer from consumption of nitrates, which are a nitrogen-based compound. Finally, large amounts of nitrogen in the air can cause breathing problems and harm trees, plants, soil, and water.
>
> For the most part, the text's details helped me determine the main idea by stating, reiterating, and providing more information about important points. For example, to explain the benefits of nitrogen and phosphorous, the author writes that these nutrients "support the growth of algae and aquatic plants, which provide food and habitat for fish, shellfish and smaller organisms that live in water." The author then provides numerous details about the harm caused by nutrient pollution, beginning with its impact on "streams, rivers, lakes, bays and coastal waters." The author explains that nutrient pollution "causes algae to grow faster than ecosystems can handle," and he or she notes specific negative outcomes—a "decrease [in] the oxygen that fish and other aquatic life need to survive" and "elevated toxins and bacterial growth." The only idea that is mentioned only once (in the second paragraph) but is not reiterated is the economic impact of nutrient pollution. I had to make inferences from the details. For example, I inferred that the loss of fish affects the seafood industry, poisoned water increases the need for cleanup or water treatment, and human health problems take a financial toll on businesses that lose workers to illness.

# Lesson 3.1

## Identifying Connotative and Figurative Meanings, p. 67

**1.** A    Pony Express riders didn't actually gallop into history. "Gallop into history" is a metaphor used to create an image in the reader's mind.

**2.** G    The reader most likely feels a sense of excitement. Phrases such as "breakneck speed" and "glorious history" are word choices that set the mood of excitement.

**3.** A    The author uses word choices to indicate that his or her attitude about the subject is complimentary. Only positive aspects of the Pony Express are described in this passage.

**4.** G    The author compares the Pony Express period in history to a chapter in a book. This is a metaphor.

**5.** B    "Breakneck" evokes the image of someone moving so quickly that the person could break his or her neck. A Pony Express rider moving that fast was going at a dangerous speed.

**6.** J

## Understanding Connotative and Figurative Meaning in Literary Text, p. 70

**7.** C    The narrator describes Dame Van Winkel as constantly nagging Rip. This is meant to make the reader sympathetic toward him.

**8. G** In paragraph 2, "adherent" is used when talking about Wolf, Rips faithful dog. In paragraph 4, "adherents" refers to a group of men. In both cases, the word could be replaced by "friend" or "friends." "Adherent" is always used in a positive sense, so it cannot mean "enemy." Neither Rip Van Winkel nor Nicholas Vedder served as teachers.

**9. A** In the fourth paragraph, the author paints a picture of the men idly chatting and Nicholas Vedder tranquilly smoking his pipe. In the fifth paragraph however, Dame Van Winkel suddenly breaks into the men's gathering, criticizes the men, and then attacks Vedder for encouraging her husband to sit idly.

**10. F** Dame Van Winkle dominates her husband by always nagging at him and telling him what to do. She also dominates the men of the village when she storms into the "philosopher's club."

**11. C** The first paragraph describes Dame Van Winkle's constant nagging. Rip is so "henpecked" that he is forced to go outside.

## Language Practice, p. 71

**12. G**

**13. D**

## Writing Practice, p. 71

Your explanatory text should provide examples of connotative and figurative language from "Rip Van Winkle" and explain how they affect the story. Your essay also should also clearly explain how different word choices might change the tone of the story. Include details, quotations, and examples to support your ideas.

> Answers will vary. Sample answer: Irving's language in "Rip van Winkle" makes readers sympathize with Rip rather than with his wife. Irving uses phrases such as "He would have whistled life away in perfect contentment" to portray Rip as a good-natured, harmless fellow. His wife, on the other hand, lets out "a torrent of criticism," attacking Rip with "the terrors of a woman's tongue." Rip, clearly the victim, has to "console himself" by visiting a club in the village. If Irving had used different language, he might have made readers much less sympathetic toward Rip. For example, Irving might have called Rip "lazy as a sloth," or "useless as a stump." At the same time, Irving might have increased readers' sympathy for Rip's wife by saying she was "understandably frustrated" rather than referring to her "continual harping." That would make "Rip van Winkle" into an entirely different story.

# Lesson 3.2

## Identifying Author's Tone in an Informational Text, p. 74

**1. B** The topic of the letter is a complaint, so the tone is negative. Anger and frustration are appropriate tones for letters of complaint.

**2. G** The author of the letter uses the word *headaches* as a metaphor to describe the problems he had at the hotel. This word has a negative connotation that helps reveal the tone of the letter.

**3. D** "Imagine my surprise" is the author's way of saying, "Can you believe this?" The other sentences explain what happened, but they do not express the writer's frustration.

**4. G** The writer uses the phrases "a number of problems" and "all of these problems" to emphasize that several things went wrong during his hotel stay. The hotel manager would most likely feel embarrassed that a guest at his hotel had so many problems.

**5. D** The tone reveals how the author feels about a subject. Changing "As the cherry on top" to "Thankfully" would demonstrate a change in the author's feelings from irritation to appreciation.

## Analyzing Tone in a Literary Text, p. 76

**6. H** The genre of the story is mystery. The tone of a mystery is commonly suspenseful.

**7. C**

**8. J** Short, terse phrases and sentences build tension in the story. This pushes the reader to move forward to find out what happens next.

**9. C** The mystery itself and the short sentences contribute to the intense tone.

**10. G** Mr. Sedgwick's lengthy inner monologue adds tension to the story. The reader must stop and wait while Mr. Sedgwick thinks about his guests. The paragraph does not describe the butler's search, and it does not actually name Darrow as the thief. The brief description of Mr. Blake at the end is part of Mr. Sedgwick's inner thoughts.

**11. B** The speaker of the sentence is uncertain and possibly a little afraid. If she boldly, proudly, or loudly offered her opinion, it would change the tone of the paragraph.

## Writing Practice, p. 78

Your explanatory text should describe how the use of connotative words, figurative language, and sentence structures expresses a writer's tone and matches his or her purpose for writing.

Answers will vary. Sample answer: The writer of the letter to the hotel manager uses words with strong connotation to show his angry tone. Mr. Walters is trying to persuade the hotel manager to refund the cost of his stay, so the language and structure of Mr. Walters' sentences are intended to evoke emotion and be persuasive. For example, Mr. Walters uses words like "headache," "disaster," and "uncomfortable" to show how much difficulty the room and hotel staff caused him. He also uses figurative language like "As the cherry on top" to show that the problems at the hotel were building up to a breaking point for the guest. Mr. Walters wrote the letter in a very sequential, almost list-like way. This makes the many problems that Mr. Walters encountered at the hotel very clear to the reader.

In "The Thief," the author is not being persuasive; rather, her intent is to entertain. Greene's tone is very different from Mr. Walters. Instead of being angry, she is mysterious and creates suspense. Greene describes the guests with words like "timidly," "nervous," "not sufficiently sure of their voices," and "distressed." These terms help build the tension in the mystery. Greene also varies her sentence structure significantly. This makes the writing interesting and adds to the mystery, and the reader does not fall into a tedious pattern of reading similar sentences repeatedly. She adds dialogue to show how the various characters speak. She also includes very short paragraphs along with longer ones. These short paragraphs cause the reader to pause and think about the story. This builds suspense.

# Lesson 3.3

## Choosing the Right Word, p. 80

**1. C** Bush uses words such as "nightmare" and "murdered" to describe the atrocities occurring in Iraq. These details are meant to persuade the American public that war is necessary. The other word choices do not have strong negative connotations, so they would not be as persuasive.

**2. F** Bush calls the people working with Saddam Hussein "thugs" because he wants listeners to picture them as criminals. Bush does not imply that Hussein's soldiers were in prison or that they came from any other countries, nor does he mention any attempts at diplomacy.

**3. C** The term "military equipment" is neutral and therefore does not convey negative feelings. The other options convey Bush's negative feelings toward Saddam Hussein.

**4. J** The word "protections" describes the efforts that the US government will take to keep US cities safe. None of the other options pertains specifically to safety.

**5. D** "Attacked" has a negative connotation. It brings to mind acts of violence that deserve revenge. None of the other choices describes these same negative feelings.

## Analyzing and Evaluating Word Choice in Various Texts, p. 82

**6. J** Anthony used persuasive language in her speech as she detailed what the preamble to the Constitution really means. Her explanations were meant to show the discrepancies between rights for men and rights for all.

**7. C** Anthony began her speech by addressing "friends and fellow citizens." She wanted the entire American public to rally behind the idea of votes for women. None of the other choices describe all the people she was trying to reach with her speech.

**8. J**

**9. B** Nothing was actually being thrown to the wind. This phrase is an example of figurative language. It provides the reader or listener with a visual image. All the other phrases are literal expressions; they mean exactly what the words say.

**10. H** "Mockery" has a negative connotation; it conveys the idea that talk of liberty has no meaning for people who cannot vote. *Silly* makes women's plight seem unimportant. *Difficult* does not express Anthony's scorn. *Encouraging* ignores the frustration women might feel when it is implied that those who cannot vote can enjoy "liberty."

**11. A** Anthony wanted other people to become angry and to take up the cause of suffrage for women. She was not describing a hopeful situation for women who wanted to vote. She did not want people to become depressed. And although her speech might have excited some people, Anthony's intention was clearly to get people angry enough to change the law.

## Writing Practice, p. 84

In your response, clearly state whether the speech persuaded you, and explain how word choices help shape your viewpoint. Include significant and relevant details from the speech to support your response.

> Answers will vary. Sample answer: Bush's speech persuaded me that Operation Iraqi Freedom was necessary to stop Saddam Hussein. In the speech, Bush describes Saddam Hussein as a "sponsor of terror" whose regime "uses fear as a tool of domination." Bush says Saddam Hussein's "thugs" murdered civilians "in cold blood." These words and phrases paint a vivid picture of a ruthless dictator who needed to be stopped. Bush also notes that civilians were "shot and shelled from behind"—a phrase that makes Saddam's troops sound cowardly as well as purely evil. In the speech, Bush also refers to the people of Iraq as "long-suffering" and says they lived in a "nightmare world." This forceful language convinced me that the Iraqi people desperately needed liberation from Saddam Hussein's regime and that Operation Iraqi Freedom was, therefore, essential.

# Lesson 4.1

## Identifying Text Structure, p. 86

**1. A** The passage uses sequence to narrate the events of the *Titanic*'s first trip.

**2. F** The size of the *Titanic* is contrasted with other ships. The *Titanic* was much larger than any other ship in the harbor.

**3. C** The word *next* is commonly used when the text structure is sequence. It helps point out the order of events.

**4. G** Many people gathered at the harbor because they wanted to say farewell to their friends and relatives.

## Variations in Organization, p. 88

**5. B** The events in the paragraph are told from start to finish. This is known as chronological order, or time order.

**6. F**

**7. A** Holmes uses flashbacks to organize the ideas in the paragraph. He refers to events that happened "last night" and "four weeks ago."

**8. J** When the passage begins, Holmes is brewing something. Then Holmes describes the missing links of the simple chain of events. Next, Mr. Hilton Cubitt rings the doorbell. Finally, Holmes holds up a piece of paper.

## Language Practice, p. 90

**9. C**

**10. F**

**11. D**

**12. J**

## Writing Practice, p. 91

Make sure your explanatory text uses a compare-and-contrast text structure to analyze the similarities and differences in the ways the authors develop their ideas using the characters of Sherlock Holmes and Hercule Poirot. You should include compare-and-contrast words such as *both, similarly, however,* and *in contrast* and relevant details to support your analysis.

Answers will vary. Sample answer: In "The Adventure of the Dancing Men" and *The Mysterious Affair at Styles*, the authors use the main character of a detective to explain the thought process behind solving a mystery. The approach of the two authors is similar. Both main characters describe their thinking to a first-person narrator. Sherlock Holmes shares his thoughts with his colleague, Watson, while Hercule Poirot speaks with an unnamed friend or acquaintance. In addition, both authors use the metaphor of links in a chain to explain how their detectives piece together clues to solve a mystery. Sherlock Holmes describes his thought process as "construct[ing] a series of inferences, each dependent upon its predecessor and each simple in itself." Hercule Poirot explains that "we will arrange the facts, neatly, each in his proper place. We will examine—and reject. Those of importance we will put on one side; those of no importance, pouf!"

Another similarity between Holmes and Poirot is that they consider no detail too small. For example, Holmes draws conclusions about Watson's investments on the basis of a "groove between [Watson's] left forefinger and thumb." Poirot's solution to the mystery comes together with information about what the deceased woman ate for dinner.

Although the main characters have similar approaches, their personalities differ. Even though both authors present their detectives as eccentric, Holmes is a "strange . . . bird" with "curious facilities," while Poirot is a kind, "cherub-like" man. Holmes seems to respect Watson, but he is somewhat condescending to his colleague. In describing how he solves a mystery, he says it is "not really difficult" and "very simple." In contrast, Poirot patiently and kindly explains to the narrator how to determine which details are significant. Despite these differences, though, both authors convey that the deductive reasoning displayed by their detectives is accessible to anyone.

# Lesson 4.2

## Identifying Text Structures, p. 96

1. **A** The numbered list establishes the order of steps that GDL systems require teenagers to complete. These steps must be completed in order, so sequence is the way this text is organized.

2. **J** One solution to the problem of teen drivers' high-crash risk is giving teen drivers more driving experience. Research proves that this solution makes teens safer drivers.

3. **C** Paragraph 5 presents possible causes for why teens have difficulty managing risky behavior behind the wheel. Paragraph 2 describes the benefits of the GDL systems, paragraph 3 describes the three stages of licensure, and paragraph 7 explains the need for more driving experience.

4. **F** A reduction in teen crashes is a direct effect of the GDL systems. The other choices do not describe an effect of the GDL.

## Text Structure and Key Ideas, p. 98

5. **C** The writer begins the passage with frog and toad sightings (effects) and introduces the possible causes for these events later.

6. **J** The first sentence of paragraph 10 emphasizes that the author is uncertain about why frogs and toads seem to fall from the sky at times. In the other paragraphs, the author is citing the opinions of other authors or experts.

7. **D**

8. **J** A whirlwind is cited as a possible cause of frogs and toads falling from the sky. The other answer choices describe the effects, or results, of storms.

Writing Practice, p. 99

Make sure your informative text clearly compares and contrasts the structure of the two passages and evaluates how well the structure of each passage conveys key ideas. You should include relevant examples from the texts as evidence.

> Answers will vary. Sample answer: The two passages use different structures to convey their ideas effectively. The passage about Graduated Driver Licensing (GDL) uses a problem-and-solution format. The author's goal is to convince readers that the GDL system helps solve the problem of dangerous teen driving, so the problem-and-solution structure works well to convey key ideas. The author states the main idea of the passage at the start and then follows it with a series of problems and solutions related to that idea. In one paragraph, for example, the author states that teenage driving is risky because teenagers are not yet physically and mentally mature. In the following paragraph, the author explains how one course in the GDL system helps solve this problem by teaching teens to regulate their behavior. Each time the author outlines a problem, a solution follows, which makes the passage's ideas effective and persuasive.

> In contrast, the passage about falling frogs and toads is written with a cause-and-effect structure. The author first shares news stories explaining the effect—falling toads. He then shares possible explanations of what caused the falling toads, such as the *Leisure Hours* and *Notes and Queries* theory that the frogs and toads fell from "trees or other places overhead." By providing proof of the effect and then various explanations for the cause, the reader is allowed to determine which makes the most sense to him or her.

# Lesson 4.3

## Locating Transitions, p. 101

1. **B** "In addition" is a signal phrase. The transition indicates that the writer is providing more information about something. The other answer choices are not considered to be signal phrases.

2. **G** According to the text, the first step in selecting the proper dog is thinking about the best breeds for your family. The signal word "first" should help you figure this out.

3. **D** The signal phrase "on the other hand" indicates a contrast between the small Chihuahua breed and larger or aggressive breeds. This phrase indicates a difference between the two types of dogs. It is not used to compare these dogs, to provide examples, or to show the effects of purchasing a small dog.

4. **J** The signal phrase "for instance" points to examples of dogs that might or might not be appropriate for families with small children. The paragraph suggests that families who have playful children might like a larger dog and that a Chihuahua would not be appropriate. This phrase does not indicate other transitions such as cause and effect, time order, or location.

5. **B** The signal word "after" explains what to do following your decision about which puppy you want to own. This transition reveals a shift in time from the preceding paragraph. The transition word "after" is not used in this paragraph to contrast information, to present examples, or to reveal a conclusion.

## Analyzing Transitions, p. 103

6. **F** The first paragraph provides important information about NASA's history. The list at the end of the second paragraph provides examples of NASA's technological inventions.

7. **B**

8. **H** This sentence provides examples of NASA's impact on technological inventions. The signal phrase "for instance" would highlight this relationship. The term "in brief" is not appropriate here because the sentence does not provide a summary. "By contrast" indicates that something will be contrasted, which does not happen in this sentence. "In conclusion" would indicate that the paragraph or passage is coming to a conclusion, which is not correct.

9. **B** The signal word "finally" shows that the writer is arriving at a conclusion. It does not indicate relative location. The term "whatever" is not a signal word that is used to reveal a shift in ideas.

10. **F** The signal word "moreover" shows an addition. It does not signal a cause, a conclusion, or an effect.

## Writing Practice, p. 104

Make sure you include examples from the texts to support your argument, and use appropriate and varied transitions and signal words to connect your ideas.

> Answers will vary. Sample answer: I am strongly in favor of continued funding for NASA. First of all, I agree with the statement in the first passage: "it is a mistake to think of NASA's budget as a waste of money that would be better spent on Earth." As the author of this passage states, the money *is* spent on Earth. It's clear from this passage that many of the technologies we depend on today would not exist if not for the space program. An example is the cell phone. Try to imagine your daily life without it.
>
> Secondly, I agree that it's important to look for other habitable planets. As the first passage states, there will be more than 9 billion humans on Earth by 2050. Soon enough, there will be no more room. Therefore, it only makes sense to continue space exploration. I agree to some extent with the argument in the second passage that many spaceflights can be done without humans. However, I believe that the human element is still essential, particularly if space is to be our future residence.

# Lesson 5.1

## Identifying an Author's Purpose, p. 108

1. **A** You can tell that this text is written to inform because it contains many facts and definitions of key vocabulary. The writing style is unbiased. This scientific article is not meant to persuade, entertain, or express emotion.

2. **H** The purpose of this text is to inform the reader about sound waves. This sentence provides an example of how compression can be heard in sound waves. This is the only answer that relates to the author's purpose.

3. **A** This sentence provides an example of transverse waves. In an informative text, the author's goal is to explain. Informative texts contain facts, definitions, and examples. Their primary goal is not persuading, entertaining, or sparking the imagination.

4. **F**

## Recognizing an Author's Point of View, p. 110

5. **C** This passage outlines George W. Bush's plans for reforming education. His point of view is that there are problems with the education system that need to be changed.

6. **F** Bush lists a series of problems with the education system, including poorly performing schools and lack of accountability. His point of view about the US education system is negative.

7. **D** Bush states in the first paragraph, "It's time to come together to get it done. . . ." Bush is trying to convince the American people that No Child Left Behind should be put into law. He is not trying to entertain. Although he does explain and inform, his primary purpose is to convince the audience that No Child Left Behind is a good plan.

8. **J** Bush lists changes that he believes need to occur in the US education system. Therefore, his point of view is that the education system needs reform.

9. **A** Bush uses the transition words *first, second, third,* and *fourth* to list his four main points. Creating a uniform educational system is not one of these points.

## Language Practice, p. 111

10. **F**
11. **B**
12. **F**
13. **D**

## Writing Practice, p. 113

Make sure your argument clearly states your point of view, and includes valid reasoning and relevant and sufficient evidence to support it.

> Answers will vary. Sample answer: I agree wholeheartedly with George W. Bush when he states that we must confront the blight of illiteracy in America. As Bush notes, nearly 70 percent of fourth graders in high-poverty schools cannot read at a basic level. That is indeed a scandal, and it affects not just a portion of our population but the entire nation. Without well-educated citizens, the United States cannot hope to maintain its status as a world leader. Unless we want to sink to the bottom, educational failure is not an option.

> I also agree with Bush that we need sweeping change, and immediately. As he remarks, "If we work only at the edges, our influence will be confined to the margins." Increased testing may be one such necessary change. However, I don't think the federal government should decide how often students are tested. Bush may be right when he says that yearly testing is most effective, but I believe testing decisions should be made at the state or local level.

# Lesson 5.2

## Text Structure in Informational Texts, p. 115

1. **A** The facts, boldfaced terms, section headings, and straightforward style are clues that this text was written to inform.
2. **G** The author defines and then describes various concepts that are important to Earth science, so the text structure is description.
3. **B** The text structure makes it easy for readers to understand which topics are studied in Earth science.
4. **H** In the excerpt, the author explains the effect of the events that are parts of the big bang theory, the open theory, and the closed universe theory, so the structure that best describes the paragraph is cause and effect.

## Text Structure in Literary Texts, p. 116

5. **B** The descriptive details of the setting and figurative language are clues that this text was written to entertain.
6. **F** The events are told in the order in which they occur, so the story has a sequence structure.
7. **A** Presenting the events in sequence allows readers to follow the plot.
8. **H** The author's use of time-order words such as *then* and *when* helps support the text structure by showing the sequence of key events.
9. **B**
10. **J** The correct sequence of events is as follows: First, the party gets quiet when the music stops. Next, people notice a masked character, and then they are troubled by his appearance. Finally, the prince becomes angry.

## Writing Practice, p. 118

Make sure you clearly explain how and why you would tell Poe's story using your chosen structure and which special techniques you would use. Detail ways in which your new version would differ from the original, and note whether the purpose would change. Be sure to include relevant and significant evidence from the text in your response.

> Answers will vary. Sample answer: I would retell Poe's story using a descriptive structure and differing points of view. I would start by describing the figure of the Red Death as he enters the ballroom, rather than starting with a description of the ball as it winds toward midnight. Poe's sequence structure leads up to a surprise when the figure of the Red Death enters the ballroom. Poe's description of the "assembly of phantasms" helps readers understand that not just any scary costume could upset the crowd, so it effectively sets the stage for the Red Death. Then Poe describes the outraged reaction of Prince Prospero, who emerges as one of the two main figures in the passage.

In my new structure, readers would learn the reactions of several attendees at the ball, so they would get a range of points of view. Rather than simply noting that the Red Death "excited such a sensation," I would describe attendees' specific reactions. This would shift the focus of the story from two individuals to the entire party, and give the story a broader sweep. The overall purpose, to entertain by creating suspense, would remain the same as in Poe's version.

# Lesson 5.3

## Inferring the Author's Purpose, p. 120

**1. A** The straightforward approach and bulleted text are clues that the author's purpose is to inform.

**2. J** The bullet points indicate the many times when it is appropriate to wash one's hands, implying that hands can become contaminated in many ways. It is true that people who are sick can spread disease and that hands are susceptible to getting dirty, but these are just two of the many reasons for washing one's hands. Although animals are mentioned, their presence in the workplace is not.

**3. A**

**4. G** The memo does not mention the work of researchers, training costs, or patient complaints.

**5. B** The text was written to inform the reader about the hand-washing policy and to persuade the readers to use the guidelines. The word *crucial* could be added to the memo to stress the importance of the guidelines and to persuade the reader that following them is important.

## Using Context to Infer Implicit Purpose, p. 121

**6. H** The fact that it is the president's responsibility to guide the nation and the military—and thus plan for the future—is the most relevant detail. The responsibility for signing legislation, the presidential election cycle, and the leadership of political parties are not relevant to the speech.

**7. A** The fact that the speech was written toward the end of the Vietnam War helps you understand that Ford wanted the American people to set aside their feelings about the war and to focus instead on the future of the United States. The fact that Ford gave the speech on a college campus explains why he refers to "your generation," but it does not hint at his main purpose. Ford's service in the United States Navy is not related to the purpose of his speech. The upcoming bicentennial was not directly related to Ford's main purpose.

**8. J** The knowledge that the president's responsibility is to set the nation's agenda helps you understand that Ford's implied purpose was to focus people on moving forward after the Vietnam War. Choices F and H are details that support Ford's purpose, but they do not convey the purpose itself. With choice G, Ford acknowledges the events in Vietnam (Indochina), but feelings about Vietnam are not his focus.

**9. C** Ford's use of persuasive language and phrases such as "join me" and "assume the challenge" are clues that he is speaking to persuade.

## Writing Practice, p. 122

Be sure you support your argument with relevant evidence from both the memo and the speech, including precise language and specific examples of rhetoric that helped you form your opinion.

Answers will vary. Sample answer: I strongly agree with Gerald Ford's statement. As he said, "We can and should help others to help themselves." In other words, we should offer assistance when warranted, but those we assist are ultimately responsible for their own welfare. Their fate "rests in their hands, not ours," as Ford remarked.

The United States should not become embroiled in another situation in which those we aid cannot, or will not, stand up for themselves. During the Vietnam War, as the State Department notes, the United States "allowed saving South Viet-Nam to become more important to us than it was for the South Vietnamese themselves." Although the United States had the best intentions, we ultimately were unable to win a war *for* rather than *with* our allies. The State Department repeats the term "judgment," reinforcing the idea that the United States made a bad decision that it can avoid in the future. The passage also repeatedly uses the word "control," hammering home the idea that the United States lost its way in the Vietnam War—and must not lose its way again. As the State

Department wrote, "In the future, we should gauge our support to our allies' efforts, and their successes. If they cannot do the job, we will be unable to do it for them." The State Department also noted, with powerful rhetoric, "We should not profess to see lights at the end of tunnels. We should not employ short-term rationales, out of short-term expediency." In other words, the United States needs to look very carefully before it leaps into another war.

# Lesson 5.4

## Identifying an Author's Position, p. 126

**1. B** Although college and the government are mentioned, the author is arguing that women should be granted the right to vote. Peaceful protests are not mentioned in the passage.

**2. F** The author begins paragraph 7 with the statement "It is argued that all women do not wish to vote." To refute the validity of this argument, the author states that men have the right to vote but not all men want to vote. The author does not claim that opponents doubt women's intelligence and morals, nor that women cannot vote in other countries. In fact, he uses the fact that women *can* vote in other countries to support his position.

**3. B** The author uses the evidence that California prisons have many more men than women to support his opinion that women have stronger morals than men. He does not use the statement to refute, summarize, or acknowledge the assertion.

**4. F**

## Analyzing Support for an Author's Position, p. 128

**5. D** Lyndon Johnson's position is that Congress should pass the voting rights bill. He does say Congress must work hard, but that is not his main point. Johnson wants Congress to pass *this* bill, not draft a new one. And although he refers to states' rights, that is not the primary issue here.

**6. F** Johnson refutes the opposing argument that election laws are issues governed solely by the states. He claims that the freedom to vote is an issue far more important than states' rights versus national rights.

**7. A** By acknowledging and then refuting opposing viewpoints, Johnson strengthens his position. He does not create, ignore, or support opposing viewpoints.

**8. H** In paragraph 11, Johnson describes what happened when Congress previously considered a similar bill. This experience explains why Johnson is insisting that Congress pass the current bill with all provisions intact. Paragraph 5 hints at this incident but does not provide details. Johnson refutes the opposition's argument in paragraph 9 and refers to bigotry in paragraph 15, but he does not provide evidence.

## Writing Practice, p. 129

Your argument should clearly establish the significance of your claim and support it with evidence. To strengthen your argument, your essay should acknowledge an opposing position and explain, through the use of evidence, why that position is not valid.

Answers will vary. Sample answer: Burning the flag should not be considered "protected speech" under the First Amendment. The reasons are clear: As Justice Rehnquist argues, the American flag is "not simply another 'idea' or 'point of view' competing for recognition in the marketplace of ideas." It is the ultimate symbol of our nation, one that "uniquely symbolizes" the "ideas of liberty and equality," as Justice Stevens notes, and therefore "worthy of protection from unnecessary desecration." Congress and 48 out of 50 states have criminalized public flag burning, and, like Justice Rehnquist, I "cannot agree that the First Amendment invalidates" this.

Justices Brennan and Kennedy argue that burning the flag is protected speech. They believe, as do I, that the flag itself expresses the belief in "that freedom which sustains the human spirit." Then they conclude that, as a symbol of freedom, "the flag protects those who hold it in contempt." However, the flag is not simply *a* symbol of freedom in the United States. It is *the* symbol of freedom for millions of citizens. As Justice Rehnquist notes, Americans' "profound regard" for the flag results from 200 years of history, and the government is simply recognizing that fact "when it enacts statutes prohibiting the disrespectful public burning of the flag." Destroying it is a crime—both a legal and a moral one.

# Lesson 5.5

## Identifying Rhetorical Devices, p. 134

1. **A** Using an analogy, the author compares the water to steel. By comparing the water to something readers can picture, the author helps create a strong visual of the setting. Because the sentence does not list items or repeat phrases or ideas, the author has not used the rhetorical devices of enumeration, repetition, or parallelism.

2. **H** The second part of the sentence provides more information to convey why nightfall was so dangerous. Because the author does not make a comparison, list items, or present two opposing ideas or situations, he has not used the rhetorical devices of analogy, enumeration, or juxtaposition of opposites.

3. **D** This excerpt lists various buildings that were close to where the mauled body was found. Through enumeration, the reader can understand how serious the wolf attack was to the community. None of the other excerpts lists a series of examples or details.

4. **J**

## Identifying an Author's Intention and Effect, p. 136

5. **C** The author uses rhetorical devices such as enumeration and juxtaposition of opposites, as well as vivid descriptions of the life of a slave, to convey how unfairly slaves were treated. The author conveys that the slaves were glad that Mr. Severe died but does not indicate that the death was deserved. Although the slaves work on a farm, the passage does not include any details about what the work was like. The passage is not a tale about his childhood but a description of what life was like for slaves.

6. **G** The author's use of rhetorical devices helps create an emotional response in the reader. Skepticism is not a likely response. Readers might discuss life in the rural south, but the topic is more specific than that. And the passage is not a cautionary tale that would prompt readers to make changes in their lives.

7. **B** The author uses enumeration when he lists different groups of people (old and young, male and female, married and single). The author does not compare the people in an analogy, ask any questions, or provide further information in a qualifying statement.

8. **J** This excerpt, unlike the others, does not convey the inhumane circumstances in which the slaves lived.

## Language Practice, p. 136

9. **D**

10. **J**

11. **B**

12. **H**

## Writing Practice, p. 137

Make sure your explanatory text clearly and accurately conveys the author's intent and effect and mentions the use of rhetorical devices.

> Answers will vary. Sample answer: In the excerpt from *Narrative of the Life of Frederick Douglass an American Slave*, Douglass describes a certain period from his life as a slave. He and the other slaves had little time to sleep, and when they did sleep, it was on the floor. They spent most of their time working in the fields and doing chores. They were overseen by the cruel, appropriately named Mr. Severe, who swore and whipped slaves liberally. Douglass describes Mr. Severe's untimely death as a relief. The author's intentions are to inform readers about his life as a slave and to persuade readers of, or at least help them understand, the unfair treatment of slaves. He communicates his intentions by describing the conditions with negative language and using rhetorical devices. For example, he describes the slaves' blankets as "coarse" and "miserable" and Mr. Severe as a "cruel man" who took "pleasure in manifesting his fiendish barbarity" in a "frightful manner." Douglass uses

the rhetorical devices of repetition and parallelism to emphasize the discomfort and exhaustion the slaves felt: "They find less difficulty from the want of beds, than from the want of time to sleep. . . ." The repetition of "from the want of" underscores that sleep deprivation was even worse than the uncomfortable sleeping conditions. Another rhetorical device Douglass uses is enumeration, as in the phrase "old and young, male and female, married and single, drop down side by side, on one common bed—the cold, damp floor. . . ." Listing the range of slaves emphasizes that no one, regardless of age, gender, or marital status, was exempt from sleeping in a group on the floor. These rhetorical devices and the many rich details have the desired effect of helping readers feel sympathy for the slaves and angry about the way they were treated.

# Lesson 6.1

### Developing an Argument, p. 140

**1. D** One of Paine's main claims is that England's constitution does not encourage liberty. The fact that the king can reject bills that the commons passes and that the members of the peers are part of the old tyranny are ideas that support Paine's claim. The fact that members of the commons are elected is a fact, not a claim.

**2. F**

**3. A** The evidence that Paine presents is relevant to his claim. All the information in the passage relates to Paine's criticism of the English constitution.

**4. G** The constitution of England allowed the king to reject bills passed by the commons. This is a fact that can be checked in historical references. The other statements are opinions. They contain biased words such as "should be," "wiser," and "ancient tyranny." Loaded vocabulary is often a sign that an opinion is being expressed.

**5. C** Paine's conclusion is a restatement of the ideas he presented. He does not add new information or call colonists to action.

### Analyzing Argument Development, p. 142

**6. F** Answer F explains the claim made in the passage. The other sentences express reasons and facts provided as evidence.

**7. C** Palma says he has no patience for people who protest this right. The other sentences are untrue, or they do not accurately express the author's opinion.

**8. H** Palma provides examples of women's success in education as proof that women belong in public life. Facts about women's suffrage, expert opinions about women's intelligence, and personal opinions about women are not part of his argument.

**9. B** Palma states his claim and supports it with facts, reasons, and examples. Answers A and C describe ways that an argument could be supported, but the author does not use these methods. Answer D describes a solution to a problem. This is not what Palma does in this passage.

**10. F** Palma connects his ideas logically. He does not present ideas chronologically, in the form of questions and answers, or through comparison and contrast.

**11. C** Palma concludes that it is only logical for women, who are allowed to participate in every other aspect of public life, to be allowed to fully participate. This includes voting. The other statements are summaries of evidence.

### Language Practice, p. 143

**12. H**

**13. B**

**14. J**

**15. A**

Make sure your argument clearly states your claim. Provide facts, reasons, and examples from the passages as relevant and sufficient evidence to back up your claim. Conclude by restating your opinion and summarizing the evidence that backs up your claim.

> Answers will vary. Sample answer: I am opposed to the food labels proposed in Initiative Measure I-522 for one simple reason: They would result in confusion, not clarity, for consumers. As stated in the passage's "against" argument, only certain supermarket foods would receive the labels, leaving consumers clueless when it comes to many meat and dairy products produced in the United States. Many, if not all, imported foods would go label-free, since manufacturers can claim these foods to be exempt at will. Restaurants would be exempt too. Yet this half-measure would cost consumers hundreds of dollars a year and hurt local farmers too. Given that this labeling would be ineffective and costly, I strongly oppose Initiative Measure I-522 and urge others to do likewise.

# Lesson 6.2

## Supporting Evidence, p. 148

1. **A** The author claims the mayor is avoiding his responsibilities. The other statements are claims made by the mayor himself.

2. **J** The mayor claims he cannot remove people from government positions for misconduct. The other statements are claims that the author is making about the mayor's powers and responsibilities.

3. **D** The fact that the mayor can remove offenders with the approval of the Board is logical evidence that the author uses. Answers A and C are arguments that the mayor gives for not being held responsible for misconduct. Answer B does not relate to the author's claim that the mayor is responsible for what happens in the city.

4. **H** The mayor states that he has no power, but then he says that he can remove people from their positions if he has the approval of the Board of Aldermen. This is an example of how the mayor's statements contradict one another. The other answer options do not describe the mayor's statements accurately.

5. **B** The mayor's logic is faulty because he contradicts himself. The other answer choices would describe sensible arguments.

## Connecting Claims and Evidence, p. 150

6. **G** Nixon admitted that he received $18,000, but he claimed that he used the money for political, not personal, expenses. The other answer choices are false.

7. **D** Nixon offered this supporting reason for why politicians need contributions from supporters. He believed that the government should not finance political business. The statement is not an example of political expenses. It is not a fact, and it does not make a strong emotional appeal.

8. **G**

9. **C** Nixon said that the records, which were then in the hands of the government, showed how he spent the money. The other answer options do not offer support for how he spent the money.

10. **F** Nixon had no proof that he did not grant special favors to supporters. The lack of proof makes this argument faulty. The other options would describe sound arguments.

## Language Practice, p. 152

11. **B**

12. **F**

13. **D**

14. **G**

# Answer Key

## Writing Practice, p. 153

Make sure that you support your claim with valid reasoning, significant and relevant facts, and examples from the text. Do not include emotional appeals or faulty reasoning.

> Answers will vary. Sample answer: Government officials should be held accountable for corruption within their administration. Although Mayor Wood of New York City argued that there was "no general head; . . . no chief executive," a mayor is considered to be the head of a city; he or she is a government official who acts on behalf of the entire community. The author of "The One Man Rule" states that the city charter "makes the heads of nearly all the departments directly responsible to the mayor." Therefore, if the mayor, along with city council members, appoints the heads of various city departments, it is only logical that he or she should be responsible for ensuring that those individuals are carrying out their respective duties. As in any workplace, a city's mayor must oversee employees and make sure that each is meeting the requirements of the job. If not, the mayor must take action to correct the problem, whether that means providing additional support or removing the employee from his or her position. In fact, as the author notes, "Any malfeasance or neglect of duty on the part of [corrupt officers] . . . entitles the mayor instantly to supersede them." According to the author of the editorial, the mayor claims to be "without power." This statement is absurd in that the position of mayor is, by definition, one of power. The author states that the mayor "has power in every case of misconduct to remove the offender from office. . . ." I agree completely. If this were not the case, then why should we elect a mayor at all?

# Lesson 6.3

## Building a Case, p. 155

1. **B**   The fact that the company cannot afford mandatory sick leave is evidence given to support the claim that employees should vote against the legislation. The other answer choices provide information about the legislation or the company's position on the legislation, but these statements do not give reasons to support the claim.

2. **F**   The fact that this company already provides sick leave for employees demonstrates its commitment to employee health.

3. **C**   The effect on employee benefits and job security is directly relevant to the audience. The other answer options are general information about the company.

4. **F**   The financial information shows that the new law would be too costly for the company and that it would force the company to lay off employees. This information is relevant to the claim that employees should vote against the new law. The other options are not relevant to the claim.

5. **C**   The author provides several pieces of evidence directly related to the company's cost for sick leave.

6. **J**   The author provides relevant evidence and states the effect of this legislation on employees. This makes the claim persuasive. The other options are false or do not support the claim.

## Evaluating Evidence in Various Texts, p. 158

7. **A**   Reagan uses this example from history as relevant evidence for his claim that his actions are necessary. The other options are other elements of an argument.

8. **F**   Reagan states that the private sector is more successful at running social programs in order to justify his claim that the Department of Education and other social programs can be cut from the government's budget. The other statements are not directly related to the claim.

9. **A**

10. **H**   The promise to not raise taxes is relevant to the claim. Reagan believes that not increasing taxes will help people and businesses recover from the recession. The other statements do not support the claim.

11. **A**   The lack of specific examples makes the evidence insufficient. The other options do not describe how the lack of specific examples categorizes the evidence.

**12. J**    The president briefly provides relevant evidence that the recession caused the budget deficit (it lowered revenues and increased costs), but those two details are not sufficient evidence to support his claim.

## Writing Practice, p. 159

Make sure your claim clearly states your position and includes valid reasoning and sufficient and relevant supporting evidence from the memo in your argument.

> Answers will vary. Sample answer: If I were a company CEO, I would urge my employees to vote against standardized sick days. As the corporate memo makes clear, standardizing sick days would most likely result in serious financial losses to the company. Under standardized sick days, as the memo notes, employees would be paid even for unused sick days. The memo cites a 2010 Department of Labor Statistics report stating that sick leave can cost 81 cents per hour per employee. No matter the size of the company, this can add up to a large yearly expense. Such an expense could, in turn, lead to cost-cutting layoffs and reduced salaries. Obviously that would not benefit employees.
>
> In the case of influenza or another disease outbreak, I would instead support following CDC guidelines, as the memo indicates, and providing sick days on an as-needed basis. This safeguards the employees' health and the company's financial health. As CEO, I would be responsible for protecting my company and those who work for it, so I feel it is ethical and essential to counsel employees on matters that could negatively affect them as individuals and as workers.

# Lesson 6.4

## Understanding Validity and Reasoning, p. 161

**1. A**

**2. H**    The defeat of the Sanford bill can be verified in historical records. The other statements are the author's opinions.

**3. D**    The evidence used to support the claim is not reasonable because it cannot be verified as supporting his claim. It is not logically sound because it is based on personal opinions rather than facts. The other descriptions of this author's evidence are inaccurate.

**4. G**    The writer's argument as a whole is biased because it is based solely on his unsupported opinion; therefore, it is invalid. Even his factual evidence about the reasons for the suffrage bill's defeat cannot be fully verified—there may have been other aspects of the bill that were not acceptable and that led to its being voted down. The other descriptions of the author's argument are inaccurate.

## Evaluating Validity and Reasoning in Texts, p. 163

**5. C**    Obama's tax cut is a verifiable fact. The other sentences are opinions. Words such as *best* and *want* are clues that these statements are opinions.

**6. J**    Obama uses Romney's plan to support his claim that trickle-down economics doesn't work at all. He describes the plan as "fairy dust," and he says it didn't work (in the past) and it won't work (in the future). The other statements support Romney's plan.

**7. C**    Obama is connecting the idea that the economy improves when the middle class has more money to spend with the idea that raising taxes on the middle class does not help the economy. The other ideas do not support Obama's claim.

**8. G**    Obama connects his ideas logically and produces verifiable facts, providing sound reasoning and valid evidence for his claim that he should be reelected to continue the progress he started.

**9. B**    The last sentence states that Obama has a plan, which supports his claim that he should be reelected. The other sentences describe the opponent's actions but do not directly support Obama's claim that he will be the best person to move the economy in a positive direction.

## Language Practice, p. 164

**10.** G
**11.** C
**12.** H
**13.** A

## Writing Practice, p. 165

Make sure you support your argument with relevant and sufficient evidence from the text. Explain why the author's claim is valid or invalid, evaluating evidence and noting any examples of fallacious reasoning.

> Answers will vary. Sample answer: J.B. Sanford's position is invalid and poorly argued. He starts his argument by stating, "Suffrage is not a right. It is a privilege that may or may not be granted." Sanford states this as fact, though it is simply one person's opinion. For another view of the matter, consider that the US Constitution mentions the "right to vote" five times.

> Sanford states his opinions as fact throughout his argument. "Politics is no place for a woman, consequently the privilege should not be granted to her," he writes. He produces no evidence to support this claim. His next statement, "The mother's influence is needed in the home," is simply another opinion. Later in his argument, Sanford writes, "Do women have to vote in order to receive the protection of men?" This question is based on fallacious reasoning. Sanford may believe that women seek the right to vote so they can "receive the protection of men," but he has no evidence to back up this opinion. Therefore, his argument that women will receive "more protection and more consideration" as long as she "keeps her place"—that is, as long as she stays out of politics—is irrelevant as well as questionable. Finally, Sanford writes, "Woman suffrage has been proven a failure in states that have tried it." Rather than providing facts to back this up, he simply adds that "It is wrong." It is Sanford who is wrong, and his empty argument makes that plain.

# Lesson 6.5

## Evaluating Arguments Founded on Logical Reasoning, p. 167

**1.** D    The author claims there are too many causes of obesity for doctors to be able to suggest just one solution to solve the problem. The other answer options are evidence and reasoning that support the claim at the start of the argument.

**2.** F    The author makes the assumption that obesity is a medical problem that needs to be solved. The other answer options define terms and explain causes of obesity.

**3.** C    The explanation of the set-point theory serves as a deduction in a series of deductions that support the claim that obesity is a complex problem to solve. The other answer options are other parts of an argument.

**4.** G

**5.** C    The author formulates deductions from the results of the studies and uses them to support the argument. The other options are not part of the author's argument.

## Evaluating Arguments Based on Hidden Assumptions, p. 168

**6.** J    The author claims that Shakespeare's work should have obscene words taken out to clean it up and make it more beautiful. The other choices are statements he makes to build his argument.

**7.** B    The author bases his argument on the unstated assumption that offensive words lower the artistic quality of literature. The other answer options are stated ideas.

**8.** J    The author's argument depends upon the reader accepting that changing literature does not damage the original work or change it in an unacceptable way.

**9.** B    The author bases his idea that Shakespeare's work would be more beautiful if it were censored on the invalid assumption that literature can be censored and not damaged in the process.

**10.** F    The author presents as a fact the idea that Shakespeare's work is defective, and assumes that everyone will agree with him, but it is his personal opinion.

**11.** A

**12.** G

**13.** D

**14.** G

## Writing Practice, p. 171

Make sure you clearly explain the hidden assumption of the text and cite significant and relevant details that helped you determine the assumption. In your evaluation, be sure to assess the validity of the reasoning and the relevance and sufficiency of the evidence.

> Answers will vary. Sample answer: The underlying assumption in Elizabeth Warren's speech is that her listeners agree with her view that the actions of certain government officials, lobbying groups, and large corporations are hurting most Americans and must be stopped. Although she does not say it outright, this assumption is clear from the title itself: "Our Agenda Is America's Agenda." Warren's repeated use of the words "our," "we," and "us" is also a clue that she believes she and her listeners are on the same side. For example, she makes statements such as "We have had to fight for what we've achieved," "[O]ur work is uphill," and "[W]e know that America agrees with us."
>
> Whether listeners and readers consider Warren's reasoning to be valid depends on whether they side with Warren and accept that the actions of the groups Warren criticizes are harmful to the American people. Warren relies heavily on rhetorical devices such as repetition and parallelism. For example, she claims, "Powerful interests have . . . attacked Social Security and Medicare. They attacked pensions and public employees. They attacked bank regulation and consumer protection. . . . [They] . . . have attacked so many of the basic foundations that built a strong middle class. . . ." She does provide some details to support her assertions, such as the big banks standing in the way of the government's enforcement of Dodd-Frank regulations. However, Warren does not cite specific examples or provide solid proof that this has happened. In addition, she claims that "our values are America's values, and our agenda is America's agenda," but she does not provide facts to back up this statement. Warren's speech seems to have been written not to prove her position but to evoke an emotional response from people who already agree with her.

# Lesson 7.1

## Comparing Texts on Similar Topics, p. 176

**1.** A Both passages are about Mammoth Cave. The genre of the first passage is memoir; the second passage is a nonfiction, informational text. The format of the first passage is all text; however, the second passage includes text and tables. The first passage has a first-person narrator; the second passage has a third-person narrator.

**2.** J Knowing that passage 1 was written in the late 19th century helps readers understand why words such as *torch* (paragraph 1), *oxen* (paragraph 2), and *lantern* (paragraph 3) were used. The other choices might provide readers with information, but they would not affect understanding the text.

**3.** C Passage 2 provides information about the park and fees associated with visiting. The information is probably more general than historians or conservationists would need. The text addresses all park visitors, not just families.

**4.** G Passage 1 uses vivid, connotative language to describe Mammoth Cave. Its main purpose is to entertain readers with fascinating information about the cave. Passage 2 provides facts and pricing information about the park. Its main purpose is to inform. Passage 1 may have also been written to inform readers about the cave's wonder and beauty and to persuade readers to visit the park, but passage 2 is strictly informational.

## Comparing Fiction and Nonfiction, p. 178

**5.** A Passage 1 is a factual account of the torture methods used during the Spanish Inquisition. Passage 2 details the thoughts and feelings of one of the torture victims. Neither passage mentions the people who created the Spanish Inquisition, the purposes behind its formation, or the events that led to its end.

**6. H** Passage 1 is entirely fact based; passage 2 details the narrator's emotions and thoughts during his experience. Passage 1 does not reveal the author's opinion about the methods of torture, does not detail the torture experienced by one man, and is not written from the point of view of the inquisitor. In passage 2, Poe describes the experience of only one prisoner.

**7. B** Passage 1 is an informational text written mainly to inform people about what happened during the Spanish Inquisition. It was not written to help, to entertain, or to persuade readers.

**8. F**

**9. B** "The Pit and the Pendulum" presents the inner emotions and struggles of the prisoner to help readers identify with him. These are characteristics of fiction.

## Writing Practice, p. 179

Make sure you note similarities and differences between the two passages' formats, context, and content. Remember to draw a conclusion about the subject based on significant and relevant details from both passages.

> Answers will vary. Sample answer: The first passage is a description of Mammoth Cave based on one person's visit. The writer gives his impressions of the cave rather than writing facts about it, and he focuses only on what interests him most. His language is colorful and sometimes poetic. For example, he writes that "the silence is of a kind never experienced on the surface of the earth. . . . This, and the absolute darkness, to a person with eyes makes him feel as if he were face to face with the primordial nothingness." Details such as this provide little or no practical information about the cave, but they give readers a vivid sense of what it's like to visit.
>
> The second passage, on the other hand, is strictly informational and objective rather than personal. It provides a fact-based description of Mammoth Cave and its surroundings, in straightforward rather than poetic prose. After the description comes practical information about visiting the cave. The author provides tables with prices for visiting the caves and camping or picnicking nearby, making the information easy to find and understand.
>
> Although the passages are very different, readers can draw a similar conclusion from the descriptive details in the first and the factual details in the second: Mammoth Cave is a fascinating natural feature that's well worth a visit.

# Lesson 7.2

## Identifying Genre, p. 181

**1. C** Passage 1 is an essay; the author's viewpoint is clearly stated, and facts backup this viewpoint. Passage 2 is a historical article; it contains facts and figures, rather than opinions, about a historical topic.

**2. G** The purpose of both passages is to inform the reader about an aspect of Japanese culture.

**3. D** Passage 1 is an essay describing the development of the Japanese tea culture, and passage 2 is a historical article highlighting facts related to Japanese immigration to the United States. The dates and topics in the passages are details of content, not literary techniques. Passage 1 does not contain a plot.

**4. G** Passage 1 explains why tea became such an important part of Japanese culture. Passage 2 discusses US immigration rules that affected the Japanese. The other statements are incorrect or only half correct.

## Comparing Texts from Similar Genres, p. 183

**5. D** Passage 2 is a letter. It is addressed to one particular person.

**6. F** Lewis writes about his experience in nature with amusement, including events such as landing in the creek four times. On the other hand, Muir seems astonished by the variations in California's climate and scenery.

**7. B**

**8. G** Both authors use the first-person point of view to tell their narratives.

Your explanatory text should include concrete details and examples of literary techniques and tone from both passages. Be sure you also focus on the authors' attitudes toward their experiences in nature.

Answers will vary. Sample answer: Lewis R. Freeman and John Muir write about their experiences in nature, but each author conveys a different tone, and thus a different attitude, toward his experiences. In *Down the Yellowstone*, Freeman begins by vividly describing his experience in Yellowstone in somewhat magical terms. He recounts seeing three rainbows that appeared "in the mist clouds as they floated up out of the shadowed depths." A "patch of bright saffron sand" makes the author think of the mythical pot of gold at the end of the rainbow. However, Freeman's admiration of the place's beauty gives way to a tone of frustration, with details about the hazardous nighttime journey. Twice, Freeman uses the word *bad* to describe the experience. In the dark, in which "a fog obscured the moon," Freeman and his companion, Carr, got lost. Later, Carr fell over a snow bank, and both fell into a creek. They were tired and sore by the time the sun rose and they crossed Mud Geyser. Although Freeman's descriptions indicate that the journey was dangerous, the passage ends in a tone of amusement. The tone is set with language such as "a boatload of seasick tourists" and "I felt just about like the Mud Geyser sounded." Freeman's vivid descriptions and figurative language help readers understand that he enjoys the beauty of nature but does not enjoy the hazards of a nighttime hike.

In *Letters to a Friend*, Muir describes his travels to Yosemite to a friend who might move to California. His descriptions are as vivid as Freeman's. Although Muir includes more facts than Freeman, he uses an extended metaphor to tell his friend about California's variety "in climate and scenery." Muir describes the weather in terms of the seasons: "March is the springtime of the plains, April the summer, and May the autumn. The other months are dry and wet winter." He then relates his journey "across the seasons": "After riding for two days in this autumn I found summer again. . . . Forty or fifty miles further into the mountains, I came to spring. . . . A few miles farther 'onward and upward' I found the edge of winter. . . . Descending these higher mountains toward the Yosemite, . . . I once more found spring." Muir contrasts the dead flowers in the plains with the blossoming flowers of the foothills and the waving grasses of the foothills with a snowy mountain where "scarce a grass could be seen." Muir's appreciation for nature comes through in a tone of admiration and awe.

# Lesson 7.3

## Comparing and Contrasting Two Arguments p. 187

1. **B** The author implicitly conveys the claim in the first paragraph by explaining how a human embryo is much like embryos of other species. In the second paragraph, he says, "I do not think we could ask nature for more complete proof that human beings have evolved from one-cell ancestors as simple as modern protozoa. . . ." He concludes the fourth paragraph with ". . . we cannot do away with the facts of structure and development and fossil history, nor is there any other explanation more reasonable than evolution for these facts." Answers A, C, and D are details that support Crampton's claim.

2. **F** Crampton supports his claim with facts about the fossilized remains of *Pithecanthropus*.

3. **B**

4. **H** Crampton believes that Darwin's theories of evolution and natural selection are valid; therefore, he would believe that unused traits would disappear as a species evolves.

5. **D** Dennert begins by saying that "Darwinism is doomed to decay." Then he goes on to cite an article stating that Darwinism cannot be defended because it cannot be proved. Dennert uses answers A and C to support his claim. He does state that Darwinism goes against Christianity, but this is one of his reasons for opposing Darwinism. It is not his primary claim.

6. **F** Dennert refutes Crampton's argument, so he is disputing Darwin's theory of evolution.

## Analyzing Evidence in Two Arguments, p. 188

7. **C** Crampton uses the *Pithecanthropus* to show that apes evolved (for example, their skulls changed shape) until eventually the ape-man evolved to become a human. Crampton does not say that scientists support Darwin's theory. Crampton does not use the example to show how highly evolved humans are, but rather he uses it to show how closely humans are related to apes. He believes that *Pithecanthropus* is the missing link for understanding evolution.

**8. J** Crampton uses scientific research and analysis for the basis of his evidence. Crampton does not use opinions, biblical support, or witness statements.

**9. B** Dennert uses only opinion to defend his claim. It is not based on logic because it does not take into account evidence that supports the theory of evolution. His argument merely explains the opinion of another writer. He does not cite research or a record of events.

**10. F** The evidence of a "missing link" is used as proof that Darwinism has basis in fact. While Crampton mentions the other points, those statements do not contradict Dennert's claim.

## Writing Practice, p. 189

Make sure that your argument clearly supports one side of the debate about raising the minimum wage. Your writing should cite relevant and sufficient evidence from the text as well as refute the argument from the opposing essay.

The minimum wage should be increased. People who are willing to work hard deserve a living wage.

As the White House points out, the minimum wage has not kept up with inflation. This means that that money earned by people who work for minimum wage doesn't go as far as it used to. The cost of things we buy changes with inflation. People who receive Social Security get adjustments in their benefits based on the cost of living. People making the lowest wages should get the same financial consideration.

The Senate Republican Policy Committee says that the minimum wage doesn't need to increase because half of those minimum-wage earners are under age 25. They believe that young workers don't need the same wage as older workers. There are two problems with this reasoning. If half of the minimum wage workers are under 25, the other half of those workers are over age 25. These are people more likely to be supporting a family. These older, low-income earners are the people that the committee claims to want to protect.

The other flaw with the argument is that the Senate Republican Policy Committee seems to imply that younger workers don't need or deserve a higher wage. People in their late teens and twenties are often supporting parents, siblings, children, and themselves. They would need and deserve a living wage just as much as older workers.

A higher minimum wage would also give more money to people to spend in businesses. Although the Senate Republican Policy Committee says that higher wages would hurt families and businesses alike, it would actually do the opposite. More people would have money to spend at these businesses. And families would have more funds available for the things they need.

Therefore, an increase in the minimum wage would benefit the well-being of individuals, families, and businesses.

# Lesson 7.4

## Comparing Textual and Visual Genres, p. 195

**1. D** The two passages and the time line are about Niagara Falls. The time line, fact list, and narrative have different formats and genres. The time line and fact list do not have speakers.

**2. H**

**3. B** "Niagara, June 10, 1843" is a personal narrative. The author's purpose in writing the text about a trip to Niagara Falls is to entertain. She uses vivid descriptions, figurative language, and sensory details to accomplish this purpose. The author is not writing to persuade, inform, or explain.

**4. J** The time line visually communicates the history of the falls, and the passage describes the writer's experience. The time line does not contain interesting facts about the waters or tell of a person's trip. The passage does not describe the history, nor does it discuss the best sites to visit.

### Evaluating Differences between Genres, p. 197

**5.** **D** "The Story of an Eye-Witness" uses vivid descriptions to evoke compassion. "Evacuating Yourself and Your Family" offers facts, information, and practical advice about what to do during a disaster.

**6.** **H** Although readers might have experienced a natural disaster, want to learn about the weather, or work for the Federal Emergency Management Agency, the intended audience is people who might need to prepare for a future natural disaster. The passage contains information that can help these people plan for an evacuation. It does not talk in detail about past natural disasters, weather in general, or working for FEMA.

**7.** **C** The purpose of this text is to entertain and inform. The use of a narrative allows the writer to provide rich descriptive details that appeal to the reader's emotions. The passage does not explain key concepts about earthquakes. It is not meant to persuade readers about earthquake preparedness. Although the narrative is told sequentially, conveying the sequence of events is not the author's main purpose.

**8.** **H** Passage 1 has a broader scope than passage 2. Passage 1 provides details about how to prepare for and carry out an evacuation during several kinds of natural disasters. Passage 2 describes one event.

### Language Practice, p. 199

**9.** B

**10.** G

**11.** A

**12.** F

**13.** B

**14.** J

### Writing Practice, p. 200

Be sure to use valid reasoning and relevant and sufficient evidence from both passages to support your claim, and remember to explain which passage was most helpful in supporting your argument, and why.

> Answers will vary. Sample answer: I think the government is justified in forcing people to evacuate their homes when natural disasters are predicted. Mandatory evacuation is a safety precaution that saves lives and may also save towns and cities millions of dollars in rescue efforts and emergency aid after disaster strikes. As "Evacuating Yourself and Your Family" makes clear, information about natural disasters reaches federal and local officials before it reaches the public, so officials know best when an evacuation is necessary. The passage shows that the government has given careful thought to when and how people should evacuate during an emergency and has mapped out evacuation routes and planned for emergency shelters. However, the only way to ensure that people use these safety measures is through mandatory evacuation.
>
> "The Story of an Eye-Witness" uses vivid language to describe the terrifying results of a natural disaster. As an eyewitness to the San Francisco earthquake, the author is uniquely qualified to persuade readers that mandatory evacuation is essential to save lives—even if that wasn't his purpose when he wrote this passage. I was more convinced by "The Story of an Eye-Witness" than by the memo from the Federal Emergency Management Agency because the personal description made the effects of a natural disaster seem so immediate and devastating.